THE BIG WILD SOUL
OF TERRENCE COLE

THE BIG WILD SOUL
OF TERRENCE COLE

An Eclectic Collection to Honor Alaska's Public Historian
edited by Frank Soos and Mary Ehrlander

University of Alaska Press

Published by
University of Alaska Press
P.O. Box 756240
Fairbanks, AK 99775-6240

Cover and interior design by UA Press
Interior layout by Rachel Fudge

Cover image: Aurora Betula © Kesler Woodward 2017.
Acrylic on canvas. www.keslerwoodward. com

Library of Congress Cataloging in Publication Data

Names: Soos, Frank, editor of compilation. | Ehrlander, Mary F., editor of
    compilation. | Cole, Terrence, 1953- honouree.
Title: The big wild soul of Terrence Cole : an eclectic collection to honor
    Alaska's public historian / edited by Frank Soos and Mary Ehrlander.
Other titles: Eclectic collection to honor Alaska's public historian
Description: Fairbanks, AK : University of Alaska Press, [2019] |
    "Contributors include: Dermot Cole, Gerald McBeath, Mary F. Ehrlander,
    Ronald K. Inouye, Carolyn Kozak Loeffler, Sherry Simpson, Frank Soos, John
    Straley, Kes Woodward, Chris Allan, Ross Coen, Stephen Haycox, Lee Huskey,
    David Eric Jessup, Dan O'Neill, Leighton M. Quarles, Katherine Ringsmuth,
    Dirk Tordoff, Russ Vanderlugt and Heath Twichell." | Includes
    bibliographical references and index. |
Identifiers: LCCN 2018029038 (print) | LCCN 2018033103 (ebook) | ISBN
    9781602233812 (ebook) | ISBN 9781602233805 (pbk. : alk. paper)
Subjects: LCSH: Cole, Terrence, 1953|Alaska—Civilization. |
    Alaska—History. | Historians—Alaska—Biography.
Classification: LCC F904 (ebook) | LCC F904 .B54 2019 (print) | DDC
    979.8—dc23
LC record available at https://lccn.loc.gov/2018029038

The University of Alaska Press and The Rasmuson Foundation
are pleased to support and present, on behalf of the editors and authors herein,
this publication in honor of Terrence Cole,
who has been a friend, a mentor, and an inspiration to all of us.

CONTENTS

I GOT OFF THE BUS

Dermot Cole

I got off the bus on an August night after a long ride up the Alaska Highway to Fairbanks and started walking to find my brother's cabin. I had a backpack and a hand-drawn map that directed me to follow College Road, past the University of Alaska campus to the Nenana Highway. It was about 11 P.M., in 1973, and it was dark and warm.

I'd just left the bus station when a guy I'd never seen pulled up on a motorcycle and shouted, "Hi, Terrence."

What followed was the first conversation I ever had with anyone in Fairbanks. The biker gave me a ride and a place to stay that night, and I discovered that Fairbanks was the kind of place where you stood a good chance of being mistaken for your twin brother within ten minutes of your arrival.

The stranger thing is that it's now forty-five years and it's still happening. I was in the electronics section at Fred Meyer a few weeks ago, looking for a computer cable, and a clerk stopped to ask me if I was still teaching. She said she had taken a history class from me as a freshman, she said, when her life centered on three words: "party, party, party." She pronounced each one as an exaggerated "par-tee."

She didn't hold the F against me, because she said she figured she deserved about 80 percent of the credit.

I told her I didn't deserve any of the credit, but that I had known that professor all my life. And then some. The first lesson I remember hearing from Terrence took place one night when I was five or six and couldn't go to sleep. We had twin beds, of course. I told him I didn't know how to go to sleep.

"Just close your eyes," he said.

Growing up on a small farm in eastern Pennsylvania, with our two older brothers and two younger sisters, we each got used to being considered half of a whole.

We were born September 23, 1953—an important date, as all twins born in the U.S. that day won a washer and dryer set as part of the second annual "Westinghouse Blessed Event Day." The company said we were among the 233 sets of twins whose parents applied for a free LS-7 washer and a DS-7 dryer, a one-year supply of baby food, and other items. Westinghouse also said it ended up giving away a couple hundred more washers and dryers than it had expected, as the 23rds of September in 1952 and 1953 somehow came with many more blessed events than normal.

We had that washer and dryer for a long time. It was one of the only things I knew about our early days.

While our parents didn't dress us in identical clothes, there were always the "which one are you?" moments of daily life.

Our folks thought they had selected distinct names, until someone destroyed their illusion with the words: "Derry and Terry, how cute!"

I look at the pictures now and even I can't tell Derry from Terry.

Perhaps the strangest childhood experience came when our mom was in failing health. Our dad decided that what we really needed was not counseling but boxing lessons.

Every Sunday after mass we would retreat to the living room for the laying on of hands.

Dad arranged the couch, chairs, and tables to create a rectangle that served as a boxing ring, and his four boys would strap on the gloves and receive instructions to wallop each other. He lectured us on the Marquess of Queensbury Rules and said that hitting below the belt was not allowed.

Our sisters watched from outside the ring, granted a waiver from this educational experience. One of my older brothers, Kevin, now thinks this was our dad's misguided effort to toughen us up. Dad had grown up in a tough neighborhood in New York, and had been through the nightmare of seeing his family evicted from a tenement.

My sister Maureen said the boxing bouts were one of those things that even a small child could recognize as a bad idea.

Our dad didn't know how to box any more than he knew how to ice skate, but he tried to teach us how to do both. While we learned how to skate on the pond and loved it, at some point he must have realized that none of us wanted to hit each other, so we hung up the gloves.

In school, my sparring partner always sat behind me, as we had assigned seats, and education took place in alphabetical order.

We traded places only once in high school and it was no big thrill, since no one at all could tell us apart.

We both got weekend jobs at fourteen, working thirteen hours every Saturday at a fruit stand for a dollar an hour. Phil, our boss, never learned our names and treated us like identical cogs in his workforce of child laborers.

He would shout things like, "Yo, twin. Push peaches," which meant we had to shout at customers to get them to buy peaches, telling them how beautiful, sweet, and inexpensive they were.

This was the start of my brother's public speaking career, and greatly helped to improve his classroom performance.

He landed at the University of Alaska after our oldest brother, Pat, moved to Fairbanks to attend college in 1970, lured by the mystique of The Great Land.

Terrence did his undergraduate work in geography and northern studies at UAF, and earned a master's degree in history in 1978.

The guidance of Norma Bowkett in the English department and Bill Hunt and Claus Naske in the history department prompted him to settle on writing and research as a career. He came under the influence of writers as varied as E. B. White, Samuel Eliot Morison, J. Frank Dobey, Catherine Drinker Bowen, and George Orwell.

He completed his doctorate in history in 1983 at the University of Washington, where Professor Robert Burke described him as one of the greatest young scholars he'd ever had the pleasure of working with.

Terrence's approach to writing history owes something to the advice of Plutarch, who said his goal was "not to write histories, but lives. And the most glorious exploits do not always furnish us with the clearest discoveries of virtue or vice in men; sometimes a matter of less moment, an expression or a jest, informs us better of their characters or inclinations, than the most famous sieges or the bloodiest battles whatsoever."

Academic writers often look only at glorious exploits and produce weighty books without a pulse, but my brother has avoided that trap. His publishing record was described as "prodigious" even before he began as a history professor.

Terrence's master's thesis, published as "Crooked Past: The History of a Frontier Mining Camp: Fairbanks, Alaska," remains the best early history of our Golden Heart City and the scoundrel named E. T. Barnette.

Terrence accomplished something similar with *Nome: City of the Golden Beaches*, a lively version of his doctoral dissertation.

He wrote a study of navigable waters in Alaska, about indoor baseball in Nome, the history of the Alaska Equal Rights Act, wartime in Anchorage, the history of the Alaska Highway, and the twists and turns of the Alaska statehood movement. Over the years he has written dozens of papers and a shelf full of books and reports.

He's edited the *Alaska Journal* quarterly, written an economic history of Alaska, and published a weekly history column for the *Fairbanks Daily News-Miner*. He worked with leading Alaskans such as publisher Bob Henning and banker Elmer Rasmuson.

Henning was right when he said my brother had a "compulsion to dig out stories and tell them to others." At home in his library, surrounded by thousands of biographies, history books about every nation and region, novels, and government reports, he has these words from Samuel Johnson's dictionary preface posted just above his computer: "In this work, when it shall be found that much is omitted, let it not be forgotten that much likewise is performed..."

Beyond his own research and writing, he has been generous with time and ideas. I've heard countless testimonials about this from former students who have gone on to careers in history, government, business, education, and science.

This is also true in my case. My first two books would never have been written and published without his encouragement and commitment. He gave me the ideas for both books and suggestions on how to approach the material to capture readers' interest. It was at his insistence that I opened my book on the 1908 auto race from New York to Paris with the words, "It began in Times Square."

"You have to have a strong opening and everybody knows about Times Square," he told me more than once. At the University of Alaska Fairbanks, Terrence has won lots of awards and praise from students and fellow faculty members, though at times he encountered faculty members who figured that he was too enthusiastic and energetic for a historian.

"There is an eclectic quality to Terrence's work," one of his academic critics said early on, opposing a bid for tenure with what I think is actually a great compliment. The funniest complaint was from a fellow professor who faulted him because he "seems always to be in such a hurry," another unintended compliment from someone trying to rest on a laurel or two.

But when a faculty committee recommended him for tenure after just a couple of years on the job, they said he had uniformly positive comments from students and that his enthusiasm was a key ingredient. The committee said he was "one of the very best teachers at UAF."

For many years he taught Modern World History 100, an introductory offering that was also the largest class in the College of Liberal Arts. Terrence liked teaching this required class to freshmen because it provided a chance to demonstrate that history need not be dry and dull. At times that meant taking steps to provoke people to think and see the world in a new light.

"I hope my younger sister gets to take your course," a former History 100 student once wrote to him. "I am glad the university required it for me."

Terrence has had roughly 12,000 students over the years, never teaching the same course exactly the same way twice. The idea of recycling the same material over and over again never held any appeal.

His approach to lecturing is more a matter of improvisation, founded on preparation, which can lead to digressions that usually—but not always—relate to the material at hand.

Terrence has worked hard to get financial support for students who needed it and given his own money to the William R. Hunt History Scholarship and the Cole family scholarship we have set up in memory of our father, Bill Cole, and our oldest brother, Pat.

It is not the brilliant students that impress him the most, but those who work the hardest and find the energy for continual improvement. Education is not a passive experience, Terrence will tell you.

If he ran the university he would give every graduate a copy of *Walden* by Henry David Thoreau. It's a book that he recommends to Henry and Desmond, his sons, and one that he hopes that his daughter, Elizabeth, will learn to appreciate when she is older.

"I think it's another American Declaration of Independence," he said. "Every page of his book has some unbelievable stunning insights about human nature."

Nearly fifty years after coming to Alaska, here is one of those timeless insights from Thoreau that I think applies to my twin brother: "I learned this, at least, by my experiment: that if one advances confidently in the direction of his dreams, and endeavors to live the life which he has imagined, he will meet with a success unexpected in common hours."

A Note from Gerald McBeath

I first met Terrence in 1986 as a member of the UAF hiring committee that brought him to our campus, and was a member of the peer review committee when he was tenured. As interim dean of CLA in 1992, I selected Terrence to be Department Chair of History; later I served as chair of the social science peer review committee when he was a candidate for promotion to full professor in 1997–98. I recognized his potential then and observed his talents unfold as he moved through faculty ranks. The lives of academicians are usually uneventful and sometimes boring. Terrence's life has been different and more colorful, especially in his marriage to Gay Salisbury. Gay, with a plan to write about Balto (whose statue graces New York's Central Park), came to Fairbanks to learn about Alaska history, met Terrence the acclaimed expert, and they fell in love. This reminds me of a Chinese adage, in which elders encouraged young men to study diligently and become scholars, since wealth and maidens can be found in books. Terrence and Gay's marriage is an illustration of that Chinese wisdom.

During the last twenty years, my friendship with Terrence has grown. He has helped me in my transition from UAF political science to new projects, including some on Alaska history and biography. He is the kind of friend to others that I aspire to someday become myself.

TERRENCE COLE AS RESEARCHER AND WRITER

Gerald McBeath

Professor Terrence Cole has had a remarkable and distinctive career. Characteristics often associated with his work include breadth, border-crossing, exciting, enthusiastic, and engaging. We consider four areas where Terrence has marked out new territory in social science research, with examples drawn from his publications.

BORDER-CROSSING

Most academics are narrow specialists, working within one discipline and no more than one or two specializations throughout their careers. Terrence is distinctive because he has worked in five separate disciplinary areas: history, political science, economics, geography, and pedagogy.

Terrence took MA and PhD degrees in history, and his academic appointments have primarily been as professor of history at the University of Alaska Fairbanks. Many of his reports, articles, and books focus on history, an example of which is his most recent study: *Fighting for the 49th Star: C. W. Snedden and the Crusade for Alaska Statehood.*[1] Snedden was a long-term publisher of the *Fairbanks Daily News-Miner*, the farthest North newspaper, and one of the most active participants in the Alaska statehood movement. He had a strong relationship with

---

[1] Terrence Cole, *Fighting for the Forty-ninth Star: C. W. Snedden and the Crusade for Alaska Statehood* (Fairbanks: University of Alaska Foundation, 2010).

Fred Seaton, secretary of interior in the Eisenhower administration. From this base he was able to mobilize a national press campaign to move statehood legislation in Congress, against the entrenched opposition of political leaders of the deep South, who sought to stymie statehood efforts of Alaska and Hawaii, to ensure that segregation continued and civil rights legislation failed. Cole's volume tells another story, of the relationship between Snedden and Ted Stevens, his protégé (whom he mentored through the rest of his career).

Snedden's view was that the *News-Miner's* mission was "to remind friend and foe alike of the need to keep the promises of statehood alive."[2] Ted Stevens remarked on Snedden's influence when he told him in 1958: "(T)he only reason we really did anything this year . . . is that we would really have caught hell from you if we didn't."[3] While they joined forces on statehood, they had a longer-term influence on development of Alaska's oil resources and the creation of ANWR.

Many historians emphasize political history in their research and writing, and that is one basis for Terrence's work in political science. Political science emphasizes leadership, from global to local, and Terrence has had an unerring eye for tales of leaders, including their foibles. One good example is the *Pacific Northwest Quarterly* piece he wrote regarding "Wally Hickel's Big Garden Hose: The Alaska Water Pipeline to California."[4] This interesting article analyzes Governor Hickel's plan to bring Alaska water to thirsty California. Cole notes that most Alaskans thought the plan was preposterous and impractical, but many of Hickel's opponents, including environmentalists, admired his "imagination, energy, and initiative, even if they believed him prone to big project hallucinations."[5] A shorter piece, written for *American Heritage* in 1981, was titled "The Strange Story of the President's Desk."[6] This recounts the curious provenance of a desk

---

2   Cole, *Forty-ninth Star*, 453.
3   Ibid.
4   Terrence Cole, "Wally Hickel's Big Garden Hose: The Alaska Water Pipeline to California," *Pacific Northwest Quarterly*, v. 86, no. 2 (Spring 1995), 57–71.
5   Cole, "Garden Hose," 70.
6   Terrence Cole, "The Strange Story of the President's Desk," *American Heritage*, Vol. 32, No. 6 (October/November 1981), 62–64.

used in the Oval Office since the time of Rutherford Hayes. The timbers from which it was made came from an abandoned British ship, the *Resolute*, which had been sent to find a trace of explorer Sir John Franklin, whose crew disappeared in the late 1840s. Found by an American whaling crew in 1855, the ship was returned to the United Kingdom in the following year. Twenty years later, Queen Victoria ordered that timbers from the ship be made into a large desk and given to President Rutherford Hayes as a token of thanks. Lastly, Cole has also offered some very traditional political science analysis, as found in a report to the city of Fairbanks on "Cities and Boroughs: The Dual System of Local Government in Alaska."[7] This is bread-and-butter work, serving people in local governments who deal with the tangled jurisdictional lines of cities and boroughs under the Alaska Constitution.

Economics is another subject Professor Cole learned much about in pursuit of his interests, and on which he has written prolifically. This includes a monumental study of the National Bank of Alaska, on which he worked for several years with Elmer Rasmuson, long-term bank president. Titled *Banking on Alaska: The Story of the National Bank of Alaska* (published by the University of Alaska Press in 2001), Cole wrote the first volume of the bank's history, and then assisted Rasmuson in compilation of the second.[8] That expansive first volume covers the founders of the bank (Arthur Anderson and then the Rasmusons). It recounts the history of the Bank of Alaska from 1916 to 1950, and then the National Bank of Alaska to the present. Cole also discusses major events of Alaska's economic history during the same period, as it is difficult to disentangle the bank from major events such as the Great Depression, the Second World War, and the 1964 Earthquake. By 1990, NBA was the state's largest bank, holding close to 50 percent of all Alaska bank assets.

---

7   Terrence Cole, *Cities and Boroughs: The Dual System of Local Government in Alaska*, report, City Attorney's Office, City of Fairbanks (Fairbanks, August 2000).

8   Terrence Cole and Elmer E. Rasmuson, *Banking on Alaska: The Story of the National Bank of Alaska* (Fairbanks: University of Alaska Press, 2001).

Already in 1978, NBA operated thirty-four branches in nineteen communities. An important innovation of the bank was to change banking law to permit statewide branching. This enabled the bank to address the unique nature of Alaska: a very small population spread over an area one-fifth the size of the contiguous-forty-eight states, in which most communities had just one or two economic endeavors. In 1999, NBA assets were sold to Wells Fargo.

A second impressive study is Cole's analysis of what the state did with wealth brought to Alaska by the discovery of oil and gas at Prudhoe Bay in 1968. The paper emphasizes revenues, resources, and taxation.[9] At statehood, federal revenues declined somewhat, and natural resource production (of gold, copper, fish, and oil) was unstable. The territorial legislature had been reluctant to establish an income tax, and only did so under duress (at Governor Gruening's claim that the territory was nearly bankrupt). The Prudhoe Bay oil discovery in 1968, development of the Trans-Alaska Pipeline System (TAPS), and production beginning in 1977 at high oil prices were a boon to the state. In 1976 voters established the Alaska Permanent Fund, which became a stable source of wealth generation.

Cole concludes his study by stating:

(T)he State of Alaska was created as an economic development machine, with a wide variety of resources and powers, so that it could generate enough funds from natural resources production to sustain itself. Everyone accepted the fact that government services in Alaska would always be extraordinarily costly compared to those in smaller, more settled, less remote regions, and therefore the state would need to garner more revenues in proportion.

This strategy paid off handsomely with the oil strike on the North Slope in the 1960s, and thanks to the wisdom of the Permanent Fund, a significant portion of the one-time only oil dollars have been saved for posterity. But the fantastic size of the lucky oil

---

9   Terrence Cole, *Blinded by Riches: The Permanent Funding Problem and the Prudhoe Bay Effect* (Anchorage: Institute of Social and Economic Research, University of Alaska Anchorage, 2004).

bonanza tended to camouflage the underlying weaknesses of the Alaskan economy, a natural resource based economy dependent on fluctuating prices and the production of diminishing supplies of raw materials. No matter how much oil it ultimately produces, Prudhoe Bay is not permanent any more than the Kennecott copper mine was permanent. The antidote to the Kennecott Syndrome and the permanent funding problem was the creation of the Alaska Permanent Fund, which turned a portion of Prudhoe Bay into an infinitely renewable resource.[10]

Several chronicles of Alaska fiscal policy since completion of the pipeline have been written, and Terrence's work is among the best.

Dr. Cole's economic writings also touch on the issues of "federal neglect." He introduces Ernest Walker Sawyer, the first U.S. official hired specifically to promote Alaska's economic development. Sawyer believed that expansion of the Alaska Railroad was essential to growing the economy. Yet four years' effort to increase business for the government-built railway demonstrated lack of success, even with robust and sympathetic federal support.[11]

A fourth area of expertise is in geography and northern studies, which Terrence studied during his undergraduate years at UAF (1973–1976). Many works express the professor's fascination with geography over the last four decades. One example is *Nome: City of the Golden Beaches*.[12] This volume reviews the colorful history of the most famous gold rush town in Alaska, tracing its story from 1900. This book is accompanied by several descriptions of gold mining in Alaska, which he has kept alive through the UA Press Classic Reprint Series. For each of these gold discovery volumes, he has written introductions or forewords. His articles on geography also answered puzzles, such as accounting for the place names assigned spots in the wilderness lacking them. One piece explains how Robert Marshall, the first leader

---

10   Cole, *Blinded by Riches*, 112–13.

11   Terrence Cole, "Ernest Walker Sawyer and Alaska: The Dilemma of Northern Economic Development," *Pacific Northwest Quarterly* 82, no. 2 (April 1991).

12   Terrence Cole, *Nome: City of the Golden Beaches*, 1st ed., vol. 11, no. 1, Alaska Geographic (Anchorage: Alaska Geographic Society, 1984).

of the Wilderness Society, gave names based on traditional signs and orientations to a swath of the central Brooks Range.[13]

Even this does not exhaust the crossings Professor Cole has made into other disciplines and subdisciplines. For example, he ventured into ethnic studies in 1993,[14] as well as reference work on the Alaska-Yukon gold rush for an encyclopedia about Irish-Americans.[15]

Cole's teaching, research, and writing also cross over into pedagogy. In several forms, his work in this area expresses his duty to the next generation of teachers, researchers, and writers. In 2013 he printed a guide for teachers to use in making sense of the Alaska Constitution.[16] He also prepared materials for the new Alaska Studies curricular requirement in all Alaska schools. These efforts included development of a "history day" for students at the college and high school levels throughout the state, where students would present their work and be assessed by panels of judges. Terrence has taken students to academic conferences to present their original work, and he shepherds their work as an effective mentor, in what is an extremely time-consuming enterprise.

BREADTH OF PRINT MATERIAL

In the course of his career, Terrence has produced a very broad range of print materials. Part of his output reflects what one would expect of productive faculty members: books and monographs, refereed

---

13   Terrence Cole, "Placenames in Paradise: Robert Marshall and the Naming of the Alaska Wilderness," *Names: Journal of the American Name Society* 40, no. 2 (June 1992).

14   Terrence Cole, "The Hard Road to Klondike: Irish Pioneers in the Alaska-Yukon Gold Rush," edited by Tim Sarbaugh and James Walsh, "The Irish of the West," Special issue, *Journal of the West* (Manhattan, KS: Sunflower University Press): 93–102.

15   Terrence Cole, "Alaska-Yukon Gold Rush," in *The Encyclopedia of the Irish in America*, ed. Michael Glazer (Notre Dame, IN: University of Notre Dame Press, 1999).

16   Terrence Cole, "Hearing History: A Teacher's Guide to the Recordings of the Alaska Constitutional Convention, 1955–1956," Alaska Constitutional Convention Teacher's Guide, 2013, accessed April 5, 2018, http://www.accteachers guide.com.

journal articles, book chapters, and the like. Where Terrence's work diverges is in the books he has contributed to, edited, or compiled. There are a full twenty of these, mostly part of the UA Press Classic Reprint Series, and Cole has written forewords, prefaces, or introductions to each of them. The original authors include important political figures, explorers, and navigators such as Judge James Wickersham, Noel Wien, Knud Rasmussen, Charlie Brower, and Hudson Stuck. Bringing these works into the modern era is a service to the state. Cole has also written roughly forty short articles for journals such as the *Alaska Journal, Alaska Geographic, Alaskafest Magazine, Alaska Today*, and *Anchorage Magazine*. These are popular pieces covering a range of topics, including the various Alaska connections of lawman and gunslinger Wyatt Earp, novelists Dashiell Hammett and Jack London, and of course, baseball.[17] As a baseball fan, Cole describes the game's Alaska associations, the rugged northern conditions for the sport (including frozen tundra in Nome), and long summer nights during the early training of major league ballplayers. General readers are more easily drawn to such pieces than to refereed journal articles; these readers are informed as well as entertained.

Terrence has also prepared nearly twenty reports to government agencies or to satisfy research contracts. These answer questions asked by funders, such as a report on the University of Alaska's land grant issues in 1993.[18] Other reports have provided historical assessments of important streets in Fairbanks, such as the Illinois Street and Minnie Street corridors.[19] Such corridor analysis is critical for

---

17 Terrence Cole, "Wyatt Earp in Alaska: The Story of an Old Gunfighter," *Alaskafest Magazine*, January 1980; "Dashiell Hammett: Author in Alaska," *Anchorage Magazine*, May 1979; "Go Up O Elam': The Story of Jack London's Burning Daylight," *Alaska Journal* 6, no. 4 (Autumn 1976); "Baseball Above and Below Zero," *Alaska Journal* 13, no. 3 (Summer 1983).

18 Terrence Cole, *A Land Grant College Without the Land: A History of the University of Alaska's Federal Land Grant*, report, Statewide Office of Land Management, University of Alaska (1993).

19 Terrence Cole, *The Illinois Street Corridor: An Historical Assessment, Report to the Dept. of Transportation and Public Facilities*, report, Department of Transportation and Public Facilities, State of Alaska (June 1990); *Historic Resources of the Minnie Street Corridor, Fairbanks, Alaska*, report, Department of Transportation and Public Facilities, State of Alaska (August 1989).

state planning purposes, to protect historical sites among other reasons.

Others look at watersheds such as the Talkeetna/Susitna River drainages or the Beluga Study Region (prepared for USDA's Soil Conservation Service); still more examine historic uses of rivers such as the Chisana and Nabesna Rivers and the Upper Susitna River (prepared for the Department of Natural Resources). His work for DNR supported its RS 2477 claims to rights of way across federal land and waters, which cover 60 percent of Alaska lands. When RS 2477 was repealed in 1976, significantly changing federal land management policy, the state DNR sought to ensure that as many routes qualified for the RS 2477 statute as possible. Professor Cole's studies of river basins included shore lands (land under navigable waters such as the Yukon), tidelands, and submerged lands, and he was able to establish previous use of "public highways" crossing public lands. This is indeed a broad and important range of topics to do research and writing on.

Finally, Terrence has popularized exhibitions, such as his 1992 monograph, *Alaska or Bust: The Promise of the Road North; A Catalog of an Exhibit on the History of the Alaska Highway* (1992).[20]

EXCITING USES OF OTHER MEDIA

Like other scholars, Cole has presented his research to local, state, and national professional associations. He goes well beyond in his extensive list of TV broadcasts and shows—for PBS, regional stations such as WGBH and WQED, the History Channel, and even the BBC. These topics cover important events in Alaska's development such as statehood, the Alaska Pipeline, the Alaska Highway, and Gold Fever. Cole also served as a history advisor to the first BBC broadcast of the mountain-climbing documentary *Mountain Men*.[21]

Another film, for which Cole was a co-writer and which has been very popular and frequently played (including in my classes in Alaska

---

20 Terrence Cole, *Alaska or Bust: The Promise of the Road North* (Fairbanks: University of Alaska Museum, 1992).

21 *Mountain Men*, prod. Mike Conefrey (United Kingdom: British Broadcasting Company (BBC), 2001), TV movie.

politics and government) is *The 49th Star*, Alaska's statehood story.[22] And another, focusing on the relationship between Alaska and the federal union, for which Cole was also an important resource, was *Mr. Alaska: Bob Bartlett Goes to Washington*.[23] A continuation of *The 49th Star*, this documentary chronicles Bartlett's roots as a small-town reporter and gold miner to his position as Alaska's Territorial Delegate. When Bartlett (by then a U.S. senator) died in 1968, he was the most respected and beloved political leader in the state.

Cole was also the initiator of the "Alaska Statehood pioneers" video recordings, produced by 360 North, in which pioneer Alaskans recounted their contributions and involvement in forming the state. Subjects talked about their lives in Alaska and reminisced about territorial Alaska and the campaign for statehood. Terrence interviewed surviving members of the Constitutional Convention—Vic Fischer, Tom Stewart, Jack Coghill, George Rogers, Katie Hurley, Maynard Londberg, George Sundborg, and Jay Hammond. He continued interviewing prominent Alaskans for several years, thereby helping preserve Alaska's history.

Another creative use of other media is Terrence's collection and exposition of caricatures and cartoons (which he also uses extensively in his classes).[24]

BALANCED AND ENGAGED

Professor Cole's high level of energy and enthusiasm does not concentrate dominantly on people, or places, or things (events). Instead, the body of his research work and writing reflects a balance among all three.

As noted above, the people Terrence writes about do include notable figures from Alaska's past. Yet they also incorporate lesser-known

---

22   *The 49th Star*, dir. Michael Letzring (United States: KUAC-TV/University of Alaska Fairbanks, 2006), DVD.

23   *Mr. Alaska: Bob Bartlett Goes to Washington*, dir. Michael Letzring (United States: Fairbanks: KUAC-TV, 2009), DVD.

24   One strong example: Terrence Cole, "Polar Cartoon Characters: Cook, Peary and the Race to the Pole," *Alaska History* 11, no. 2 (Fall 1996).

characters such as Brian Garfield, the novelist and screenwriter who crafted *The Thousand-Mile War*, describing conflict between Japan and the U.S. in the Aleutian campaign of World War II; William Haskell's *Two Years in the Klondike and Alaskan Gold Fields*, the narrative of the life of a gold-seeker including its dangers, hardships, and privations; and Joseph Grinnell's *Gold Hunting in Alaska*—his accounting as an American field biologist and zoologist of exploration in the Kotzebue Sound region where he discovered more than seven hundred new bird specimens.[25] The way in which Cole selects and writes about these figures enlarges the record of Alaska's development, acknowledging the state was formed by multiple forces and personalities.

Places occupy an equally large part of Terrence's repertoire. Nome, frontier Fairbanks, Anchorage, Copper Center, Arctic Village, and the Klondike are all featured, among many others. As mentioned above, Dr. Cole spends great attention on streets, rivers, and highways.

Finally, important events at the global, national, regional, and local level further attract Dr. Cole's interest. These include books and articles on the air war and the world war in Alaska, literature on polar exploration, smaller expeditions, and even the landing of a Zeppelin.

It is the rare social scientist who attempts and achieves the kind of balance that Terrence Cole does in his work.

CONCLUSION

The result of the four patterns here is that Terrence is one of the best-known Alaska writers in history, geography, political science, and economics. Already he has received the main awards available to a University of Alaska Fairbanks professor: Several ASUAF awards for being an outstanding professor, the Emil Usibelli Distinguished Teaching Award (1994), and the Edith R. Bullock Award for

---

25 Brian Garfield, *Thousand-Mile War: World War II in Alaska and the Aleutians* (Fairbanks: University of Alaska Press, 2010); William B. Haskell, *Two Years in the Klondike and Alaskan Gold-fields, 1896–1898: A Thrilling Narrative of Life in the Gold Mines and Camps*(Fairbanks: University of Alaska Press, 1998); Joseph Grinnell, *Gold Hunting in Alaska* (Anchorage: Alaska Northwest Publishing, 1983).

outstanding service to the University of Alaska (1998). He received the Governor's Award for the Humanities in 2006, the Alaska Historian of the Year award in 2011, and with his brother Dermot, the Boy Scouts of America award as Fairbanks Citizen of the Year (2011).

Terrence has had a professional life filled with accomplishments, and has set an exceptionally high standard for the contributions we academics should seek to make to the public.

BIBLIOGRAPHY

Cole, Terrence. "The Hard Road to Klondike: Irish Pioneers in the Alaska." In *Journal of the West*, 93–102. The Irish of the West. Manhattan, KS: Sunflower University Press.

———. "Go Up O Elam': The Story of Jack London's Burning Daylight." *Alaska Journal* 16, no. 4 (Autumn 1976): 235–41.

———. "Dashiell Hammett: Author in Alaska." *Anchorage Magazine*, May 1979, 33–35.

———. "Wyatt Earp in Alaska: The Story of an Old Gunfighter." *Alaskafest Magazine*, January 1980, 31.

———. "Baseball Above and Below Zero." *Alaska Journal* 13, no. 3 (Summer 1983): 129–35.

———. *Nome: City of the Golden Beaches*. 1st ed. Vol. 11, No. 1. Alaska Geographic. Anchorage: Alaska Geographic Society, 1984.

———. "Ernest Walker Sawyer and Alaska: The Dilemma of Northern Economic Development." *Pacific Northwest Quarterly* 82, no. 2 (April 1991): 42–50.

———. "Placenames in Paradise: Robert Marshall and the Naming of the Alaska Wilderness." *Names: Journal of the American Name Society* 40, no. 2 (June 1992): 99–116.

———. *Alaska or Bust: The Promise of the Road North*. Fairbanks: University of Alaska Museum, 1992.

———. *A Land Grant College Without the Land: A History of the University of Alaska's Federal Land Grant*. Report. Statewide Office of Land Management, University of Alaska. 1993.

———. "Polar Cartoon Characters: Cook, Peary and the Race to the Pole." *Alaska History* 11, no. 2 (Fall 1996).

———. "Alaska-Yukon Gold Rush." In *The Encyclopedia of the Irish in America*, edited by Michael Glazer, 9–11. Notre Dame, IN: University of Notre Dame Press, 1999.

Cole, Terrence, and Elmer E. Rasmuson. *Banking on Alaska: The Story of the National Bank of Alaska*. Fairbanks: University of Alaska Press, 2001.

———. *Blinded by Riches: The Permanent Funding Problem and the Prudhoe Bay Effect*. Anchorage: Institute of Social and Economic Research, University of Alaska Anchorage, 2004.

———. *Fighting for the Forty-ninth Star*. Fairbanks: University of Alaska Foundation, 2010.

———. "Hearing History: A Teacher's Guide to the Recordings of the Alaska Constitutional Convention, 1955–1956." Alaska Constitutional Convention Teacher's Guide. 2013. Accessed April 5, 2018. http://www.accteachersguide.com/.

———. *Historic Resources of the Minnie Street Corridor, Fairbanks, Alaska*. Report. Department of Transportation and Public Facilities, State of Alaska. August 1989. 1–46.

———. *Cities and Boroughs: The Dual System of Local Government in Alaska*. Report. City Attorney's Office, City of Fairbanks. Fairbanks, August 2000.

———. *The Illinois Street Corridor: An Historical Assessment, Report to the Dept. of Transportation and Public Facilities*. Report. Department of Transportation and Public Facilities, State of Alaska. June 1990. 1–20.

Garfield, Brian. *Thousand-Mile War: World War II in Alaska and the Aleutians*. Fairbanks: University of Alaska Press, 2010.

Grinnell, Joseph. *Gold Hunting in Alaska*. Anchorage: Alaska Northwest Publishing, 1983.

Haskell, William B. *Two Years in the Klondike and Alaskan Gold-fields, 1896–1898: A Thrilling Narrative of Life in the Gold Mines and Camps*. Fairbanks: University of Alaska Press, 1998.

Mountain Men. Produced by Mike Conefrey. United Kingdom: British Broadcasting Company (BBC), 2001. TV Movie.

Mr. Alaska: Bob Bartlett Goes to Washington. Directed by Michael Letzring. United States: Fairbanks: KUAC-TV, 2009. DVD.

The 49th Star. Directed by Michael Letzring. United States: KUAC-TV/University of Alaska Fairbanks, 2006. DVD.

A Note from Mary F. Ehrlander

I first met Terrence Cole when I enrolled in his U.S. history course in spring 1990. I found his teaching style so engaging that I remember thinking *if only all the boys' (my three sons') teachers could be just like this.* Later I took a graduate course from him, one of those that prepared me well for my PhD program at the University of Virginia. When I returned to UAF in 2001 as a faculty member in the History Department and Northern Studies Program, Terrence became a colleague of mine. I benefited from his mentorship and especially appreciated his encouragement of various research projects I took on. Over the years he's become a dear friend. I appreciate his intellect and enjoy his goofy sense of humor, but most of all, I have always admired his devotion to students' learning and well-being.

THE INIMITABLE PROFESSOR TERRENCE COLE

Mary F. Ehrlander

In the past thirty years, I have learned to know Terrence Cole as a professor, colleague, mentor, and treasured friend. As our relationship has evolved and matured, I have never lost sight of my first impressions of him as *my* professor. But having worked alongside him for seventeen years, I have developed a deeper appreciation of his commitment to students and his love of learning. I know of no faculty member more dedicated to students' education and well-being. His infectious enthusiasm has spurred countless students to pursue research culminating in university degrees, publications, and careers. As former student Hild Peters puts it: "Dr. Cole creates his own weather patterns; a simple encounter with him could be a transformational moment in a person's life." Of the twenty Northern Studies MA alumni whose advisory committees he chaired, seven earned PhDs in history, and an eighth is now an interdisciplinary PhD student. No other former or current Arctic & Northern Studies faculty member has a record that matches his. The impacts of his thirty-year teaching career reach far beyond the university, multiplying through the lives and work of his students.

Terrence's celebrity status extends from the elementary, middle, and high school students who have participated in local History Day competitions; to nationwide viewers of his appearances on PBS and the History Channel; to audiences at his conference lectures in Alaska, the Lower Forty-Eight, and worldwide; to passengers on Alaska cruise ships. Of his public service endeavors, National History Day has unquestionably most gratified him and has had the broadest impact. He and Fairbanks teacher Maida Buckley initiated the local program twenty years ago in 1998, and since then tens of thousands of Fairbanks youngsters have known the satisfaction of solving mysteries and producing knowledge through their own diligence. National History Day accepts only middle and high school student projects, but several years ago, Terrence and Maida created a Novice category in Fairbanks to accommodate elementary school students' interest in the event. This move encapsulated Terrence's can-do spirit, his penchant for improvisation, and his tenderness for children. His encouragement of the love of history, research, and scholarship has left an indelible mark on a generation of young Alaskans, inspiring them to believe in themselves and their dreams, while also reminding them that excellence requires hard work.

My first experience with Professor Terrence Cole occurred in 1988, when I enrolled in his U.S. history course. His lectures, punctuated with anecdotes and wisecracks, kept us alert. He typically rushed into the classroom, carrying a jumble of transparencies, mostly historical political cartoons and maps, to illustrate his points. He regularly committed blunders, such as spilling his coffee on the overhead projector, tripping on its cord, writing on its glass plate with a permanent marker, and once breaking a faucet in the room. These moments provided entertainment, but the course's true value lay in the life that he brought to the subject matter, and its relevance to our own.

Later I took a graduate-level course from him, which turned out to be the most challenging course I had ever taken. In it, we were required to read a book and write a "précis" on it once a week. When he returned our first assignments, we learned that few of us knew what a précis was. Terrence distributed copies of the one submission that had met the mark. This put us on track, but he kept up the pressure, week after week, always demanding more of us. Three years later, Terrence's knack for engaging and educating students won him UAF's Emil Usibelli Distinguished Teaching Award. Eventually, his teaching methods and tactics would become legendary.

For many years, Terrence taught *20th Century World History*, a course in UAF's core curriculum. This freshman-level course requirement enrolled many students who were neither prepared to do well nor pleased to be taking the class. Terrence tried to connect with each of them, and for them to grasp the opportunities that a college degree could bring. Much of the wisdom he dispensed pertained to life skills, rather than history *per se*. For some years, he began the course with his "Don't Blame the Teacher" lecture. "Can't make it to class? Not the teacher's fault. Can't understand the assignment? Get help, it's not the teacher's fault," he repeated. His former teaching assistant Brittany Retherford muses: "I loved that lecture...he encouraged students from day one to be responsible for themselves. It was a wonderful way to set a standard for them." She clarifies, "Of course, Terrence is so sweet and lenient, and he really admires his students who are juggling life struggles...One semester, a pregnant student was so nervous about missing the final exam because it coincided with her due date. When she told Terrence, he just gave her such a warm smile and made some joke, and I could see her nervousness melt away. They came up with a solution."

His animated lectures often incorporated both visual and sound effects. Former graduate student David Jessup, who sat in on Terrence's world history class for three semesters, recalls: "On the day when Dr. Cole described the Japanese attack on Pearl Harbor, he played a recording of Franklin Roosevelt's December 8th address to Congress. As Roosevelt, in his speech, mentioned one Japanese bombing target after another, Dr. Cole kept perfect pace, circling one location after another on a map of the Pacific projected on the front screen from an overhead projector. While letting President Roosevelt do all the talking, Dr. Cole made an unforgettable visual display of the extent of the Japanese attacks on December 7, 1941. Everyone left the room with a better understanding of the scale of the Pacific War." Jessup recollects that Terrence is "a master" of the visual aid. "During his lecture on the atomic bombings of Hiroshima and Nagasaki, he left an image projected behind him of an utterly devastated city. Only at the end of the lecture did he tell us that we were not looking at Hiroshima or

Nagasaki. We had been looking at an image of Tokyo after American firebombing with 'conventional' weapons."

Dirk Tordoff describes his classroom experience with Terrence similarly: "As an instructor Terrence is immersed in a subject so completely it's as if he just stepped out of that era. His lectures are an enthusiastic ride through time, complete with short detours to visit interesting personalities and events pertinent to the time that are often overlooked by other historians."

Knowing that many students not only disliked reading but did not know *how* to read for meaning, Terrence assigned Mortimer Adler and Charles Van Doren's classic, *How to Read a Book*. Meanwhile, he regularly referred to books he had read, bringing the authors to life and inviting students to engage, as if in conversation with them. In recent years he required Victor Frankl's *Man's Search for Meaning* in his World History class, not so much to teach about the Holocaust as to urge his students to seek meaning in their own lives. If Frankl could find purpose in his life at Auschwitz, surely we can discover meaning in our own lives today, he insisted.

Terrence's choice of literature for this first-year history class illustrates his philosophy of teaching: his mission is to inspire the love of learning, to facilitate students' intellectual growth, and to guide them in attaining their educational and life goals.

An avid proponent of a liberal education, Terrence typically began his *20th Century World History* course centuries earlier in the Scientific Revolution and the Age of Enlightenment, when questioning previously held truths led to dramatic changes in humans' understanding of the world and to the belief in our right and capacity for self-government. Students typically indulged such detours, finding the notion of questioning, especially challenging authority, familiar and appealing. His pushing them to reconsider their own assumptions, however, led to discomfort. His reasoning and examples unsettled, and even angered, some students.

He railed against irrational thinking, including nationalism and religious parochialism, because it leads us to diminish the humanity of others and to dismiss competing ideas outright. The brilliance of the liberties enshrined in our First Amendment, he insisted, lay not only in the foundation they laid for self-governance and the protection of individual rights, but in the space they provided for the advancement of knowledge and understanding. Irmelin Gram-Hanssen, a former teaching assistant, recalls: "Terrence always knew how to make an impression and how to make the students rethink what they thought they knew...the class was about so much more than history...He gave his students a solid introduction to critical thinking...He wanted (them) to be wary of simple answers to complex questions and to engage in critical reflection before reaching their conclusions." She concludes: "At the end of the day, his teaching style and methods were a result of his solid belief in the ability of each and every student to connect the dots, to question assumptions and explore history as a lens to understand their own time. This was his gift to his students (whether they recognized it as such or not!)." Brittany Retherford recollects: "A lot of students who went through his class would tell me that Terrence was the first professor they'd had who made them think. And he did."

Students sometimes became lost in his scene setting, big ideas, dramatic stories, and asides. Some were never sure whether his antics are merely part of his shtick, or whether they related to a key point in the day's lecture. Charity Curlee vividly remembers Terrence knocking the clock off the wall the first day of class, although his purpose eludes her. For several semesters he lugged around a six-foot pencil a student had given him. Did he use it to make a point about Henry Petroski's microhistory *The Pencil: A History of Design and Circumstance*?

Such seeming digressions caused more than a few students anxiety. Occasionally one raised a hand to ask: "Is this going to be on the test?" While some mistook his rabbit trails for absentmindedness, Chris Cannon recognized that it was actually his *intense focus* that sometimes gave the impression of distractedness. One evening years ago in his *Polar Exploration and Its Literature* class, for instance, Terrence began his lecture with the overhead projector cord in his hand. "Time ticked away as he lectured with that projector cord waving around in his hand. Some students reminded him several times to turn around and plug the cord into the wall, but he was too absorbed in the class to make it to the wall to plug in the cord. With only a few minutes left one student said something like 'Terrence, stop and go plug in the projector.' At that point Terrence said... 'Ah, screw it.' We never did see those visual materials... I just remember how his ability to cater to emergent topics that arose in class (whatever they were) was sometimes more important than following the lesson plan. Terrence is very good at living in the present."

Hild Peters, with wonder: "He could never find the one paper he thought he brought to class, but he could tell you what book, what edition, and on what page an interesting quote was located."

Terrence's immense knowledge and recall of Alaskana and polar exploration literature generates frequent requests for advice from both seasoned and budding historians. Pinning him down to pick his brain can be challenging. Those who succeed are in for an unforgettable ride. He has sat with students for hours, his laptop at hand, suggesting one publication after the other, and emailing links to the works. Students leave such encounters with not only a lasting impression of the remarkable scope of his knowledge, but an appreciation of the rare privilege they have enjoyed in capturing the undivided attention of this learned man.

His devotion to students' writing evokes similar awe. Carolyn Kozak Loeffler prizes the gift of his writing mentorship: "Although a conversation with Terrence can feel like a wild ride down endless rabbit holes, he is hyper focused with your paper in front of him. The time he's spent combing through my writing sentence by sentence, sometimes focusing on a single word, has proved invaluable to my writing." Brittany Retherford treasures the warmth a simple gesture conveyed. As she struggled with polishing her thesis, Terrence sent her Samuel Eliot Morison's essay "History as a Literary Art." She noted: "Terrence always looks for how to relate complex ideas to people in a simpler way... It truly is an art."

Victoria Smith, Director of Student Support Services at UAF, whom Terrence has guided both as an undergraduate and graduate student, says of his role in her academic life: "Terrence is the ultimate mentor... He sees the best in you, even when you can't see it in yourself—perhaps especially when you can't see it in yourself... Some of the times that I've felt most welcome/intelligent/worthy have been when I'm around Terrence. I think we knowingly, and sometimes unknowingly, surround ourselves with people we admire and want to emulate. If I can be even a fraction of the advisor to others that he's been to me, then I will know that I've made him proud."

Terrence's student-centered teaching philosophy extends to exposing learners to unique and memorable experiences outside the classroom. A 1999 special topics course on the *Exxon Valdez* oil spill included travel to two conferences marking the tenth anniversary of the disaster, one in Valdez and one in Anchorage. David Jessup recalls: "The class took two university SUVs from Fairbanks to Valdez, where we spent the night in the local school, attended the conference, and watched spill response vessels demonstrating their speed and maneuverability in the Sound. Then we headed toward Anchorage, stopping for dinner at a motel restaurant in Glennallen." The excursion derailed for half of the group when the van carrying Terrence and David broke down there in Glenallen. "There was only one room available at the motel that night. We all crowded into it, and most of us slept on the floor... a vehicle and driver (came) to fetch us and bring us back to Fairbanks. Dr. Cole was not happy. But the *Exxon Valdez* course is an example of his taking the opportunity to provide students with an experience that they would never have had otherwise."

One year he took his *Polar Exploration and Its Literature* class on a field trip to the UAF Institute of Arctic Biology's Toolik Field Station, which provides facilities and support for Arctic research. Terrence and students piled into a twelve-passenger van to make the 285-mile trek up the Dalton Highway. Snowfall delayed their return home, but the students made the most of it, watching *The Big Lebowski* and having a snowball fight in Wiseman. "But we also learned a lot about fascinating research from the scientists on the ground," Brittany Retherford remembers. "We toured the buildings that were constructed to withstand the harsh climate. It was perfect—this is today's polar exploration research, and Terrence was excited about sharing it with us."

For many years Terrence mentored the UAF History honors society and raised money to take students to Phi Alpha Theta's annual conference to present their research. One year he took eighteen students to the conference. Often he has opened doors for students, providing them with educational and career-enhancing opportunities they never could have imagined. For instance, he recently pushed past bureaucratic tape to take graduate students Katie Hayden and Anne Rittgers to a UArctic program on extractive industries in Mirny and Yakutsk in the Sakha Republic. As Anne relates: "To hell with rules, or deadlines, or other barriers; Terrence never hesitated to find a way—even when there seemed to be no way—for his students to follow their wildest dreams." When he accepted an invitation to provide a lecture on the construction of the DEW Line at a fall 2017 NORAD symposium in Colorado Springs, he asked if his PhD student Lt. Col. Russ Vanderlugt could accompany him. Illness kept Terrence from the conference, but Russ moderated a panel of Canadian academics and high-ranking defense officials discussing Canada's new defense policy. The conference proved invaluable as Russ prepares for a future as a Department of Defense strategist with expertise in North America and northern latitudes. He explains: "The NORAD Symposium was a high-level 'by invitation only' conference on North American defense. (It) provided excellent international exposure and networking opportunities with senior academics and military officers, along with U.S. and Canadian State and Defense Department officials." Russ's experience exemplifies Terrence's tireless efforts to elevate and showcase students.

Terrence's interest in his students reaches beyond academics to finances. He counsels students to avoid taking more loans than necessary. He once invited a student couple to live in his basement for a year, to spare them the cost of rent. He and his siblings have endowed a scholarship at UAF, and Terrence donates regularly to this and other scholarships. He has secured grants for history projects that fund graduate students' tuition. His vast network of professionals have sometimes provided summer employment for his students. Former student Cary Curlee recalls an incident that exemplifies Terrence's preoccupation with student welfare: "I was walking with him on campus, on the first day of the semester, and we ran into some high-ranking staff members. He spoke with them about a small number of students who still didn't have funding. I was impressed with these folks, relatively important people by all appearances, putting their heads together to think of ways to obtain funding for a few students who needed it. It occurred to me these folks were putting students first. Ultimately, helping people should be everyone's primary goal. Terrence's sure is."

Co-teaching Terrence's *Polar Exploration and Its Literature* course in spring 2018 allowed me to observe and reflect on the qualities and practices of this remarkable intellect and educator. To be clear, I was not *actually* co-teaching the course, but rather providing a bit of structure and standing prepared to fill in as needed. We issued an invitation to former students and the public at large to join us whenever they please, as Terrence taught his signature class this last time. I sensed that he was at his inspirational best this semester. Although he jokingly attributed occasional lapses of memory to "chemo-brain," his memory of polar exploration events, actors, and literature astonished us. Even more captivating were his tales about the books he brought to class each week—works he has collected over the years in used bookstores, library sales, and online. Some pertain to polar exploration, others not at all. As he opened each work, he recounted the story of when he purchased it, sometimes noting the price, and then imparted the work's special meaning to him. Often, he turned to a memorable passage and read it aloud, as if poring over the book for the hundredth time. His treatment of George Hamlin Fitch's 1916 *Comfort Found in Good Old Books* perfectly portrayed his own sentiments about the written word.

His cancer diagnosis has prompted Terrence to reflect upon the meaning of life and how he wants to spend the precious interval that remains to him. That he chooses to revisit the literary treasures he has collected over the years and share them with his students testifies not only to his affection for the books but to his devotion to his students. Consciously or unconsciously, as he performed this weekly ritual, Terrence modeled the habits of mind of the consummate scholar, as he encourages his listeners to consider a more intimate relationship with their own books. I suspect that twenty, thirty, and forty years from now, students and guests who have partaken in this rite will remember little of the readings on our syllabus, but they will retain a vision of Professor Terrence Cole regaling them with stories of the books that have piqued his imagination and enriched his life.

I HAVE KNOWN TERRENCE COLE

Ronald K. Inouye

I have known Terrence Cole in many roles: teacher, colleague, researcher, advocate, cajoler, chronicler, and jester to those who may be otherwise unreachable. Through the years, we have worked together on conferences, workshops, and lectures for students as well as off-campus community events.

The annual Alaska Historical Society conferences have provided me a glimpse into Terrence's UAF history professor role. Always encouraging students to present papers, he shepherds them through the processes of researching, presenting, and publication. These conferences become occasions when current and past students, some now professional historians themselves, gather to learn and celebrate together and extend UAF relationships into many museums, historical societies, and communities beyond Fairbanks.

Historically, university presses publish significant scholarly works, frequently requiring subsidies. As an advocate for the University of Alaska Press and series editor for its Classic Reprint Series, Terrence sought to reissue Judge James Wickersham's 1938 memoir, *Old Yukon*. The University of Alaska Press was interested in the project, but needed external financial underwriting. Terrence successfully obtained a $10,000 grant from the local Tanana-Yukon Historical Society, penned a foreword, and edited and abridged the volume, reissued in 2009 as *Old Yukon: Tales, Trails, and Trials—Memoirs of Judge Wickersham*.

Camaraderie is another distinctive Terrence Cole hallmark. When the infamous History Department troika of Claus-M Naske, Bill Hunt, and Terrence Cole, as well as students and hangers-on, were in Anchorage awaiting a plane departure to the annual Historical Society conference, the decision was made to kill time at the local "Book Cache." The group entered the bookstore, and the three authors immediately stalked the shelves looking for their titles. Within minutes, Claus loudly summoned a clerk and demanded his titles be shifted to more trafficked aisles. Challenged by such leadership, Bill similarly requested prominence for his titles. The clerks were befuddled! Then Claus and Bill ordered Terrence to follow suit. We were amused—and embarrassed—and the clerks panicked! Terrence then turned on his seniors; knowingly amused and yet embarrassed himself by the behavior, he attempted to calm them down, which intensified their efforts before this willing audience of minions.

Fortunately, airplane departure time was near, so the group departed. The clerks were glad to see us leave. Terrence earned the moniker of "negotiator," and the rest of us had just witnessed the camaraderie of the "Gang of Three."

Teacher, colleague, researcher, advocate, cajoler, chronicler, jester, and negotiator—these all aptly describe Terrence Cole.

A Note from Carolyn Kozak Loeffler

I sat down with Terrence Cole early in my first semester at UAF. I had heard many stories about his humor, energy, and eccentric teaching style from my colleagues at the Anchorage Museum, and I was eager to meet him in person, albeit a little nervous. His reputation preceded him, and I—having been away from academia for almost seven years—felt insecure about my new hat as a graduate student. I had read his books. I loved his narrative style. Imposter syndrome aside, I knew I wanted Terrence Cole on my graduate advisory committee.

We met in the Wood Center in early January. Terrence's smile and laugh immediately put me at ease. We talked about long-term goals and professional ambitions, research interests, and previous projects. I rambled on excitedly about visual imagery, propaganda, and national identities. Terrence patiently listened, nodding his head. When I was done, he looked at me and said, "I think you should write about the polar bear." Admittedly, this wasn't the thesis I had in mind. It seemed too far removed from the ideas that made me tick. But I started seeing polar bears everywhere—selling political agendas and consumer products alike. "He's right," I thought. "There's something happening here."

Even aside from his academic guidance, Terrence is a beloved mentor. Countless conversations in parking lots and driveways and coffee shops have helped me navigate through big transitions—from coping with grief and mourning to celebrating my new married life. There is something oddly reassuring about a man in a bike helmet, covered with hi-viz flashing safety lights, gesturing wildly about some deep interest he and I have shared. Despite chronic overbookings and always running late, Terrence still manages to find time to check in and provide support for all of his students. He goes above and beyond to set others up for success—an example I hope I can replicate in my own life.

Thank you for your generosity, Terrence. It is a thing of wonder. It fills my cup—I always have more to give to others when I think of you.

ARCTIC TERROR

The Polar Bear in American Visual Culture (thesis excerpt)

Carolyn Kozak Loeffler

It is paradoxical that new opportunities are opening for our nations at the same time we understand that the threat of carbon emissions is imminent.[1]
—Olafur Ragnar Grimsson, President of Iceland (1996–2016)

Apart from uncertainty regarding the progress of climate change in the North, perhaps the greatest source of befuddlement is our proverbial desire to have our cake there and to eat it too.[2]
—John McCannon, American historian

By virtually any standard of measurement, the Arctic is hotter than ever before—physically, politically, and emotionally. Rising ocean temperatures, opening sea lanes, disappearing pack ice, and global fear of environmental devastation have combined to make the Arctic Ocean the great question mark of the future of the human race, with *Ursus maritimus*, the "sea bear," at least for now, standing in as a substitute for *Homo sapiens*.

In human eyes the polar bear has long been a paradoxical creature, mirroring the same paradox at the center of America's relationship to the Arctic today, with the region seeming to offer two widely

---

1   Andrew E. Kramer, "Warming Revives Dream of Sea Route in Russian Arctic," *New York Times*, October 17, 2011.
2   John McCannon, *A History of the Arctic: Nature, Exploration and Exploitation* (London: Reaktion Books Ltd., 2012), 306.

divergent paths to the future. Stretches of uninterrupted ecosystems and wilderness areas are framed as resource warehouses on the one hand, or sacred environmental preserves on the other, pitting historical frontier identities against moral obligations to future generations. Both perspectives expound futurity, either promising deliverance from future energy crises and resource shortages, or further instances of environmental and moral degradation. They also illustrate the frequent tension between citizenship and consumerism. The polar bear—in its transition from ferocious to vulnerable, from a symbol of cold to a symbol of melt—illuminates the shifting historical perspectives of humanity's environmental responsibilities and the roots of this ideological divide.

As a charismatic but contentious symbol, the polar bear illustrates the ideological conflict over climate change between competing stakeholders, who deliberately frame their perspective to appeal to either the citizen identity or the consumer identity. Formally, the act of framing may be defined as "conscious and strategic efforts by groups of people to fashion shared understandings of the world and of themselves that legitimate and motivate collective action."[3] Framing processes help draw boundaries around a given problem, outline its causes, and, most importantly, identify responses or remedies. Framing a complex issue like climate change increases its accessibility and saliency to policy makers and the public alike, functioning to highlight linkages between issues, and thereby galvanize political action. Framing occurs in all forms of media—including photographs, charts, graphs, cartoons, illustrations, and the moving image—and spreads through magazines, television, films, radio, an ever-growing number of websites, and ubiquitous social media platforms. This chapter explores how various stakeholders have used polar bear imagery to frame Arctic and environmental issues to shape public perceptions and sell specific ideologies. Image and discourse analysis, communications theory, and semiotic theory reveal how the polar bear became a symbol of melt.

---

3   Kate O'Neill, *The Environment and International Relations, Themes in International Relations* (Cambridge: Cambridge University Press, 2009), 31.

With countless images now available in the palms of our hands, it is more important than ever to recognize that despite the old adage, seeing is not believing. As Susan Sontag famously states in *On Photography*: "photographs are as much an interpretation of the world as paintings and drawings are."[4] Problem definition itself *is* a process of image making, through which the images attribute cause, blame, and responsibility. Because climate change impacts in the Arctic remain abstract and distant to the vast majority of Americans, widely distributed imagery plays a vital role in framing public opinions of the region's issues and furthering understanding of the region itself.

UNDERSTANDING FRAMING EFFECTS: THE ARCTIC REFUGE

The ongoing debate and controversy surrounding the Arctic National Wildlife Refuge (ANWR, the Refuge) demonstrates the ways in which opposing stakeholders frame specific issues to sway public opinion. As in any political campaign, unbiased analyses about Arctic drilling are difficult to find. Some economic studies demonstrate that ANWR's oil reserves will save America from future high oil prices and foreign oil dependency. Some support the contrary. Some environmental impact studies conclude that oil and gas development would be disastrous for the Porcupine Caribou Herd and vulnerable polar bear populations, and other studies conclude responsible practices would result in negligible effects.

The largely uninformed American public relies on this contradictory evidence to form opinions about a place few will ever see or understand. Under these circumstances, emotional arguments and images compete over whether drilling for oil should be permitted, with the stakes being nothing short of life or death on either side, no matter if the goal is to protect pristine lands for future generations or to ensure the economic security of the United States.

Opinion polls conducted in the early 2000s regarding U.S. energy policy and opening the Arctic National Wildlife Refuge to oil

---

4   Susan Sontag, *On Photography* (New York: Straus and Giroux, 1977), 6–7.

development clearly demonstrate the potent effects of framing to sway participants one direction or another. Survey researchers frequently asked Americans whether they supported an increase in domestic oil production. The results ranged wildly, affected by a number of framing factors. When framed as a way "to reduce the country's dependence on imports of Middle East oil," 73 percent approved of "increasing oil drilling in the U.S."[5] However, support for drilling diminished when the question was reframed to balance national security concerns with reminders of environmental impacts, or when pollsters encouraged respondents to consider "other solutions," like energy conservation.[6] Interest in expanded oil production also waned when attention shifted from the general to the specific. Respondents endorsed drilling when the location was vaguely defined within U.S. borders, but they expressed reluctance to support it in any number of places mentioned specifically by name, including public lands in the Rocky Mountains, the Great Lakes, Florida's Gulf Coast, or, most notably, Alaska's Arctic National Wildlife Refuge.[7]

A 2006 General Social Survey questioned a representative sample of more than 1,800 U.S. adults about their knowledge and opinions concerning the polar regions. Polar knowledge among adults proved to be limited, but not entirely lacking. Polar knowledge, general science knowledge, and education—together with individual background characteristics like age, sex, political alignment, and income—predicted policy-relevant opinions.[8] Because Americans prove relatively uninformed about the Arctic, they are highly susceptible to changing their opinions regarding oil and gas development in ANWR based on the framing of survey questions.[9] The strong and demonstrable effects of framing on polling responses led the staff at the

---

5   Deborah Lynn Guber and Christopher Bosso, "Framing A.N.W.R.: Citizens, Consumers, and the Privileged Position of Business," in *American Political Science Association* (Washington, D.C., 2005), 9.

6   Ibid.

7   Ibid.

8   Lawrence C. Hamilton, "Who Cares About Polar Regions? Results from a Survey of U.S. Public Opinion," *Arctic, Antarctic, and Alpine Research* 40, no. 4 (2008): 671.

9   Ibid.

Environmental News Service to complain, "you get what you poll for."[10]

Given the powerful effects of framing, unsurprisingly, opponents and proponents of opening the Arctic National Wildlife Refuge to drilling employ images that appeal to one or the other side of the citizen-consumer divide. When oil prices spiked during the George W. Bush administration, pro-drilling interests effectively used the narrative "American consumers are paying the price" for keeping ANWR protected.[11] They assigned blame for the high cost of gas to Congress and partisan politics. This rhetoric was amplified after the terrorist attacks on September 11, 2001, and found new strength under the frames of "energy security" and "national security." A fearful American public found great consumer appeal in the positive frames of "freedom," "choice," and "security" regarding drilling in the Refuge. Similar frames have found new strength under the Trump adminis- tration: policies which could encourage deregulation and greater domestic production, while conceivably easing the State of Alaska's ongoing fiscal crisis.

Several tactics characterize pro-industry images: high-altitude shots that diminish detail, prevalent use of winter images, and large groups of animals comingling with oil and gas infrastructure. The messages downplay the fragile ecosystem of the coastal plain by removing environmental details like plants and small animals, focus- ing on the winter months, and emphasizing the peaceful (and plentiful) coexistence of animals with roads, pipelines, and drilling platforms. The deliberate depiction of large numbers of animals responds to the "identifiable victim" effect. Psychological studies suggest that images of single individuals or animals evoke the greatest emotive or affective feeling, while affect begins to decline at two or more and completely collapses in larger groupings, at which point "psychic numbing" or "turning off" leads to "apathy and inaction."[12]

---

10   David W. Moore, "Conflicting Polls Show an Uncertain Public on A.N.W.R." (news.gallup.com: Gallup, 2005).

11   Guber and Bosso.

12   Kate Manzo, "Beyond Polar Bears? Re-Envisioning Climate Change," *Meteorological Applications* 17 (2010): 198.

Pro-development images deliberately minimize the ecological and environmental significance of the coastal plain of the Refuge. These images assure the American public that development of this zone will not compromise any "national treasures" currently protected under federal law. Images of animals and industry thriving together respond to concerns for the well-being of the Porcupine Caribou Herd. Even the use of the acronym ANWR represents a deliberate framing decision, purposefully divorcing the region from the emotional associations of "wildlife" and "refuge," which suggests *sanctuary*.

In contrast to the images used by pro-drilling advocates, images used by environmentalists typically face south, capturing the mountain range in the summer with a variety of flora and fauna. The images depict caribou, polar bears, wolves, migratory birds, grizzly bears, and more, in a manner consistent with the "identifiable victim" theory. These photographs capture intimate moments amid the landscape or between animals, and sweeping vistas showcasing the Refuge's abundant wildlife. They evoke tenderness, empathy, awe, and reverence in the viewer and provide a face to what is at stake. The ANWR that opponents of oil and gas development present could not be farther removed from Senator Frank Murkowski's blank piece of paper. For environmentalists, the Refuge is a place of unparalleled natural wonder. Protecting it from exploitation in perpetuity is a moral imperative. Development of the coastal plain would fundamentally change the wildness of the entire refuge, they argue, at a cost that would greatly outweigh any monetary benefit.

Environmentalists and other opponents of oil and gas development make an emotional appeal to civic-minded citizens. Because the Arctic National Wildlife Refuge contains the full range of Arctic and Subarctic ecosystems uninterrupted by roads or infrastructure, opponents of oil and gas development frame ANWR as America's last frontier, "a sacred domain not yet corrupted by civilization."[13]

---

13   Finis Dunaway, "Reframing the Last Frontier: Subhankar Banerjee and the Visual Politics of the Arctic National Wildlife Refuge," review of *Arctic National Wildlife Refuge: Seasons of Life and Land*, Gail H. Hull, *American Quarterly* 58, no. 1 (2006): 162.

They argue that this is where the real value of ANWR lies, not in oil and gas revenues. The frame places the onus of responsibility on the American public to do their civic duty and protect the priceless landscape, whose value cannot be calculated with money. Not only does this message appeal to the citizen's emotions, it actively shames the consumer.

Increasingly, this narrative has amplified and broadened in the twenty-first century as international attention shifts to the impacts and causes of global climate change. The Arctic National Wildlife Refuge, as a pristine place in the region of the world experiencing the effects of climate change most acutely, has come to symbolize the politicized tensions between economic development and environmental protection—that is, the tension between being the global consumer and the global citizen. In the eyes of conservationists, the battle to protect ANWR now represents a battle to protect the world from global climate change. Opponents of oil and gas development argue in favor of greater efficiency and increased use of alternative energy sources, to reduce our reliance on oil and overall carbon footprint. Although they continue to emphasize the value of wilderness in framing their arguments, linkages with broader concerns of climate change have enhanced their cause's political saliency. Notably, conservationist imagery no longer identifies the Porcupine Caribou Herd as the most vulnerable victim of oil and gas development. Marketing campaigns have shifted to the most iconic victim of global climate change: the polar bear.

As the Arctic warms and changes, the polar bear stands as the ultimate identifiable victim. The bears—dependent on pack ice—face mounting travel and hunting challenges as their frozen habitat disappears. The image of a solitary, exhausted, or starving megafauna has become the most recognized casualty of global climate change, and as such, opponents of developing the Refuge were quick to adopt the polar bear as its poster child. Nearly every pro-protection website for the Refuge features a full-page spread on the polar bear.

Without mandated permanent federal protection, the Arctic National Wildlife Refuge remains a political hotspot. Numerous stakeholders from federal, state, tribal, local, and outsider industries continue to advocate for their competing causes. The manner in which they frame these causes depends on the political climate and will adjust accordingly to sympathetic causes and beneficial linkages. By aligning themselves with the global concern of climate change and framing the Refuge as a symbolic battleground for an impending global crisis, opponents of developing ANWR have capitalized on the political sway of an international movement to strengthen their appeal to the civic-minded identities of the American public.

SELLING THE POLAR BEAR, BUYING SALVATION

Just as commercial advertising of the early twentieth century incorporated popular Arctic images and themes to catch the eyes of consumers, environmentalists and advertisers alike tap into green and climate change sentiments to sell products and ideologies today. Because of the bear's association with global climate change and related politics, the polar bear in the early twenty-first century has moved beyond basic consumer advertising and into the more complex arenas of corporate image and environmental activism.

As natural heritage sites and wildlife became increasingly understood as globally owned resources—that is, as globalization shifted environmental thought beyond national boundaries—consumer preferences and demands changed. By the 1990s, polls indicated that companies' environmental records influenced consumer purchases.[14] Sustainability practices mattered to consumers following decades of environmental disaster images broadcast directly into their living rooms, from Ohio's Cuyahoga River catching fire in 1969 to the Exxon Valdez oil spill in Prince William Sound in 1989. Ideas of environmental protection shifted from an infrequent conversation to a moral obligation in every citizen's life.[15]

---

14   Jack Doyle, "'Enviro Imaging' for Market Share: Corporations Take to the Ad Pages to Brush Up Their Images," in *Not Man Apart* (Friends of the Earth, 1990).

15   Walker Kent and Wan Fang, "The Harm of Symbolic Actions and Green-Washing: Corporate Actions and Communications on Environmental Performance and Their Financial Implications," *Journal of Business Ethics*, no. 2 (2012).

This new public discourse and market trend toward environmental sustainability incentivizes corporations to follow suit. As a result, new marketing strategies and initiatives have been developing since the 1990s to boost companies' public images and environmental reputations. Some companies take an active role in environmental management, a few going as far as lobbying governments for greater environmental regulations (e.g., Patagonia). Others engage in carbon offsetting, a voluntary program in which companies and individuals alike can participate that entails paying for activities that prevent emissions from other sources, or those that attempt to remove CO_2 from the atmosphere, rather than reducing one's own CO_2 emissions.[16]

In the rush to "green up" corporate images, more dubious tactics have also emerged, including green-washing, the practice of engaging in symbolic communications of environmental concern without substantially addressing them through actions.[17] Notorious examples of green-washing from the late 1980s and '90s include Chevron's "People Do" campaign, featuring Chevron employees protecting a variety of charismatic animals including bears, butterflies, and sea turtles. Critics pointed out that many of the environmental programs promoted in Chevron's campaign were mandated by law and ignored or distracted from the company's spotty environmental record, including its violations of the Clean Air Act, the Clean Water Act, and spilling oil into national wildlife refuges.[18] A 1989 advertising campaign by the chemical company DuPont followed a similar vein, featuring marine animals jubilantly clapping their wings and flippers in chorus to Beethoven's "Ode to Joy" in response to the company's new double-hulled oil tankers.[19] DuPont was the single largest corporate polluter in the United States in the early 1990s.[20] Absurdity aside,

---

16   Jules Peck, "Forgive My Carbon Sin," *Ecologist* 38, no. 4 (2008).

17   Kent and Fang.

18   David C. Korten, *When Corporations Rule the World*, 2nd ed. (San Francisco: Berrett-Koehler Publishers, 2001).

19   Ibid.

20   Jack Doyle, "Dupont's Disgraceful Deeds: The Environmental Record of E. I. Dupont De Nemour," *The Multinational Monitor* 12, no. 10 (1991).

green-washing campaigns are classic examples of misdirection. They shift the consumer's focus away from a company's actual environmental track record and redirect it toward peripheral "feel-good" initiatives. Such maneuvers illustrate that consumers *want* to feel good about the products they buy, and that companies have major profit incentives to ensure they do.

Emotional manipulation of American consumers lies at the heart of environmental historian Finis Dunaway's book *Seeing Green*. Dunaway demonstrates how media have historically blamed individual consumers for environmental degradation and have thus deflected attention from corporate and government responsibility. He argues that environmental messaging in the United States has been dominated by market forces and advertising—that American consumers are led to believe the path to greater sustainability is through personal product choices and behavior only, rather than systemic change through regulation and policy.

For example, after ninety-six minutes of illustrating a catastrophic future of climate change impacts, Al Gore's *An Inconvenient Truth* ends with what Dunaway calls "a consumerist fantasy of green salvation through carbon off-setting."[21] Food writer and environmentalist Michael Pollan elaborates:

> I don't know about you, but for me the most upsetting moment in *An Inconvenient Truth* came long after Al Gore scared the hell out of me, constructing an utterly convincing case that the very survival of life on earth as we know it is threatened by climate change. No, the really dark moment came during the closing credits, when we are asked to . . . change our light bulbs. That's when it got really depressing. The immense disproportion between the magnitude of the problem Gore had described and the puniness of what he was asking us to do about it was enough to sink your heart.[22]

---

21   Finis Dunaway, *Seeing Green: The Use and Abuse of American Environmental Images* (Chicago: University of Chicago Press, 2015), 271.
22   Michael Pollan, "Why Bother?," *New York Times Magazine*, April 20, 2008.

Gore—through promoting the use of energy efficient light bulbs, reusable grocery bags, and hybrid vehicles—*equated* green consumerism with environmental citizenship, thus resolving these conflicting identities and providing an American public with feel-good product options that require no monumental changes in public policy or lifestyle. Similarly, companies worldwide can now buy their way into perceived environmental sustainability through the purchase of carbon offsets, in lieu of reducing their own emissions. Many environmentalists argue that offset programs are "band-aid" solutions that prevent funding and innovation capital from being invested in real emission reductions. Cheap carbon offsets depend on partnerships with developing nations, leading some critics to conclude that carbon offset programs are little more than colonial profiteering.[23]

Thus, in the twenty-first century, environmental salvation is achieved through consumerism. While greater and greener market choices certainly constitute progress, critics argue that the focus on consumerism distracts from industry-wide solutions, perpetuates inequity, discourages the emergence of collective responsibility, and undermines the likelihood of both collective grassroots changes and public pressure on governments to act.

Companies employing green advertising have become somewhat more self-aware in recent decades. They recognize that ignoring the environmental and social impacts of their businesses risks damaging their reputations, which could potentially cripple their brands for years.[24] Given the market growth in a host of sustainable brands and the organic food market in the last ten years, companies have monetary incentives to cultivate a business culture (or perceived business culture) of green or environmentally sustainable practices. In the early 2000s, Phillips Oil (now Conoco-Phillips) released an advertising campaign directly addressing concerns about Arctic drilling. The ad features a sleeping sow polar bear with a small cub sleeping on her back. The caption paired with this image reassures the viewer that

---

23 Peck.
24 "Green Is the Way to Go for Marketers," *Marketing Week* 29, no. 19 (2006).

Phillips' business practices do not disturb the animals; in fact, it claims, "it's like we've never been there at all."

Coca-Cola has used the polar bear as a lovable trade character since the 1920s in France, but the bears became truly iconic for the brand in the early 1990s with the launch of their television commercial "Northern Lights." The animated commercial anthropomorphized the bears, depicting them enjoying Coca-Cola and viewing the northern lights like a human family at the movies. "That's really what we were trying to do," said the creator of the commercial, Ken Stewart, "create a character that's innocent, fun, and reflects the best attributes we like to call 'human.'"[25]

In 2007, Coca-Cola aligned itself strategically with the World Wildlife Fund (WWF) and pledged $2 million toward WWF's conservation efforts over two years. To increase visibility of the partnership and sell more product, Coca-Cola released a limited-edition beverage label featuring polar bears. An additional $3 million in direct donations from customers supplemented the funding to WWF.[26] Given the brand's estimated worth of $80 billion and pending accusations of human rights violations, charges of green-washing soon followed. Coca-Cola has since modified its partnership with WWF to focus on clean water initiatives and "measurably improving environmental performance across the company's supply chain, integrating the value of nature into decision-making processes, and convening influential partners to solve global environmental challenges."[27]

The backlash against Coca-Cola's support of polar bear research highlights the politically contentious nature of the polar bear within the frame of global climate change and poses the question—would any amount of money have been enough? While monetary support of organizations working toward systemic change is undoubtedly valuable, the case of Coca-Cola and WWF raises questions about

---

25   Ted Ryan, "The Enduring History of Coca-Cola's Polar Bears," Coca-Cola, https://www.coca-colacompany.com/holidays/the-enduring-history-of-coca-colas-polar-bears.

26   Mya Frazier, "Should the Polar Bear Still Sell Coca-Cola?," The New Yorker, November 6, 2014.

27   "About Us," http://wwfcocacolapartnership.com/.

corporate motivations, as well as how and if companies can financially support environmental efforts without being accused (guilty or not) of tokenistic gestures. Coca-Cola's conscious decision to move away from emphasizing politically and emotionally charged polar bear conservation reflects the motivations behind such sustainability partnerships: public image and revenue.

Environmental activists and commercial industries alike use the polar bear to communicate green sentiments to individual consumers. Both recognize the emotional appeal of the polar bear and use the animal in advertising to manipulate emotions to spur action, be it donating money to conservation efforts, purchasing a product, or in some cases both.[28] In the shift from national to global environmentalism, the polar bear became "living heritage," a process assisted, as environmental historian Peter Coates suggests, "by the fairly widespread perception that polar regions elude national ownership and are the ultimate global commons."[29] To lose the polar bear to extinction due to environmental degradation would be a loss for all humankind, akin to destroying Leonardo Da Vinci's *Last Supper*. "As such," Coates explains, "this bear is studied, protected, appreciated, and commoditized by an international fraternity of scientists, nature preservation organizations and nature importing tourists."[30]

Groups like WWF and Greenpeace use images of the polar bear extensively in their anti–Arctic drilling campaigns. Never mind the four million people who live above the Arctic Circle whose lives would be disrupted and permanently changed due to off-shore oil development; it is the polar bear that has emerged as the poster child of choice for environmental non-government organizations

---

28   World Wildlife Fund, Defenders of Wildlife, the Sierra Club, National Wildlife Foundation, Oceana, World Animal Foundation, and Polar Bear International—that's seven different conservation organizations—offer "adopt a polar bear" shopping choices through their online gifts shops and fundraising efforts. By making a purchase or donation to one of these organizations, participants receive a plush toy polar bear and often a certificate. Shipping not included.
29   Peter Coates, "Creatures Enshrined: Wild Animals as Bearers of Heritage," *Past and Present* 226 (2015): 294.
30   Ibid.

(NGOs). Because the bear exists in the American imagination as a lovable and relatable trade character, consumers easily make the step to identifiable victim.

Environmental images of the polar bear are often up-close, tight shots with the bear appearing to gaze directly at the camera lens and into the eyes of the viewer. Bears playing with one another, an affectionate moment between a sow and her cubs, or a gesture that easily translates to common human expressions, are all typical fare for these images with an environmental message. For instance, WWF's ad reading "What on earth are we doing to our planet?" features a bear covering his face as though in painful disbelief. Greenpeace International has staged numerous demonstrations worldwide featuring protesters dressed in polar bear suits, often carrying signs that say, "ARCTIC NOT FOR SALE." Humans in costumes, likely made with plastic, protest oil-fueled consumerism through the donning of a lovable trade character created by commercial industry. Such images demonstrate how dramatically our visual lexicon has changed since 1900.

WWF's and Greenpeace's respective anti-drilling campaigns pit the survival of the polar bear against Arctic oil and gas development. These images also imply that by supporting Arctic oil and gas development, consumers are partially *to blame* for the suffering and decline of the polar bear. Churchill, Manitoba–based conservation nonprofit Polar Bear International, located on Hudson Bay in northern Canada, takes a similar approach in their social media campaigns. Several times a week they ask followers what they (the viewers) are doing to save the polar bear. The bear is further anthropomorphized by linking the well-being of polar bears with the well-being of humans and vice versa, posting contorted or resting polar bears for "yoga bear Wednesdays." Such tactics emphasize the responsibility individual citizens have to habitat and wildlife conservation.

While some of Polar Bear International's posts encourage community-based action ("We can address climate change by becoming involved in efforts in our own communities to shift to a renewable energy future"[31]), these posts predominantly target individuals to spur individual action. Polar Bear International, unlike WWF or Greenpeace, remains deliberately apolitical. It does not make calls for political action (e.g., letter writing, protests, etc.) and regularly reminds followers that "Climate change isn't a left or a right issue. It's an issue that affects all of us."[32]

Through these marketing campaigns, the polar bear has become the "Smokey Bear" of the global climate crisis: "Only you can prevent global climate change." Smokey, like the polar bear, rose to environmental fame in the 1950s due to victimization. Fire crews responding to a large forest fire in the Capitan Mountains of New Mexico found the cub treed, separated from his mother, and badly burned in the spring of 1950. The crew retrieved the cub and flew him to Santa Fe, where he received treatment for his injuries and a flurry of attention from the press. Smokey's story was broadcast nationwide, and letters of support flowed in. The state game warden presented the cub to the chief of the Forest Service and dedicated Smokey to a conservation and wildfire prevention publicity program. Smokey lived the rest of his life at the National Zoo in Washington, D.C.[33] The bear's message of "Only you can prevent forest fires!" exemplifies the tendency of environmental messaging in the United States to focus on the responsibility of individuals.

Commercial marketing employs the same tactics to sell products to consumers. In a review of "Green Sentiments and the Human-Animal Relationship in Print Advertising During the 20th Century" conducted by marketing researchers Nancy Spears and Richard Germain, the authors note that as consumers expand their preferences for environmentally responsible brands, "it is imperative for marketers to identify practical ways to tap the commercial potential stemming from this environmentally sensitive zeitgeist in ways that

---

31 Text quoted from a Polar Bear International Instagram post from March 12, 2018.

32 Text quoted from a Polar Bear International Instagram post from March 26, 2018.

33 The Ad Council, "Story of Smokey," https://smokeybear.com/en/smokeys-history/story-of-smokey.

do not overplay the green appeal."[34] Spears and Germain's study proposes a theoretical model based on positionality—the constantly evolving relationship between humans and other creatures—examining "the culturally understood position that humans hold in relation to animals and how this position adapts to ever-changing societal demands."[35] This model proposes that consumer values are either self-focused or society-focused—that is, values may focus primarily on the self and how the environment beyond oneself can be fitted to the self, or values may focus on the environment and how the self can be fitted to the environment. This model is useful when examining how commercial marketing uses climate change narratives and the polar bear to sell products or to sell environmentalism.

Whereas human domination over nature characterized the early years of the century, the expression of green sentiments in the latter years projected value in nature for nature itself. The findings of the study concluded that "diminishing the centrality of humans and forwarding the inherent value of animals can focus consumers on environmentally friendly aspects of products."[36] Similarly, the study concludes that showcasing society-focused values stirs customers to reflect on the environmentally supportive stance of the advertised product.

Advertisers today tap into the cultural sentiment that the self can be fitted to the environment. From energy-efficient light bulbs, to items made of recycled plastic, to biodegradable cleaning items, evidence of products designed (or at least advertised) to fit green sentiments is found almost everywhere in the market. As previously discussed, consumers want to feel good about the products they purchase and use. Studies have found that buyers say they are willing to pay more for sustainable products, and as Spears and Germain suggest, this may be due to the product's perceived ability to fit consumers to their surrounding environments. The polar bear, as a victim

---

34 Nancy E. Spears and Richard Germain, "A Note on Green Sentiments and the Human-Animal Relationship in Print Advertising During the 20th Century," *Journal of Current Issues and Research in Advertising* 29, no. 2 (2007): 53.

35 Ibid., 54.

36 Ibid., 60.

of global climate change, taps into these emotional market drivers and serves to remind consumers of the effects of their participation in a fossil fuel–based economy. A market of "environmentally friendly" products allows consumers to alleviate the guilt often associated with this participation through perceived individual choice: grocery shopping as daily environmental activism.

Environmental salvation through consumerism is perhaps most succinctly illustrated in a 2011 Nissan Leaf electric car commercial. The commercial opens with a polar bear in the Arctic, surrounded by glaciers collapsing into the water. The bear rises, dives into the water, and swims ashore. Accompanied by the emotional soundtrack of a single piano, the bear makes his way south through woods, highways, railroads, and cities. The huge white predator is uncomfortably out of place in these scenes, drinking out of puddles and entering the urban environment. He eventually wanders into a tidy suburban neighborhood and up to a man about to leave for work in his electric vehicle. The bear rears up on two legs and embraces the man in a hug. The man leans in and returns the embrace. The scene is one of absolution, ending with a voiceover saying, "Innovation for the planet. Innovation for all." The message is clear: spend your money on a Nissan Leaf, and both the polar bear and the planet will thank you.

BIBLIOGRAPHY

"About Us." http://wwfcocacolapartnership.com/.

Ad Council, The. "Story of Smokey." https://smokeybear.com/en/smokeys-history/story-of-smokey.

Coates, Peter. "Creatures Enshrined: Wild Animals as Bearers of Heritage." *Past and Present* 226 (01 / 01 / 2015): 272–98.

Doyle, Jack. "Dupont's Disgraceful Deeds: The Environmental Record of E. I. Dupont De Nemour." *The Multinational Monitor* 12, no. 10 (1991).

———. "'Enviro Imaging' for Market Share: Corporations Take to the Ad Pages to Brush up Their Images." In *Not Man Apart*. Friends of the Earth, 1990.

Dunaway, Finis. "Reframing the Last Frontier: Subhankar Banerjee and the Visual Politics of the Arctic National Wildlife Refuge." Review of

Arctic National Wildlife Refuge: Seasons of Life and Land, Gail H. Hull. *American Quarterly* 58, no. 1 (2006): 159–80.

———. *Seeing Green: The Use and Abuse of American Environmental Images*. Chicago: University of Chicago Press, 2015.

Frazier, Mya. "Should the Polar Bear Still Sell Coca-Cola?" *The New Yorker*, November 6, 2014.

Guber, Deborah Lynn, and Christopher Bosso. "Framing A.N.W.R.: Citizens, Consumers, and the Privileged Position of Business." In *American Political Science Association*. Washington, D.C., 2005.

Hamilton, Lawrence C. "Who Cares About Polar Regions? Results from a Survey of U.S. Public Opinion." *Arctic, Antarctic, and Alpine Research* 40, no. 4 (2008): 671–78.

Kent, Walker, and Wan Fang. "The Harm of Symbolic Actions and Green-Washing: Corporate Actions and Communications on Environmental Performance and Their Financial Implications." *Journal of Business Ethics*, no. 2 (2012): 227.

Korten, David C. *When Corporations Rule the World*. 2nd ed. San Francisco: Berrett-Koehler Publishers, 2001.

Kramer, Andrew E. "Warming Revives Dream of Sea Route in Russian Arctic." *New York Times*, October 17, 2011.

Manzo, Kate. "Beyond Polar Bears? Re-Envisioning Climate Change." *Meteorological Applications* 17 (May 4, 2010): 196–208.

McCannon, John. *A History of the Arctic: Nature, Exploration and Exploitation*. London: Reaktion Books Ltd., 2012.

Moore, David W. "Conflicting Polls Show an Uncertain Public on A.N.W.R." news.gallup.com: Gallup, 2005.

O'Neill, Kate. *The Environment and International Relations*. Themes in International Relations. Cambridge: Cambridge University Press, 2009.

Peck, Jules. "Forgive My Carbon Sin." *Ecologist* 38, no. 4 (2008): 30–35.

———. "Green Is the Way to Go for Marketers." *Marketing Week* 29, no. 19 (2006): 40–41.

Pollan, Michael. "Why Bother?" *New York Times Magazine*, April 20, 2008.

Ryan, Ted. "The Enduring History of Coca-Cola's Polar Bears." Coca-Cola, https://www.coca-colacompany.com/holidays/the-enduring-history-of-coca-colas-polar-bears.

Sontag, Susan. *On Photography*. New York: Straus and Giroux, 1977.

Spears, Nancy E., and Richard Germain. "A Note on Green Sentiments and the Human-Animal Relationship in Print Advertising During the 20th Century." *Journal of Current Issues and Research in Advertising* 29, no. 2 (2007): 53–62.

A Note from Sherry Simpson

I met Terrence in the mid-1980s at a party hosted by his twin brother, Dermot. We played some nerdy writer game, and they trounced everyone there by cheating telepathically (and by being smart). But what impressed me most was Terrence's irresistible laugh. In his classes, I discovered that the proper approach to history—to the world, really—is an intellectual exuberance, a pure delight in learning, an adventuresome curiosity, and the impulse to laugh.

My essay here draws from a research paper I wrote as a Northern Studies student, and from trawling through old files, where I found several newspaper articles scrawled with Terrence's distinctive handwriting. It reminded me of how much he's shared over the years, how generous his enthusiasm is, how irreplaceable he is.

"DOGS IS DOGS"

Savagery and Civilization in the Gold Rush Era

Sherry Simpson

Study old photographs of the unruly gold rush camps, the towns rising raw from mud and tundra, the stampeders grinding their way toward the promised land, and soon the dogs begin ghosting from the backdrop of history. They're everywhere—loitering on the fringes of crowds, lounging in saloons, posing stolidly before resuming the strain against the harness or beneath the pack. Often they're the liveliest, most familiar elements in the scene. The miners' clothing seems odd, the buildings quaint, the landscape scraped bare by people trying to pry riches from the earth and from each other, but the dogs are dogs—yawning, nosing at someone's hand, pricking up their ears at something outside the frame. They're so familiar that it's easy to overlook such ordinary creatures swept up in an extraordinary time.

The photographs document a brief but memorable episode in an ancient collaboration between humans and dogs. Archaeologists and geneticists continue deciphering the origins of modern dogs, but recent research suggests that they tacked away from wolves and toward people between 20,000 and 40,000 years ago.[1] Equally complicated is the tangled history of their migration to the New World and domestication by indigenous inhabitants. What's certain is that Alaska Natives and First Nations people had fashioned a

---

1   Rachael Lallensack, "Ancient Genomes Heat up Dog Domestication Debate," *Nature*, July 18, 2017, http://dx.doi.org/10.1038/nature.2017.22320.

E. A. Hegg photograph of dogs hauling a casket of water in Nome, ca. 1900. *Lanier McKee Photograph Collection at Alaska and Polar Regions Department, UAF.*

useful symbiosis with dogs for hunting, packing, and traveling long before Euro-American explorers, colonizers, traders, and gold-seekers introduced their versions of *Canis lupus familiaris* into the country.[2] Non-Natives quickly grasped the indispensability of dogs, likening them to the horse on the prairies, the camel in the desert, the reindeer in Lapland—"what the yak is to India or the llama to Peru," wrote Alfred Hulse Brooks.[3] They were beasts of burdens, the sinew and blood of winter travel, companions vexing and comforting, a survival tool. "Without dogs we could scarcely have existed this

---

2   David B. Anderson, *The Use of Dog Teams and the Use of Subsistence-Caught Fish for Feeding Sled Dogs in the Yukon River Drainage, Alaska*, Technical Paper No. 210 (Juneau: Division of Subsistence, Alaska Department of Fish and Game, 1992), 5.

3   Alfred Hulse Brooks, *Blazing Alaska's Trails*, 2nd ed. (Fairbanks: University of Alaska Press, 1973), 402.

winter," admitted Klondike miner Jeremiah Lynch at the turn of the twentieth century.[4]

Dawson City wasn't the first gold rush town where dogs and humans engaged in an uneasy collaboration, but it was the most dramatic. In 1897, a year after gold was discovered on Bonanza Creek, Dawson's population of 5,000 people included few women and almost no children—"in the main, a city composed of grown people and dogs," reported *Harper's Weekly* correspondent Tappan Adney.[5] All but a few of an estimated 1,500 dogs worked for a living, and those few that didn't—a bull terrier, a pug, a couple of lapdogs—formed their own little society. "Somebodies' pets they," he wrote, "but sadly out of place here, where neither dogs nor men have much time to play."[6]

Play was never part of the deal for dogs. For people, a dog's role as conscript or companion masked a more subtle, primeval function. "Symbolically the dog is the animal pivot of the human universe, lurking at the threshold between wildness and domestication, and all of the valences that these two ideals of human experience hold," writes cultural historian David Gordon White. In the North's history, dogs literally roamed back and forth across this boundary. They were of the wild yet helped people survive it. Dogs also act as the "alter ego of man himself, a reflection of both human culture and human savagery," White writes.[7] That savagery frequently erupted in people delirious with gold fever who brutalized their dogs out of frustration with the landscape's unrelenting rigors. "It just made my heart ache to see how cruelly they were treated," a woman stampeder said. "Men seemed to become heartless up there. The environment, perhaps, makes them so."[8]

The gold rush era cast in high relief humanity's deep-rooted ambivalence toward dogs as creatures of mythical stature and practical utility,

---

4   Jeremiah Lynch, *Three Years in the Klondike* (Chicago: The Lakeside Classics, 1967), 144.

5   Tappan Adney, *The Klondike Stampede* (New York: Harper & Brothers Publishers, 1900), 355.

6   Ibid., 210.

7   David Gordon White, *Myths of the Dog-Man* (Chicago: University of Chicago Press, 1991), 15.

8   William Haskell, *Two Years in the Klondike and Alaskan Gold Fields* (Washington, D.C.: Hartford Publishing Company, 1898), 342.

cultivated into docility but reviled for filthy habits, eaten by people and eaters of people.[9] The very animals so essential to opening the north to newcomers created public disorder, constant conflict, unceasing noise, and unsanitary and sometimes dangerous conditions. They exposed people's fickle hearts: they were valuable enough to steal and aggravating enough to abuse; often neglected and sometimes ennobled.

Paradoxically, the fractious presence of so many dogs helped foster the establishment of civic order—human culture—in these rough communities. The gradual surrender of frontier norms to social pressures reiterated an evolution that began long ago, a process artfully characterized by two researchers as "We Didn't Domesticate Dogs. They Domesticated Us."[9]

■ ■ ■

Argonauts from every social stratum flooded the Yukon and Alaska—perhaps 30,000 to 35,000 in the Klondike Rush of 1897–98 alone.[10] So did dogs of every breed and no particular breed. Most people sorted them into two broad groups: the valuable northern breeds and the second-class "Outside" dogs. "The class of dog we require is the 'Malamute' or the 'Husky'; they are hardier, most used to the climate, and can be depended on," advised Inspector Charles Starnes of the North-West Mounted Police.[11] Mounties preferred the lean, wolfish huskies common to Athabascan Indian tribes, but freighters and others favored the sturdy malemutes used by coastal and Arctic Native groups.

A lack of doggishness in these northern breeds confounded people inclined to see them as half-feral anyway. "I never saw them play; even

---

9 Paul Shepard, *The Others: How Animals Made Us Human* (Washington, D.C.: Island Press, 1997), 62–64. Brian Hare and Vanessa Woods, "We Didn't Domesticate Dogs. They Domesticated Us," March 3, 2013, https://news.national geographic.com/news/2013/03/130302-dog-domestic-evolution-science-wolf-wolves-human/.

10 "Gold Mining and the Creeks" (Parks, Environment Canada, n.d.).

11 C. Starnes, "Report of the North-West Mounted Police, Part III, 1900, Appendix B" (Ottawa: S. E. Dawson, 1901), 49.

Caribou Hotel, Dominion Creek, Yukon Territory. *Larss and Ducloss. MacKay Photo Collection, Accession #70-58-268, Alaska and Polar Regions Archives, Rasmuson Library, UAF.*

the puppies were grave and sedate," wrote Hamlin Garland.[12] Stampeder Basil Austin traded a rifle, fifty pounds of flour, a pound of tobacco, and five pounds of tea for a husky that spurned friendliness, refused to pull, ran away, and was the "meanest cuss of a dog that ever drew breath." Austin shot it after it stole a slab of moose. "But he was little more than a wolf," he wrote, "with savage instinct that dictated his every action; we should not have expected anything better from him."[13]

Mining engineer T. A. Rickard described malemutes as "devoid of those instincts of faithfulness that make the dog a friend of man, although Jack London can spin fanciful yarns about him." He was not the only person to make a plainly racist equation: "He is to the dog tribe what his master, the Eskimo, is to the human species."[14] Others

---

12   Hamlin Garland, *The Trail of the Goldseekers: A Record of Travel in Prose and Verse* (New York: The Macmillan Company, 1906), 104.

13   Basil Austin, *The Diary of a Ninety-Eighter* (Mount Pleasant, MI: John Cumming, 1968), 112–13.

14   T. A. Rickard, *Through the Yukon and Alaska* (San Francisco: Mining and

appreciated the intelligence and steadfastness of Native dogs. In Skagway, a sourdough told Addison Powell that his husky, Mose, had once saved his life. "I suppose you place a high value on him?" Powell asked. The old-timer replied, "Mister, don't ask me to place a value on my partner. I couldn't think of it! Why, if I should lose my poke of dust, rather than to part with Mose, we would hit the trail back and try for another raise."[15]

Few imported dogs possessed the physique, temperament, and hardy constitution necessary for rugged travel and harsh winters. (Neither did many people, for that matter.) "The poor 'outside' dog— one feels sorry for him," Adney wrote. "He is often a pet or a game dog, and the drudgery of harness is galling to his pride. One meets him on the trail, tugging hard at a load of freight for his master, with tail and head down. He casts his eyes up into yours with a shamed expression which says, 'Who ever thought that I would come to this!'"[16]

Character and quality aside, stampeders and miners regarded dogs as warm-blooded currency whose value fluctuated wildly depending upon the season, the latest strike, and supply and demand. Circle City miners knew that victory attends the swift, and word of the Klondike discovery instantly inflated the canine market as the town emptied. Dogs worth $25 to $50 apiece began selling by weight, surging from $1.50 to $2.50 per pound, wrote William Haskell.[17] One miner offered to trade three cabins worth $500 each for a single dog from musher Arthur Walden, who had delivered the news that launched the stampede.[18] The relative importance of men and dogs became clear to Klondike-bound Anna Fulcomer, who rented a dog in Circle City for $30 with the guide included for free. "The hopes of hundreds here rest on their ability to get a bob-tailed dog," she wrote

---

Scientific Press, 1909), 291–92.

15   Addison M. Powell, *Trailing and Camping in Alaska* (New York: Newold Publishing Company, 1910), 111.

16   Adney, *Klondike Stampede*, 213.

17   Haskell, *Two Years*, 285–86.

18   Arthur Treadwell Walden, *A Dog-Puncher on the Yukon* (Boston; New York: Houghton Mifflin Co., 1928), 77.

her sister.[19] Similar dickering occurred everywhere people needed dogs. Dawson City miners possessed more gold than food after a fire destroyed critical supplies in fall 1897, and dogs sold for $300 to $500 apiece to those eager to escape a hungry winter. "One man sold a team of five splendid dogs for twenty-five hundred dollars," Walden reported.[20] The spectacular Klondike strike galvanized a vigorous trade in dog-selling and stealing in Seattle as entrepreneurs mined their own fortunes from the wallets of gold-seekers. "If there are any dogs over fifty pounds in weight left in any other section of the United States, it is not the fault of the ambitious collectors who think there is a small-sized fortune in every dog shipped to this market," the *Seattle Times* remarked. But booms will bust, and inevitably the dog market collapsed so precipitously that one man purchased 106 dogs for $100, plus a free monkey.[21] A desperate opportunist who couldn't give away his inventory turned them loose under cover of night and bolted for Dawson.[22]

The sad result of this irrational exuberance was that travelers often arrived with fewer dogs than when they embarked, due to poor diets, overwork, disease, accidents, and extreme cold. Only seven of twenty-one dogs survived a 1,600-mile journey from the Yukon River to Dyea, for example.[23] Even the Mounties struggled to recruit satisfactory dogs; in 1898 a transport of 140 Labradors dwindled to nineteen by the time they reached Tagish.[24] Sometimes starving stampeders resorted to eating their teams dog by dog.

Physical abuse was another significant cause of mortality. Dog freighter Arthur Walden was appalled at the brutality he witnessed along the White Pass Trail. "The cruelty to animals was something

---

19   *The Official Guide to the Klondyke Country and the Gold Fields of Alaska* (Chicago: W. B. Conkey, 1897), 150.

20   Walden, *Dog-Puncher*, 114.

21   "Too Many Dogs in Town," *Seattle Times*, February 22, 1898, 5.

22   Michael Spellacy, "'Segura Miguel' Gold Rush Memoir" (Alaska and Polar Regions Collections and Archives, Rasmuson Library, University of Alaska Fairbanks, n.d.), Chapter 1, 1–2.

23   *Official Guide*, 248.

24   Z. T. Wood, "Report of the North-West Mounted Police, 1899, Appendix A" (Ottawa: S. E. Dawson, 1900), 21.

Picture of battleship and some fans above bar on wall, stove in foreground.
Circa 189(9?)–1900. *P.E. Larss Photograph Collection, Alaska State Library, PCA 41-072.*

terrible, and strange to say it was not practiced by the so-called rougher element who knew something about handling animals," he wrote. "The worst men were those who in former life were supposed to be of the better class. These men lost their heads completely." One man who traversed the pass inexplicably turned on his dogs, beating them before shoving them under lake ice. "Then he sat down and cried," Walden added.[25] Sometimes people of conscience or the rough justice of miners' meetings intervened. "It was recently decided at such a meeting at Circle that a man cannot lick his own dog," reported A. C. Harris in 1897.[26] On the Valdez Glacier, stampeder Basil Austin and his comrades protested the constant maltreatment of three inexperienced dogs by their owners. "They shot the poor dogs while we were

---

25   Walden, *Dog-Puncher*, 135.
26   A. C. Harris, *Alaska and the Klondike Gold Fields* (Chicago: Monroe Book Company, 1897), 467.

eating supper," he wrote. "While we were sorry for them, we felt they were better off than to be further subjected to such damnable treatment."[27] Charles Margeson described seeing three to four half-starved dogs dragging loads of 500 pounds across the glacier. "A few men were so cruel to their dogs, and beat them so much," he wrote, "that a committee was sent to wait upon them; and they were ordered to stop beating them, or they would be dealt with by the indignant miners."[28] Often dogs labored under terrible conditions only to be dispatched once old age weakened them or their usefulness ended. Chisana miners killed many of their dogs in 1901 to avoid paying to board them through an idle summer in Valdez.[29] In Circle City, white men customarily shot all but their best dogs "rather than let them go through summers of starvation and suffering as the Indians did," Walden noted.[30]

Animal abuse was so rampant in Dawson City that the *Klondike Nugget* began crusading against the ill treatment of dogs. The criminal code of Dawson City provided for the arrest and punishment of anyone found guilty of cruelty to animals, wild and domestic, but the problem was enforcement. "Dogs are aggravating, of course, and one feels like excusing a whole lot of sulphurous expletives in the drivers, but the howling of beaten dogs in our ears night and day suggests the enforcement of the Northwest ordinance against cruelty to animals," the paper hinted. "There is not a more faithful servant in the North than the dog, nor any so hardly used.

"Horses would die in a month if subject to a third of the hardships which dogs cheerfully undergo for their master's benefit. A little interference by the police would act as a wholesome restraint on the 200-pound bullies who in anger would maim a 50-pound dog."[31]

But there were also people like Ohio reporter E. Hazard Wells, who shared expensive mutton and beef with an emaciated dog that

---

27   Austin, *Diary*, 43.
28   Charles Anson Margeson, *Experiences of Gold Hunters in Alaska* (Hornellsville, NY: The Author, 1899), 78.
29   "Mushers Arrive from Chesna," *Valdez News*, May 11, 1901, 1.
30   Walden, *Dog-Puncher*, 85.
31   "Editorial on Cruelty to Dogs," *Klondike Nugget*, November 2, 1899, 4.

appeared at his cabin door. "I patted him gently on the head and he looked up in surprise," Wells wrote. "It was unexpected kindness. How quickly came the answering look of friendship and fealty from the dog's eyes. He was my devoted follower from that moment."[32] Basil Austin and his friend grew fond of three ragged dogs they bought in Klutina, selling them only out of necessity to a one-legged saloon-keeper in Forty Mile. "I could soon see he liked dogs, and although we hated to part with them we felt sure they would have good care," Austin wrote.[33] Prospector Michael Spellacy penned entertaining reminiscences of three mutts who accompanied him from Dawson to Nome. He returned to Ohio with Tilicum, a Gordon setter and collie mix he called the "best and truest 'pardner' I struck in Alaska."[34]

Dogs that managed to survive their journeys became an essential part of a camp's work force. They pulled wheeled water barrels, hauled sledges stacked with logs and firewood, carted earth in underground mines. They towed boats along riverbanks, lugged packs laden with gold or provisions, even transported coffins in sled hearses. Teams delivered mail, supplies, newspapers, shop goods, and visitors to surrounding creeks and distant towns. "Indeed, the dog-team had become the chief symbol of conspicuous wealth in the Klondike," writes historian Pierre Berton. "It was the Cadillac of its time. "[35]

But released on their own recognizance during summer, dogs devolved into agents of chaos. "They are really more of a pest than the much-advertised mosquito," one guidebook admitted.[36] They brawled in the streets and saloons, stole food, wandered in and out of buildings, slept where they wanted, raided garbage, bit people, harassed horses, howled relentlessly, killed sheep and chickens. "Dogs everywhere, day and night, howling, fighting, filthy, mangy dogs— all these and more form at present one of the worst nuisances that has

---

32   E. Hazard Wells, *Magnificence and Misery: A Firsthand Account of the 1897 Klondike Gold Rush*, ed. Randall M. Dobb (New York: Doubleday, 1984), 97.

33   Austin, *The Diary of a Ninety-Eighter*, 122.

34   Spellacy, "Segura Miguel Memoir," Chapter 13, 12.

35   Pierre Berton, *The Klondike Fever: The Life and Death of the Last Great Gold Rush* (New York: Basic Books, 2003), 399.

36   *Official Guide*, 217.

for a long time afflicted the citizens of Dawson," complained the *Dawson Daily News*.[37] The *Skaguay News* ranked dogs among unsavory civic blights: "Prostitution and mangy dogs are too common in this particular section of broad white north. Let us have less of both evils."[38] Occasionally, exasperated citizens became vigilantes, though shooters risked fines as high as $150.[39] "Quit Poisoning Dogs," admonished a Dawson newspaper. "It is generally supposed that most of the poisoning is done by cheechakoes who do not know or appreciate the value of a dog in this country, and who find their slumbers disturbed by nightly malamuting."[40]

A persistent problem in mining communities everywhere was thievery by those who did appreciate the value of a dog. "Sergeant Wilson says there is scarcely a day that he is not called upon to listen to tales of woe concerning stolen dogs," noted the *Klondike Nugget*.[41] Police rescued several purloined animals from the steamer *Monarch* one fall shortly before they were shanghaied to Nome.[42] The Iditarod stampede in 1909 emptied the Fairbanks dog pound, stimulated "fancy prices" up to $100 per canine, and inspired prospectors heading downriver to toss dogs into their skiffs "without taking the trouble to hunt up the owners."[43] A United States marshal in Nome reported that a gang of thieves was snatching dogs from Natives along the coast and selling them in town.[44]

The perpetual commotion caused by loose dogs, rampant animal abuse, and thievery encouraged mining camps and frontier communities to culture themselves into proper towns. A burst of municipal litigation against dog-stealing prospectors followed the election of a

---

37   Norm Borotin, *A Klondike Scrapbook: Ordinary People, Extraordinary Times* (San Francisco: Chronicle Books, 1987).

38   Catherine Holder Spude, *Saloons, Prostitutes, and Temperance in Alaska Territory* (Norman: University of Oklahoma Press, 2015).

39   "Appeal Denied; Will Have to Pay $150 for Shooting a Dog," Semi-weekly *Klondike Nugget*, October 18, 1900, 2.

40   "Quit Poisoning Dogs," Semi-weekly *Klondike Nugget*, September 9, 1900, 6.

41   "Dog Thieves Abroad," *Klondike Nugget*, February 18, 1900, 4.

42   "Claimed the Dogs," *Klondike Nugget*, September 27, 1899, 3.

43   "Demand for Dogs Has Caused Rise in Price," *Fairbanks Daily News-Miner*, October 6, 1909, 4.

44   "Dog Thieves Up the Coast," *Nome News*, February 29, 1901, 1.

temporary "consent government" in Nome in 1899.[45] James Wickersham's first case as district court judge in Eagle reunited Chief Charley of the Tena Indians and his stolen dog.[46] After Congress allowed Alaska towns to incorporate in 1900, the mining hubs of Douglas and Juneau approved dog licensing and animal control as their earliest ordinances.[47] A Fairbanks dog ordinance inspired these headlines: "Ill Fated Days for Stray Dogs. If Your Favorite Bow-Wow is Missing Recall Whether You Tagged Him. If Not Go to the Pound."[48] The exasperated manager of the railroad construction site of Anchorage discovered that without legal authority from the legislature or an incorporated municipality, juggling nuisance dogs and nuisance owners was a "rather ticklish proposition as well as expensive."[49]

Passing laws was easier than enforcing them in communities where ornery miners often resisted government interference. An early Dawson ordinance requiring owners to muzzle or tie up their dogs was "an unmitigated evil and flagrant imposition," declared the *Klondike Nugget*.[50] Public outrage alternated with public necessity as the law was repeatedly suspended, altered, and reinstated until an outbreak of rabies spooked everybody in 1901. The dog population dwindled to about 500 following an efficient extermination campaign and a reinvigorated pound system. "To a great extent the Dawson dog has had his day," the *Nugget* announced.[51]

■ ■ ■

But not the northern dog. They became more essential as a calmer social structure permeated the Yukon and Alaska. Stampeders became

---

45   Edward Harrison, *Nome and Seward Peninsula* (Seattle: Metropolitan Press, 1905), 56.

46   James Wickersham, *Old Yukon: Tales, Trails, and Trials* (Washington, D.C.: Washington Law Book Co., 1938), 42–45.

47   "Council Meets," *Douglas Island News*, May 28, 1902, 2.

48   "Ill Fated Days for Stray Dogs," *Fairbanks Daily News-Miner*, May 17, 1909.

49   J. G. Watts, "Records of the Alaska Railroad Animal Files, 1924–56," November 14, 1917, RG 322, Box 67, File 139.

50   "That Dog Ordinance," *Klondike Nugget*, December 14, 1898, 2.

51   "Dog Days in Dawson," Semi-weekly *Klondike Nugget*, October 19, 1901, 1.

settlers, mining camps disappeared into the past or civilized themselves into a future, and the territorial economy that emerged relied heavily on sled dogs. For a few decades after the rushes, a guild of working sled dogs conducted trappers, missionaries, doctors, marshals, judges, mail carriers, freighters, game wardens, villagers, and, yes, prospectors through winter's expansive territory. Eventually the role of sled dogs was eclipsed by planes, trains, cars, and, in the 1960s, snowmachines, cruelly nicknamed "iron dogs." The subsequent revival of dogsled racing was partly a response to the dwindling purpose of working dogs (and perhaps of a certain breed of northerner, too). Mushing dogs for fun and sport was a way to bind people to the animal that has so faithfully shadowed the human pilgrimage through time.

Nostalgia has long since gilded the nitty-gritty reality of life in the goldfields. The half-starved, overworked, mangy curs of yore have morphed into the cheerfully romantic huskies and malamutes depicted by Alaska master artist Fred Machetanz and others. Our own complicated histories, myths, and longings cloud a clear-eyed perception of the animal itself. Robert Marshall, the levelheaded chronicler of life in Wiseman, knew this.

"A great deal has been written about the dogs of the North, much of it nonsense," he wrote in his classic study, *Arctic Village*. "When I first came to the Koyukuk one of the sourdoughs told me: 'If you've read any of those books by James Oliver Curwood and Rex Beach, well, they paint a picture of dog teams like a fellow might dream about, but they don't actually come that way. Dogs is dogs and a fellow don't want to expect too much of them.'" Marshall contributed his own litany of annoyances: the barking, the fighting, the daily nuisance of harnessing and unharnessing them, the mistakes and exhaustion of the trail, the relentless demands of cooking for them and feeding them and tending them.

"Yet withal," he concluded, "there is nothing in the Arctic as valuable, and in many ways as admirable, as a good dog."[52] Stories of the gold rush remind us that, as with people, there are dogs good and

---

52 Robert Marshall, *Arctic Village* (Fairbanks: University of Alaska Press, 2000), 119.

bad, faithful and untrustworthy, industrious and lazy, heroic and savage. But like Marshall, perhaps the truest thing we can say is simply: Dogs is dogs.

BIBLIOGRAPHY (PARTIAL)

Adney, Tappan. *The Klondike Stampede*. New York: Harper & Brothers Publishers, 1900.

Anderson, David B. "The Use of Dog Teams and the Use of Subsistence-Caught Fish for Feeding Sled Dogs in the Yukon River Drainage, Alaska." Technical Paper No. 210. Juneau: Division of Subsistence, Alaska Department of Fish and Game, 1992.

Austin, Basil. *The Diary of a Ninety-Eighter*. Mount Pleasant, MI: John Cumming, 1968.

Berton, Pierre. *The Klondike Fever: The Life and Death of the Last Great Gold Rush*. New York: Basic Books, 2003.

Borotin, Norm. *A Klondike Scrapbook: Ordinary People, Extraordinary Times*. San Francisco: Chronicle Books, 1987.

Brooks, Alfred Hulse. *Blazing Alaska's Trails*. 2nd ed. Fairbanks: University of Alaska Press, 1973.

Garland, Hamlin. *The Trail of the Goldseekers: A Record of Travel in Prose and Verse*. New York: The Macmillan Company, 1906.

Harris, A. C. *Alaska and the Klondike Gold Fields*. Chicago: Monroe Book Company, 1897.

Harrison, Edward. *Nome and Seward Peninsula*. Seattle: Metropolitan Press, 1905.

Haskell, William. *Two Years in the Klondike and Alaskan Gold Fields*. Washington, D.C.: Hartford Publishing Company, 1898.

Lallensack, Rachael. "Ancient Genomes Heat up Dog Domestication Debate." *Nature*, July 18, 2017. doi:10.1038/nature.2017.22320.

Lynch, Jeremiah. *Three Years in the Klondike* Chicago: The Lakeside Classics, 1967.

Margeson, Charles Anson. *Experiences of Gold Hunters in Alaska*. Hornellsville, NY: The Author, 1899.

Marshall, Robert. *Arctic Village*. Fairbanks: University of Alaska Press, 2000.

The Official Guide to the Klondyke Country and the Gold Fields of Alaska. Chicago: W. B. Conkey, 1897.

Powell, Addison M. *Trailing and Camping in Alaska*. New York: Newold Publishing Company, 1910.

Rickard, T. A. *Through the Yukon and Alaska*. San Francisco: Mining and Scientific Press, 1909.

Shepard, Paul. *The Others: How Animals Made Us Human*. Washington, D.C.: Island Press, 1997.

Spellacy, Michael. "'Segura Miguel' Gold Rush Memoir." Alaska and Polar Regions Collections and Archives, Rasmuson Library, University of Alaska Fairbanks, n.d.

Spude, Catherine Holder. *Saloons, Prostitutes, and Temperance in Alaska Territory*. Norman: University of Oklahoma Press, 2015.

Starnes, C. "Report of the North-West Mounted Police, Part III, 1900, Appendix B." Ottawa: S. E. Dawson, 1901.

Walden, Arthur Treadwell. *A Dog-Puncher on the Yukon*. Boston; New York: Houghton Mifflin Co., 1928.

Watts, J. G. "Records of the Alaska Railroad Animal Files, 1924–56," November 14, 1917, RG 322, Box 67, File 139.

Wells, E. Hazard. *Magnificence and Misery: A Firsthand Account of the 1897 Klondike Gold Rush*, ed. Randall M. Dobb. New York: Doubleday, 1984.

White, David Gordon. *Myths of the Dog-Man*. Chicago: University of Chicago Press, 1991.

Wickersham, James. *Old Yukon: Tales, Trails, and Trials*. Washington, D.C.: Washington Law Book Co., 1938.

Wood, Z. T. "Report of the North-West Mounted Police, 1899, Appendix A." Ottawa: S. E. Dawson, 1900.

A Note from Frank Soos

When I think of Terrence Cole, I often think of a warm summer evening at an Alaska Gold Panners' baseball game years ago. We were watching from down on the third-base line, and Terrence was moved to hold forth on how the renovations to Growden Park had ruined it, followed by a brief history of the ballpark itself. That moment contained many of Terrence's best qualities: his love of history, of Fairbanks, and of baseball. And of course he had a ball cap firmly planted on his head as he spoke.

DON'T YOU KNOW THIS PLACE WILL KILL YOU?

Jack London and Jon Krakauer on Death in the Alaska Wild

Frank Soos

When I took my job teaching English and creative writing at the University of Alaska, I knew close to nothing about this state. Yes, I knew we Americans had bought the place from the Russians shortly after the Civil War, and I knew Alaska had become a state in 1959. As Cub Scouts we had placed a small commemorative version of Alaska's big dipper flag on the bulletin board of our basement den.

I truly had only the vaguest idea of what life would be like in such a place. Alaska was mysterious, inviting in its wild allure, and frightful in its harsh climate. I knew it was cold: "When it's springtime in Alaska, it's forty below,"[1] Johnny Horton sang. And I knew that kind of cold could kill a person. I knew that because I had read Jack London's "To Build a Fire." "To Build a Fire" was a regular feature of junior high and high school literature anthologies. It even appeared in college texts. I taught it myself when I was on the faculty at Virginia Tech.

■ ■ ■

After stepping into overflow on a creek, London's unnamed protagonist quickly builds a fire to warm and dry himself, but he builds it under a spruce tree laden with snow. "It was his own fault, or, rather,

---

1   Johnny Horton, "When It's Springtime in Alaska (It's Forty Below)." http://www.metrolyrics.com/when-its-springtime-in-alaska-lyrics-johnny-horton.html.

his mistake,"[2] as the narrator would have it, perhaps taking up for his man after the snow drops from the tree and smothers the fire. But finally we readers are discouraged from feeling much sympathy for the character. He has ignored the old-timer's advice; he has been indifferent and at times cruel to his dog, at one point pushing the dog onto thin ice, where it breaks through. And most importantly, this man "was without imagination."[3] He saw things, but seemed incapable of grasping their significance.

What would a person learn from "To Build a Fire"? That nature is not so much cruel as indifferent to our human presence. That one mistake can kill a person. That a person "must never travel alone in the Klondike after fifty below."[4] All registered, all noted by this "*chechaquo*" when I arrived in 1986.

Jack London may have absorbed these lessons himself. He spent only one winter in the North, but took home with him the material for a good number of stories and the well-read short novels *The Call of the Wild* and *White Fang*. His details can be hyperbolic. At minus 55° Fahrenheit, spit will not freeze in the air or even when it hits the ground, even if a person is six foot six. In the Klondike, the sun does rise briefly every day, even near winter solstice. And a temperature of 75° F, as estimated by the narrator, would have been highly unlikely even in those days before global warming. But the real dangers of overflow and warm upwellings in creekbeds are on target. This is why travelers rarely walk in small streams, but rather along them.

Maybe after just a year in the North, Jack had learned that.

It's easy to mock the character's flaws: He's ill-prepared for the cold. He seems to have no Plan B in the event he cannot reach camp in a day. He does travel alone against advice, and he makes a classic mistake in building his fire.

But the story's real drive comes from the cascade of failures as the lone traveler tries to build a second fire. With his hands out of his

---

2   London, Jack. "To Build a Fire." In *Great Short Works of Jack London*, ed. Earle Labor (New York: Perennial Classics (Harper & Row), 1965): 293.

3   Ibid., 285.

4   Ibid., 292.

mittens, his fingers quickly grow numb and stiffen. He has trouble gathering suitable kindling, and then trouble lighting a match to his piece of birch bark (an excellent fire starter), until he finally ends up lighting the entire bundle of matches at once. Burning himself, and smelling rather than feeling the burns, he gets his fire going. But too clumsy to control his feeble new fire, he watches it go out. What is there left to do but make a desperate and futile attempt to run to his fellows at their camp still miles up the trail?

London's slow and carefully detailed account of one mistake compounding into another is augmented by the constant refrain in his character's head, "The old-timer on Sulphur Creek was right...."[5]

The convincing power of "To Build a Fire" stands in contrast to the over-the-top treatment in "Love of Life," where men in the Far North are again faced with adversity of their own making. In this story, a gold miner who slips and sprains his ankle is abandoned by his traveling companion. Left to fend for himself, the man struggles on with the help of a stick for a crutch. He is gradually reduced to crawling along in near starvation, and saves himself by catching a nest of ptarmigan chicks and eating them alive. And then by a second wildly unlikely encounter with a sick she-wolf. He and the wolf stalk each other until, exhausted, he falls asleep only to wake up with the wolf's teeth on his neck. But she is too weak to make the bite that would kill him, and he is somehow able to strangle her instead. This story falls into the tradition of those found in *True* and *Stag*, magazines from my boyhood featuring men in torn shirts armed only with sheath knives facing down rampant grizzly bears. For all the tight tensioned control London exhibits in "To Build a Fire," he lets what may have been his affection for extreme Naturalism get out of hand. "Love of Life" becomes just a tall tale.[6]

Still, it's easy for any Alaskan who spends time outdoors in any season to see some of his own mistakes in "To Build a Fire." Backpack stoves become balky and won't light. Firewood has not been gathered

---

5   Ibid., 295.
6   London, Jack. "Love of Live." In *Great Short Works of Jack London*, ed. Earle Labor. (New York: Perennial Classics (Harper & Row), 1965): 327–48.

and covered before the rain comes. The tent leaks and sleeping bags become sodden. Bears and other critters steal your food or perhaps threaten you. Boats, whether small canoes on rivers or commercial fishing boats, capsize. We don't need old-timers to remind us of all the ways nature's indifference leads to the inevitable natural fact: Nature will kill us one way or another.

Which may be a way to say that reading "To Build a Fire" might not be the worst preparation for coming to this country. It made me thoughtful, probably overly cautious, in my first winter in Alaska. On the university ski trails, I stuck near to the warming hut.

Maybe a young guy named Christopher McCandless needed to read it, too. He stumbled naively and unprepared not so far into the Alaskan wilderness, but far enough and foolishly enough to die. But unlike the serves-you-right reaction readers might feel for the protagonist in "To Build a Fire," a good number of readers of Jon Krakauer's *Into the Wild* felt sympathy, and even admiration, for Chris McCandless.

Here is how Krakauer characterizes McCandless as he brings his story of this wanderer to a close:

> It would be easy to stereotype Christopher McCandless as another boy who felt too much, a loopy young man who read too many books and lacked even a modicum of common sense. But the stereotype isn't a good fit. McCandless wasn't some feckless slacker, adrift and confused, racked by existential despair. To the contrary: His life hummed with meaning and purpose. But the meaning he wrested from existence lay beyond the comfortable path: McCandless distrusted the value of things that came easily. He demanded much of himself—more, in the end, than he could deliver.[7]

This seems to me to be an overly generous appraisal of a guy who did not have the gumption to keep from starving to death. His various journal entries don't show much of deep thinking or careful self-examination; instead they offer a catalogue of bad judgments. McCandless kills a moose, but he doesn't know how to properly dress

---

7   Krakauer, Jon. *Into the Wild* (New York: Anchor Books, 1997): 184.

the animal or how to dry the meat to keep it from rot and ruin. But that is beside the point. Jon Krakauer's take on Christopher McCandless is based on his own romantic overlay, placed on top of the narrow facts of the McCandless story.

And that romantic overlay seems to have had an infectious result. Every summer since the publication of *Into the Wild* in 1996, people have made what might be called holy pilgrimages to the abandoned Fairbanks city bus out the Stampede Road, the last place McCandless was seen alive after being dropped off by the man who picked him up as a hitchhiker. The road is clearly marked, off the Parks Highway just north of Healy, and it's not a long hike to the bus. In warmer weather, the level and the water velocity of the Teklanika River can vary greatly. People have gotten into trouble out that way, have needed rescue, and at least one has drowned trying to reach the bus.

But why would reading *Into the Wild* provoke such a response? From boys' adventure books featuring risky brushes with danger and death that the protagonist survives and so becomes more of a man to *On the Road*, wherein Jack Kerouac's heroes hit the road and flout convention in some search for their true selves, the promise of romantic adventure pulls like an undertow.

Here's an entry dated April 28, 1992, from Chris McCandless's journal, where he writes using his pen name Alex Supertramp:

> I am entering the bush. I found a .22-caliber Remington, and I hope it will serve me well. I have been walking for God knows how long. I do not have much food or clothing and it seems as if I had not prepared enough for this part of my journey. Hopefully this trip into the wild will provide me with the happiness that I have for so long been looking for. I will update when and if I can.
>
> Alex[8]

True enough, he has not prepared well enough so that a few months later on August 5, 1992, he writes:

---

8   Diary of Chris McCandless. https://intothewild2016.wordpress.com.

Day 100. I am in the weakest condition I have been so far. The wind is terrible and death looms as a serious threat. I am too weak and do not have the strength to pick my body up and walk out of this bus. I have literally become trapped in the wild. I continue to yell, as if there if [*sic*] any other soul that had the rotten idea of wondering [*sic*] so far out into the wilderness.

Alex[9]

Alex/Chris is beginning to look like Jack London's unnamed protagonist at this point. Both men recognize their limits when, in fact, it has become too late to do anything about them but accept the inevitable.

As he fails, London's character thinks, "Freezing was not so bad as people thought. There were lots worse ways to die."[10] Agreed. Starving to death may be one of them.

But what is the romantic appeal that a figure such as Chris McCandless seems to hold for his admirers that overrides the harder, harsher lessons of nearly a century earlier? Here is McCandless's last journal entry:

SOS. I NEED YOUR HELP. I AM INJURED, NEAR DEATH AND TOO WEAK TO HIKE OUT OF HERE. I AM ALL ALONE, THIS IS <u>NO JOKE</u>. IN THE NAME OF GOD, PLEASE REMAIN TO SAVE ME. I AM OUT COLLECTING BERRIES CLOSE BY AND SHALL RETURN THIS EVENING. THANK YOU.[11]

And here is Jon Krakauer's final judgment of McCandless:

But if he pitied himself in those last difficult hours—because he was so young, because he was alone, because his body had betrayed him and his will had let him down—it is not apparent from the photograph. He is smiling in the picture and there is no mistaking

---

9   Ibid.
10 London, "To Build a Fire," 299.
11 Krakauer, 197–98.

the look in his eyes: Chris McCandless was at peace, serene as a monk gone to God.[12]

Jack London's narrator focuses on the now-dead protagonist's dog:

> ...it crept close to the man and caught the scent of death. This made the animal bristle and back away. A little longer it delayed, howling under the stars that leaped and danced and shone brightly in the cold sky. Then it turned and trotted up the trail in the direction of camp it knew, where were the other food providers and fire providers.[13]

London is writing fiction and Krakauer is writing nonfiction. But Chris McCandless died before Jon Krakauer could have met the man. He is working from the sketchiest details left behind. And both men are building narratives, building them with intention. For London, the universe is indifferent and cold. His character is dead and the stars still shine, the dog goes off looking for food and shelter.

Krakauer would like to see his figure as a romantic visionary rather than a foolish guy with poor outdoor skills and bad judgment.

Narrative is a powerful force. For a person reading "To Build a Fire," the impulse might be to turn up the thermostat a few degrees and put on a sweater. The outside world is a cold, unwelcoming place. We are invited to take the narrator's point of view. In this case, London earns it. In "Love of Life," one hyperbolic detail piled onto another eventually breaks the reader's faith in the narrator. Willing suspension of disbelief, which any story must rely on, is lost and the reader is lost with it.

And for a person sitting in a comfortable living room or dormitory, reading *Into the Wild* may remind him of all he may be missing, all the adventure that is waiting right out the door if he would just slough off his unneeded possessions, throw out his thumb and go. In this way, McCandless's exploits, adroitly narrated by Krakauer, draw readers

---

12   Ibid., 199.
13   London, "To Build a Fire," 300.

closer. And in this way, too, Chris McCandless becomes as much a created character as the man Jack London made up of whole cloth.

Whether McCandless achieved happiness or greater self-awareness is up for grabs, but readers seem to be eager to join with Krakauer in filling in those blanks with emphatic affirmations. So they come to make their way to the rusting old bus for a moment of oneness with the dead man.

■ ■ ■

When we track our past lives, individually or collectively, we are building a history of ourselves. But when we read fiction or the literary nonfiction of a writer such as Jon Krakauer, we are entering into a world that invites our imaginative participation. To successful writers' credit, readers gladly jump in. That happened to me when I first read "To Build a Fire." It happened to many others when they read *Into the Wild*. What we read became something almost palpable and real.

If you can catch a bunch of Alaskans who've spent some time outdoors sitting around talking, once you steer them away from tall stories about bear encounters, you might get them all to own up to their own McCandless mini-moments. We have all taken risks. But when the camp stove failed and we ate the dinner cold, shivered in our wet sleeping bags, we came back and figured out how to avoid at least that particular mistake again. In retrospect, and pushed along with a tone of ironic hyperbole, our mistakes can seem funny. Chris McCandless may have had such stories to offer himself had he had some more gumption. But there is no guarantee, neither here nor in boys' books of big adventures, that such trials will make us braver, smarter, or wiser.

What we can appreciate is the suasive power a well-told story can have. A good narrative picks up speed and carries its readers along. When we put the book down, though, we may want to let our pulses return to normal and ponder: Isn't it better to face death on the page and get over it? And maybe learn a few useful things about human nature along the way.

BIBLIOGRAPHY (PARTIAL)

Krakauer, Jon. *Into the Wild*. New York: Anchor Books, 1997, 184.

Labor, Earle, ed. *Great Short Works of Jack London*. New York: Perennial Classics (Harper & Row), 1965.

A Note from John Straley

I have been asked to describe my relationship with Professor Cole. Unlike other esteemed contributors to this book, I have neither been a student nor a teaching colleague of Terrence Cole, but have attended numerous scholarly, literary, and social gatherings where we have both been asked to "pipe down." Sometimes a host will notice loud, inappropriate laughing when nothing apparently funny has been said from the podium, sometimes there will be snoring from someone lying behind the last seats in the lecture hall, often there will be talking...or, more accurately, "Marxian" (Groucho not Karl) stage whispering of bad jokes, terribly told during somber lectures...this will almost always be one or the other of us.

JOSEPH HAZELWOOD AND
THE ONE THOUSAND DOZEN

John Straley

I am not particularly smart and I'm definitely not a scholar, but I come up with a good idea every once in a while. There was one such time, riding on a bus with Terrence Cole from Skagway to Dyea. We passed the Dyea harbor, where in 1897 and 1898 thousands of gold rush miners had offloaded their gear without benefit of a dock, and Terrence mentioned that Jack London himself had made the same trip and had used the experience to inform his Klondike stories. Terrence was dressed in that moment in a strangely cut military green jacket, and he had been telling some attractive young women at the conference we were attending that it made him look like Fidel Castro. Instead, my wife had just told him on the bus, she thought he looked like an employee of the National Park Service.

And so, trying to rapidly change the subject, Terrence continued to tell me about his interest in a little-known Jack London story called "The One Thousand Dozen," in which a man named Rasmunsen comes up with a plan to transport a thousand dozen eggs up over the pass and down the Yukon river system to Dawson City, and then sell the eggs for up to five dollars a dozen.

Rasmunsen struck Terrence as the first real tragic boom-time entrepreneur in literature, and an emblem of London's socialist dogma. Terrence then pretended to puff on a cigar and leaned toward Jan. "Fidel, Jan. Come on! Obviously!" If you have never seen Professor Cole, he is small, clean-shaven, and very pale, with almost white hair.

Frankly, a Christmas cookie looks more like Fidel Castro than Terrence Cole does, and he knows it.

This bus ride was just before Terrence learned he was sick with gastric cancer. The bay at Dyea was serene that day; there was not a single ship and not a sign of the frantic capitalist dreamers of a century before. A few gulls floated on the waves, and the waves broke softly on the rocks. Later I found a section from London's *Daughter of the Snows* that captured Jack London's impression of a more chaotic Dyea harbor:

> Everybody was in everybody else's way; nor was there one who failed to proclaim it at the top of his lungs. A thousand gold seekers were clamoring for the immediate landing of their outfits. Each hatchway gaped wide open, and from the lower depths the shrieking donkey-engines were hurrying the mis-assorted outfits skyward. On either side of the steamer, rows of scows received the flying cargo, and on each of these scows a sweating mob of men charged the descending slings and heaved bales and boxes about in frantic search. Men waved shipping receipts and shouted over the steamer-rails to them. Sometimes two and three identified the same article, and war arose.

That day as I bumped along on the bus I didn't have so much of an idea as a memory, and I tried to wrestle it into a good idea. I'm a private investigator, a storyteller, a poet sometimes; good ideas rarely come to me, but when they do they come like smoke drifting across a lake. So it helps my thought process if someone is cooking something appetizing over the fire. This memory was of a case I had worked on almost thirty years ago, and that kind of smell is always powerful in my memory—powerful if not appetizing.

Joseph Hazelwood was the captain of the *Exxon Valdez* when it went aground on Bligh Reef in Prince William Sound on March 24, 1989. Hazelwood was in his cabin doing paperwork and listening to Vivaldi's "Four Seasons" when he felt the shudder of the ship, which was drawing some fifty feet of draft, strike a reef, approximately thirty feet below the surface of the water at its shallowest. This means some twenty feet of hull was crushing like a can under his feet and all he felt was a shudder—a change in cavitation of the prop, and a sense that the ship had stopped. No one lurched to the deck or cried out. The massive ship just ground to a halt.

The captain had instructed his second in command to contact him after he had made the turn to avoid the ice coming from the glaciated inlet. That turn was never made, and the captain was never summoned. The ship's grounding caused a spill of over a million barrels of crude oil into Prince William Sound. It took more than two days to mount a response to the spill, and by that time oil had spread to hundreds of miles of coastline, causing incalculable damage to fish, wildlife, birds, intertidal and microscopic life, and marine mammals. Photographs of oiled birds and sea otters dominated the international press for weeks. The final damages are still not known. Even though far worse spills have taken place since, the backdrop of the pristine Alaska coast has caused the *Exxon Valdez* spill to become an iconic disaster in the public's imagination.

I was the investigator hired by Hazelwood's attorneys for his criminal trial. I worked out of an office in Anchorage. The captain had his main team of lawyers in New York, where his friend from the Maritime Academy, Michael Chalos, had his offices and served as his principal legal advisor. Chalos hired Dick Madsen from Fairbanks as Hazelwood's Alaska counsel. Madsen had been a former law partner of the then-governor of Alaska, Steve Cowper. Chalos also hired a young motion writer from Anchorage, Rick Friedman, who I regarded as nothing short of a genius. Rick and I had worked together on the homicide of a fishing boat skipper. Since then I had worked several homicides on fishing boats and had built a reputation as a private investigator who knew "boat crimes." I was working for the public defender covering all of southeastern Alaska, investigating mostly sexual abuse of minors and murder cases, when I got the call to work on *State v. Hazelwood*, a felony DUI case, full time and for a salary that sounded unimaginable at the time. I took the case, and that was how I made the acquaintance of Captain Joseph Hazelwood.

Joseph was his given name; his friends and family called him Jeff, and to everyone else at the time he was known simply as "Captain" or "the Captain." He was already infamous by the time of his trial, having been on the cover of nearly every major news magazine. Because he had lost his driving license in New York due to prior driving while intoxicated convictions, and because he had been seen drinking a martini hours before he got on the ship, alcohol became the focus of the initial news story. His blood collected by authorities was not preserved correctly and was collected too far outside the timeframe to be of evidentiary value to fact finders. No one who had contact with him the night of the grounding—neither his crew nor the authorities who responded to the ship—ever saw any indication of impairment. At his trial, the Captain was found not guilty of the felony "reckless discharge of oil," but guilty of the misdemeanor "negligent discharge of oil." On the day of the verdict, we were satisfied with the jury's decision; we felt we won our trial. Later in federal proceedings, it was found that the Alaska authorities had withheld information from the defense concerning the mishandling of the alcohol, and upon appeal even the misdemeanor charges were overturned, albeit after the Captain had performed the entirety of his thousand hours of community service, picking up trash on the side of Alaska highways and working in soup kitchens.

The Captain has had to carry the burden of the ship's grounding throughout his life. He was finished with his chosen career, and no one would hire him to run a tanker again. Though there had and have since been far worse spills all over the world, his name became iconic and inseparable from environmental disaster.

He always recognized the scope of the tragedy, though he hated to be its poster boy.

Joseph Hazelwood is a guarded and bookish man, fiercely intelligent, both proud and shy. Really the worst kind of personality to have this kind of notoriety visited upon him. I spent quite a bit of time with him during the trial, as part of my duties were to unofficially keep an eye on him to make sure he was not harassed or threatened. This wasn't difficult actually—in Alaska, the spill had brought employment and huge paydays. Drunks would approach him on the way to court, but mostly to thank him for the earnings they had made working on the spill—"God bless you, man, I bought my wife a Corvette with what I made in Valdez." The Captain would shake his head and say,

"Well . . . it's a nice car, and a nice sentiment, but a crappy circumstance . . .," but the guy was gone by then and bragging to his friends.

The Captain walked like a sailor. We often took the stairs in the courthouse and the hotel, and he hopped down steps bowlegged, with legs spread wide as if on a pitching vessel. He didn't like to wear shoes inside, and often picked up loose objects on the ground with his toes. I'm not sure if this is a sailor's trait or just a personal quirk, but it was notable. He was indomitable at trivia; he could tell you not only the title of a great many tunes, but also the musicians who played on a particular track. I guess he may have been wrong sometimes, but I never saw anyone challenge him and succeed. He also was well read in the literature of the sea. He was known to have taught his officers celestial navigation, and he was proud of his knowledge of seamanship and maritime history. He was clearly intelligent and had good skills in language and mathematics. To me, he seemed well balanced and a natural leader, and his crew had liked him.

My good idea kept developing over the months—at first I thought there was a connection between Jack London himself and the Captain. Or perhaps there was a certain resonance that Hazelwood might have with the story "The One Thousand Dozen." So I asked him to read the story and he agreed to talk with me about it.

I wanted to tape record an interview with the Captain about his reactions to "The One Thousand Dozen," and after he read the story he thought he didn't have anything of interest to say. I sent him a list of questions and he agreed to send me answers. I think because he was at the center of one of the most litigious events of the twentieth century, he was reluctant to go on tape. I also gave him a final cut on this article. Here is my brief interview with the Captain, conducted on February 19, 2018.

■ ■ ■

JS: I have been reading about Jack London and thinking about his experiences and yours. He grew up in Oakland and sailed a small boat as a boy. You grew up on Long Island, and I understand you sailed a small boat. What kind of boat did you sail?

JH: Having the good fortune of growing up in a house overlooking a sheltered harbor, we (myself and my contemporaries) had access to all sorts of watercraft—motor and sail. I preferred sailboats as they required a bit more thought to get from point A to point B. Started out crewing on small sailboats like Comets and Snipes, and graduated to crewing on larger sailboats owned by friends' and neighbors' parents.

JS: Where did you sail it?

JH: Initially started in the local harbors and bays and then to the Long Island Sound and thence into the Atlantic.

JS: London reports getting in all kinds of trouble with his boat— robbing oyster farms and sneaking around docks where he wasn't supposed to be. Did you have anything similar?

JH: No trouble or sneaking around. To make money I started out as a "cull boy" for local clammers, then dug hard-shelled clams from boat(s) that friends and I made. I also had the good fortune to crew on a sailboat racing from Newport, Rhode Island, to Bermuda, and found I wanted to keep on going on arrival in Bermuda. I was not a dreamy kid as such, but when I was first learning to read I was fascinated with the slot in the local post office that was labeled "All Other Places."

JS: London was very intelligent and loved to read. You were similar in this. Can you describe your reading habits as a young person?

JH: Growing up I found that reading offered my mind a more detailed mental image/interpretation that was lacking in movies, likewise I preferred radio over television. I guess I had a good but not florid imagination.

JS: What was your first experience or awareness of Alaska? Did you read Jack London as a kid?

JH: When my father explained to me navigation and showed me how "Great Circle" routes were shorter than "Rhumbline" distances, I was surprised that the shortest route from New York to Japan passed over Alaska. As a youngster I read *The Call of the Wild* and *The Sea Wolf*. I also stumbled across some Robert Service poetry that seemed to strike a chord in my young mind.

JS: Your father was a commercial pilot. When did you decide that you wanted to go to sea?

JH: As a majority of my childhood friends were the sons and daughters of commercial airline pilots (ex–World War II military fliers), in the neighborhood we all were a bit inured to the fascination with flying, other than the cheap (free) worldwide travel options that having a father in the cockpit(s) offered. I just had a natural attraction to all sorts of watercraft.

JS: Why did you want to go to sea? Did that decision have anything to do with your experience with your small boat?

JH: I found that it was a more or less natural progression from small boats and the trips I'd made on them which determined that I was going to make a living afloat.

JS: When you first considered going to sea did you think of going north to Alaska or did you first imagine crossing the Atlantic? When did you go to sea?

JH: My first "seagoing" job was cod fishing out of Point Judith, Rhode Island, as a deckhand under sail and power at fifteen.

JS: When did you first go to Alaska?

JH: Other than short stops in Fairbanks en route to and from the Far East, 1969 or 1970 to Drift River/Cook Inlet.

JS: What was your experience there?

JH: Tying up to the Christy Lee Platform at the foot of Mt. Redoubt, as it was steaming away, was an eye opener for a young deck officer.

JS: When did you first decide that you wanted to be the master of a tanker?

JH: I'd trained as a deck officer in college and considered that moving up the ranks would be a natural progression in a career. I was not overly ambitious for the captain's role without first learning the "ropes" in the ways of a commercial ship while in the subordinate billets.

JS: Why a tanker?

JH: My first attraction was "Break Bulk" freighters, with cargo handling as a real exercise in seamanship and a variety of complicated cargo configurations. But I could see that those types of vessels were on their way out and being replaced by container vessels, which didn't appeal to me. Tankers seemed to be a more challenging type of vessel.

JS: I spoke to several skippers and people in the industry who told me that you were a very good tanker captain. Is that true?

JH: I'd prefer to be thought of by my contemporaries as a competent seaman.

JS: What makes a good tanker captain?

JH: I, drawing from experiences from Master Mariners that I'd sailed under and respected, felt that looking out for one's crew is of primary importance. Taking care of the crew, keeping in mind their shortcomings and strengths goes a long way to making any Master's job easier, and by extension the operation of the vessel more efficient. I believe this applies to any type of vessel.

JS: Let's talk about "The One Thousand Dozen"—when I first read the story I couldn't help think of the parallels between transporting a very fragile cargo over a hostile landscape and the challenge of transporting crude oil from the Arctic. Is there anything about this story that resonates with you?

JH: As a tale of an adventure I found it a good read. Some of the most difficult jobs I found at sea started out as rather benign, but one has to adapt to their circumstances.

JS: You're clearly not like Rasmunsen, but how do you think you are different? Are there any ways that you are similar? Are you driven in the way he was depicted?

JH: I don't feel that I'd be so driven with pursuit of money as my motivator.

JS: It is my impression that you loved being a tanker captain, is that true?

JH: I enjoyed the going to sea and actual ship handling in different ports and the lifelong friends that I made along the way. Not just on tankers but on many different types of watercraft. As mentioned earlier, the Master's rating was a natural progression in a seagoing career, not a "Holy Grail" type of pursuit for me. But as I said, I very much liked being at sea and handling ships.

JS: On the day of the grounding, when the eggs broke so to speak, your career was over... Can you tell me what it was like when you felt the *Valdez* go aground, you went up to the bridge and you went out on the wing, what did you hear, what did you smell, what did you feel?

JH: I could see oil boiling adjacent to the hull, and I remember the smell of the oil. I knew the situation was catastrophic. My first thoughts (and by extension) were to make sure that all the crewmembers were safe and checking that the vessel on the strand was stable.

JS: Do you think you might have shared any of Rasmunsen's grief that night?

JH: On that particular evening I didn't have time for sorrow or any other "loftier" thoughts than the safety of my crew and the stability of the vessel.

JS: London's description of sailing down the lakes and rivers apparently has great similarities to his own experience in the Klondike. What did you think of those scenes, and how do you judge his seamanship?

JH: I'd (in the real world) do a little better "Voyage Planning," including cargo stowage, but that's just the old freighter mate in me. As far as his seamanship is concerned, he was in "survival mode" for much of his travel/travail, so some literary license has to be allowed.

■ ■ ■

Hazelwood's combination of pride and shyness is clear. He is not Rasmunsen. But perhaps there is a parallel to be made with the settings the two men found themselves in. They were both part of an Alaska boom and bust economy. I admit I have never seen a nineteenth-century port such as the one Jack London described, but I have witnessed the bustle of other boomtown Alaska economies: Deadhorse in the Arctic and the Valdez oil terminal. They were slightly more civilized than London's Dyea harbor, but there is violence beneath the surface, and there is pornography piped in electronically. The oil boom has lasted longer than the gold rush, but the principle has remained much the same as Rasmunsen's: solid, predictable money will be made by the lucky ones who get there first, but the scrappy money will be made by the opportunists who sell shovels and eggs.

The parallels to London's own sense of adventure still accrue in my mind. Captain Hazelwood grew up sailing a small boat on Long Island Sound, had crewed on sailboats, and had worked culling clams for commercial clam diggers. He didn't romanticize his childhood in the way Jack London had, and he wasn't as poor, but he still felt the pull of the sea and adventure.

This from *Jack London and the Klondike* by Franklin Walker:

> ...much of London's activity involved more excitement than harm. Sailing the *Razzle Dazzle* into the shallow south bay during the dark of the moon took skill, evading the guards at the oyster beds was a tricky business, and there was real sport in coming home on a spanking breeze to reach the market where saloon keepers bought readily for oyster breakfast and free lunch, caring not a whit whether the oysters came from the abandoned beds off Asparagus Island or from the inadequately guarded holding of the monopolistic company across the bay near Redwood City.

The *Razzle Dazzle* was London's small sailing skiff. Hazelwood sailed those same small boats called Comets and Snipes at first. He first stuck close to home, gradually sailing farther and farther out into the Atlantic by himself, and then as a crewman to cross the ocean in a transatlantic sailboat race. Clearly Hazelwood was drawn by the sea much as London was, though they had different backgrounds and came from different coasts.

In "The One Thousand Dozen," David Rasmunsen conceived a plan which was "figured briefly and to the point, and the adventure became iridescent-hued, splendid. That eggs would sell at Dawson for five dollars a dozen." He shares his plan with his wife in San Francisco, where it crystallizes. He weighs out the eggs with a local grocer and travels up the west coast, disembarks at Dyea, hires Tlingit packers to carry the eggs up over the pass, and then builds a boat he names *The Alma* (after his wife . . . the adventure takes a bit of a Homeric turn there). At every bend in the adventure, the difficulties, expenses, and challenges are greater than he budgeted. He gets iced in on the river, caches the eggs in the woods, goes back to San Francisco, and repeats the journey the next year to deliver the rotten eggs to Dawson. When the buyers discover they have bought rotten eggs, they corner Rasmunsen, and he can't bear to sell the poisoned eggs for dog food.

He ends the story by hanging himself.

Clearly the Captain isn't Rasmunsen. He was never motivated by greed. But there are some similarities, not in the personalities of the men but in the business where they found themselves—the Alaska boom and bust wilderness capitalism that continuously prompts disaster.

The Captain's wife plays a role in the story of his grounding. In London's story, the wife plays the role, I think, of reminding the reader of domesticity as the idealized hearth and home and the reward for the adventurer at the end of his travels, as a sailor might dream of his wife at home waiting for him, when his true love is the sea. In my investigation of the *Valdez* grounding, the Captain's domestic life was a lynchpin to understanding what happened. After Hazelwood left a Valdez pizza restaurant on the night of March 24, 1989, hours before boarding the oil tanker, he walked across the street and sent flowers to his wife. I spent some time tracking down this information because he paid for that transaction with a credit card, and because that credit card transaction was verified by long-distance call, it gave our investigation a steady time mark for when he left the restaurant and walked away from any access to alcohol. Alcohol became a non-issue to the jury as a result, largely due to the testimony of the people who were with him and those flowers for his wife.

Truthfully, my good idea was only this: the transportation of a fragile commodity always has and always will be almost foolishly risky. A single-hulled tanker has a massive bulk but a remarkably fragile skin and structure. Just loading the tanks the wrong way could twist a ship in two. When the *Exxon Valdez* grounded, it did not lurch, or crash, or throw the crew to the decks, and in truth, double hull tankers are not much better. Just as loading the tankage can break a ship in pieces, the accidental unloading that occurs after a fatal grounding can cause the unsecured part of a ship to twist away and sink into the sea. This is why the Captain, after the grounding, had to maneuver the *Valdez*, first to ascertain how it was hung on the reef, and then to secure it to prevent sinking and more spillage.

Indeed, the greed of the oil boom and the "iridescent-hued, splendid" plan does find its way into the realities I have witnessed in Deadhorse and along the Trans-Alaska Pipeline project. The American driver and fuel consumer thinks nothing of burning gasoline that originates from the Arctic or from the Gulf of Mexico or Saudi Arabia. As we pump the stuff into our cars, focused and careful not to spill it on the concrete of the gas station or the convenience store where we buy it, we take for granted that our fuel should make its extraordinary trip all the way to us, also *without spilling a drop*. Which in a way is as crazy as Rasmunsen thinking he could transport a thousand dozen eggs to Dawson.

The oil business and Rasmunsen are each motivated by profit, even if big oil has had far more capital and a larger market. The idea that we are going to transport all that liquid, all those great distances, without spilling a drop, is just as unreasonable as transporting a thousand dozen eggs over the Golden Staircase and down the river system of the Yukon at the end of the season. It's a fool's errand. This is what the Native protesters in the Dakotas, camping and picketing to stop pipeline construction on their own lands, know very surely. Crude oil carries corrosive water—considering water extraction and fracking more water than ever—and pipelines rust. I've seen it for myself in Prudhoe Bay, in the lines and in the huge balancing tanks. Corrosion—like a rotten egg you wouldn't want to feed to your dog.

I think Terrence "Fidel" Cole was right that London meant to indict capitalism in his short story. I think he meant to make the point that the promise of profit feeds on individual workers' sense of adventure to gain its own rewards. The adventurer to London was the person who lived closest to his "animal nature," and this nature animates the worker's drive—for the benefit of profit and to the detriment of the individual.

You see these themes in many of London's Klondike stories, such as *Call of the Wild* or "To Build a Fire"—the animals go back to their wild nature. Men become lost and die in pursuit of an unattainable greed, by straying from their natural animal instincts.

In my own brief interview with Captain Hazelwood, he was circumspect. He is tired of talking about the grounding, and the event that ruined his name and his career. I respect that, but I have my own memory of a conversation with him years ago, when he mentioned his feelings of loss standing out on the wing, where he described the smell of the oil as "sickening." But memory is a tricky thing. The last page of "The One Thousand Dozen," though, remains the same:

> Somebody knocked at the door, knocked again, and let himself in. "What a mess!" he remarked, as he paused and surveyed the scene. The severed eggs were beginning to thaw in the heat of the stove and the miserable odor was growing stronger.
> "Must a-happened on the steamer," he suggested.
> Rasmunsen looked at him long and blankly.
> "I'm Murray, Big Jim Murray, everybody knows me," the man volunteered. "I'm just hearin' your eggs is rotten, and I'm offerin' you two hundred for the batch. They ain't good as salmon, but still they're fair scoffin's for dogs." Rasmunsen seemed turned to stone. He did not move. "You go to hell," he said passionlessly.

Here the pride of a man is shown, the pride of a man whose life has irrevocably changed. He is not the Master of a tanker standing on the wing. It would take more than a hundred years and another age of industrial greed and industrial arrogance, but the result would be the same: one man standing on the wing with the foul smell of oil and no way of getting it back in the hull. He would act to save his ship and protect his crew, but he must have known that his career, that natural progression of mastery was over, and he, like Rasmunsen, would be a punch line. Worst of all, he was smart and sensitive enough to sense it all coming.

Today the Captain delivers yachts for wealthy clients. He takes the wheels of beautiful boats and sails them to glamorous ports, and turns them over to mostly amateur or novice seamen who will rarely take them offshore. Some of the owners have professional skippers and crews, but the Captain still smiles at the modern electric winches and the comfort of switching from the covered wheelhouses. He double-checks the electronics with his own trusted tools. He is old school, and still very proud. He is still an expert seaman, I think, and a mariner, and will always be, but the world will never really know, and that is all right with him.

I think of this now, of his mastery, when I remember back to Dyea, and that quiet day with Terrence Cole. I realize that I am out of my depth in trying to offer literary insight to a subject Terrence knows so well himself. I only want to honor an old friend with one more tale of my misspent life of crime, and only wish I could have helped him more, when we had more time for revolution, and more room to maneuver around the ice.

A Note from Kes Woodward

I promised myself some years ago that I would never write an academic paper again, so that I could spend all my time and energy in my studio, on my paintings. I wouldn't have done this for anyone but Terrence.

Beyond our longstanding personal friendship, Terrence and I have shared so many graduate students over the years, serving on their thesis committees and shepherding them through their programs. I have been continually amazed and delighted by his dedication, energy, insight, and rigorous but wholly original approach to history—both speaking about it and writing about it. More than anyone I know, Terrence makes history fun.

I've tried here to follow his example by looking in a fresh, personal way at a different element of a subject I've written and lectured about for years. Thank you, Terrence, for your friendship and inspiration, and I hope you enjoy this small tribute.

SYDNEY LAURENCE, BELLE SIMPSON, AND THE NUGGET SHOP

Kes Woodward

More than forty years ago, when I was a just-turned-twenty-six-year-old art curator at the Alaska State Museum, fresh out of graduate school and brand-new to Alaska, I was sent to visit and court for possible donations of artwork to the museum a legendary figure in Juneau history—ninety-two-year-old Belle Simpson, in her apartment across the channel in Douglas, Alaska. I knew that she had given the State Museum one Sydney Laurence painting some years before, and that she'd owned and operated a gift shop and curio store in Juneau called The Nugget Shop for much of the century, but I barely knew who Sydney Laurence had been, much less how important Belle Simpson and The Nugget Shop had been to the career of the man who became Alaska's most sought-after and celebrated Alaskan historical painter. I wish so often that I could talk with Belle Simpson today, knowing what I have learned about Sydney Laurence over the past four decades, as I still have so many questions that she might uniquely be able to answer.

Sydney Mortimer Laurence (1865–1940) was the first professionally trained artist to make Alaska his home, and he is Alaska's most widely beloved historical painter. I have written and lectured extensively about Laurence's life and work, focusing primarily on the lasting impact of the image he forged of Alaska as "The Last Frontier." Laurence composed a compelling picture of Alaska as a place where people are few and, when present at all, are small, lonely, and vulnerable, while the land is large, awesome, and indifferent to human fortunes. That romantic, "Last Frontier" image continues, for better and worse, to inspire many residents and to lure hundreds of thousands of annual visitors to Alaska today.[1]

I have argued that Sydney Laurence's paintings—the originals in museums and the homes of prominent private collectors, and the countless reproductions of them in gift shops, banks, medical centers, businesses, state offices, and everyday Alaska homes—helped lodge and cement that "Last Frontier" image of Alaska in our imagination. I had not considered until recently, however, how Sydney Laurence's work came to widespread attention, how his vision of Alaska was promulgated, and how it came to take hold. This essay examines a key element of that story—the pivotal role that Belle Simpson and her husband, Robert Simpson, owners of The Nugget Shop curio store in Juneau, played in Laurence's artistic success and in making his images widely known.

Sydney Laurence came to Alaska from England in 1903 or 1904,[2] following some success as an expatriate American painter in England and some extensive adventures as an artist-correspondent for turn-of-the-century newspapers and magazines, covering conflicts from the Spanish-American War in the United States to the Boer War in South Africa and the Boxer Rebellion in China. We don't know for certain why he suddenly left his artist wife and their two small children in England in 1903 to come to Alaska, never to see them again. Perhaps

---

1   Kesler E. Woodward, *Sydney Laurence, Painter of the North* (Seattle: University of Washington Press in Association with the Anchorage Museum of History and Art, 1990); Kesler E. Woodward, *Painting in the North: Alaskan Art in the Anchorage Museum of History and Art* (Seattle: Anchorage Museum of History and Art, 1993).

2   Even the year of Sydney Laurence's arrival in Alaska is not certain. He would later say that he arrived in 1903, but new work of his continued to be published regularly in London's *Black and White* magazine that year, and he was listed in the catalog of an exhibition of paintings at England's Cheltenham Fine Arts Society in 1904 as an Honorary Member. By late 1904, in any case, he was certainly in Tyonek, Alaska, as he received picture postcards there from his wife, Alexandrina, of herself and their two sons. For images of the postcards, now in the collection of the Anchorage Museum, and further discussion of the date of Laurence's arrival in Alaska, see Woodward 1990, 12–13, 125, 129.

his global adventures as an artist-correspondent kindled his wander-lust. He would say in a 1925 interview that it was simple—that like so many others of the era, he was drawn by the lure of gold:

> I was attracted by the same thing that attracted all the other suck-ers, gold. I didn't find any appreciable quantity of the yellow metal and then, like a lot of other fellows, I was broke and couldn't get away. So I resumed my painting. I found enough material to keep me busy the rest of my life, and I have stayed in Alaska ever since.[3]

Laurence was, however, far from an overnight artistic or financial success in Alaska. His early years on the northern frontier were hard. During most of his first two decades in the Territory, he lived hand-to-mouth, dabbling unsuccessfully in small-scale prospecting and mining, speculating on oil leases, and frequently trading some of the few paintings he had time and means to make for room and board. When artist and mountain climber Belmore Browne, on his way to try to climb Denali in 1910, encountered him in the village of Beluga on Cook Inlet, Laurence regaled him with tales of his past glories before coming to Alaska, but was impoverished and unwell, and Browne described him in his journal as "a sad relic of the frontier."[4]

Five years later, a dozen years after his arrival in the Territory, Laurence was still only painting sporadically. He was making his living as a commercial photographer in the brand-new town of Anchorage and continuing to prospect, unsuccessfully, for both gold and oil. Between 1915 and 1923, however, his fortunes would change dramatically. He was able to close his photographic studio in 1922 and pursue painting full-time, and he would become widely acknowledged as the Territory's most prominent painter. A close look at the

---

3 Interview with the *Los Angeles Times*, reported in the *Anchorage Times*, December 3, 1925.

4 Belmore Browne Papers, Box 2, Folder 4, Stefansson Manuscript no. 190. Dartmouth College Library, Hanover, New Hampshire. For more on the encounter between artist/mountain climber Belmore Browne and Laurence at Beluga in 1910, including the full text of the note concerning Laurence in Belmore Browne's 1910 journal, see Woodward, "Sydney Laurence," *Southwest Art* 20, no. 7 (December 1990): 76–77 and Woodward 1993.

chronology and details of his success makes it clear that it was due not only to the originality of his vision and the quality of his work, but to the introduction of his paintings to a wider audience and to their successful marketing.

In retrospect, it is clear that the watershed event that heralded the belated change in Laurence's fortunes was the first sale of one of his paintings in Belle and Robert Simpson's Nugget Shop in Juneau in 1919. The artist was by that time almost fifty-five years old, and his years in Alaska had been hard ones, but the big break he needed did not come too late. Belle Simpson would very soon after contact him, asking for as many paintings as he could produce.

Laurence's work and career have not historically been regarded as closely tied to Juneau and Southeast Alaska, but instead to Anchorage and Denali—the mountain he knew as Mt. McKinley. He lived and painted in and out of Valdez, Cordova, various locales along Cook Inlet, and Anchorage for two decades after his arrival in the Territory. His early Alaska paintings were primarily of Prince William Sound, Cook Inlet, and more and more frequently over time, of Denali. He began painting North America's highest peak, with the Tokositna River in the foreground, from his "outdoor studio" at a camp in the Dutch Hills west of Talkeetna, early in the second decade of the century, and he essentially made the mountain into an icon, and its image from that locale his own. Among the five thousand or more paintings Sydney Laurence is known to have made, at least a thousand are of Denali, and they are by far the most sought-after examples of his work. Though he made paintings of the Juneau area, where he stopped frequently on his travels north by ship from Seattle in the spring and south in the fall, and of other Southeast Alaska locales, they are far fewer in number than his southcentral Alaska scenes.

Laurence moved to Los Angeles in the early 1920s and later to Seattle, but he returned to Alaska nearly every summer to paint until his death in 1940. He stayed and worked in the Anchorage Hotel during those summers, making frequent trips, especially in the early years of his summer residences, to paint in the surrounding landscape. In winters in Los Angeles and later Seattle, he continued to paint almost exclusively Alaska scenes, mostly of Cook Inlet, Denali, and

Prince William Sound. The predominance of south central Alaska subject matter in the work he did in all his studios has to some extent led the significance of his Juneau images and connections to be largely overlooked. In recent years, however, the Juneau-Douglas City Museum has been able to acquire several fine examples of his Juneau-area paintings through the generosity of local donors. Following one of those acquisitions, I gave a talk about Laurence and his work there in 2012. In the fall of 2017, the museum's director, Jane Lindsey, excited about the museum's acquisition of another Juneau-area Laurence painting, asked if I could give another talk for them, specifically focusing on his paintings of that area.

It was not until I was preparing that talk that I realized fully the absolutely crucial role that Belle and Robert Simpson, owners of the early and thriving Juneau gallery and curio store The Nugget Shop, played in Laurence's success as an artist. Without the Simpsons' championing of his work and their success in selling it to Juneau residents and visitors—many of whom were traveling on early cruise ships along the Inside Passage and would never go as far north as Prince William Sound, Cook Inlet, or Anchorage, and would never see Denali—Laurence may never have been able to put aside his dabbles in gold prospecting and oil leases and his work as a commercial photographer to become a full-time painter, much less the legendary figure in Alaska historical art that he is today.

As late as the mid-1910s, Sydney Laurence was still billing himself as a commercial photographer. He opened a photography studio in Valdez in February of 1915, but in June of the same year, he moved to the more rapidly growing new town of Anchorage, opening a photography studio in the Carroll Building when it was completed in late summer. He occupied the east half of the building for a year, before moving down the street to the Harmony Theatre. In 1917 he was living in the Anchorage Hotel and was still listed in the town directory as a photographer. He was doing some painting as well, but very few paintings are known today to date from those first few years in Anchorage. In 1918–19, he was continuing to run his photography business, attempting to augment his meager income by mining on

Cache Creek and doing a bit more painting as he traveled between Cache Creek, Talkeetna, and Anchorage.

It was not until 1919 that Laurence's career as an Alaska painter really took hold. Many paintings, both large and small, date from 1919, and among them are some of his finest works. It is more than coincidental that his first sale at The Nugget Shop in Juneau was made that year.

Belle and Robert Simpson's Nugget Shop was a storied Juneau institution for more than half a century. It opened, according to various sources, in 1914, 1915, or 1917[5] in the Seward Building (built in 1913) at 145 South Franklin Street, near Front Street, and moved in 1923 to the Cheney Building, also on South Franklin Street but closer to the steamship dock. It would move again in 1947, when the Simpsons built the Simpson Building at Second and Seward Streets (that building, currently the home of Salt Restaurant, still bears the Simpson name on the façade). Robert Simpson died in 1952, but Belle continued to run the shop until it closed in 1970.

The photo of The Nugget Shop's interior accompanying this paper, full of Sydney Laurence paintings, comes from an entertaining, if largely myth-filled book, published by Sydney Laurence's second wife, Jeanne Laurence, in 1974.[6] Its caption in the book indicates it is from the early 1920s, but the photo actually dates from at least the late 1920s. In the course of my own several decades of study on Sydney Laurence's oeuvre, I have seen more than a thousand Laurence paintings in person, and at least that many more in reproduction. It's perhaps not surprising, then, that I've identified the current whereabouts of a number of the paintings on view in this photo. But it is somewhat remarkable, I think, that the locations and histories of so

---

5   Mary Lou Gerbi, "Belle Goldstein Simpson: A Nugget of Old Juneau," *Alaska Southeaster*, November 2000.

6   Jeanne Laurence, *My Life with Sydney Laurence* (Seattle: Salisbury Press, 1974). This source is an unabashed paean of praise to Jeanne Laurence's husband, Sydney, in which she repeats many of the myths and exaggerations that the much-older Sydney told her about his life and career when they met. It is the source for most of the myths and legends that our 1989 retrospective exhibition and publication on his life and art set out to test for veracity and try to correct.

Snapshot of The Nugget Shop interior, originally published in Jeanne Laurence's *My Life with Sydney Laurence* (1974).

many of the paintings in one snapshot-in-time from The Nugget Shop are even known today.

Some of the paintings in the photograph definitely date from later in the 1920s. The largest on view, a 5½-by-4-foot grand and typical Laurence view of Denali, is one of Sydney Laurence's best-known paintings. Titled *Arctic King*, it was painted in 1925. It belongs to the Anchorage School District and has been for years on loan to and on view in the Anchorage Museum.

The winter Denali scene to the left of *Arctic King* now belongs to a private Fairbanks collector, and we know from the documentation that accompanied it that it was originally purchased directly from The Nugget Shop by Carl V. S. Patterson of Towanda, Pennsylvania, in August of 1929. Another Laurence painting on view, at the upper left of the wall on the right, also lives in Fairbanks, donated to the Fairbanks North Star Borough Library by Fairbanks collector Keith Gianni just a few years ago, along with a number of other important historical and contemporary Alaska paintings.

The sailing ship on the far right of the photo, a 1928 painting titled *A Mid-Ocean Sunset*, was in an early Laurence exhibition at the Anchorage Museum in 1975.[7]

It is clear from this single snapshot that by the late 1920s, Juneau's Nugget Shop carried a wide selection from among Laurence's most popular landscape themes. Only a couple of the paintings in this photo were scenes of the Juneau area. On the lower left of the wall on the right side of the photo is a painting of Mendenhall Glacier in Juneau, the location of which is also known today, and the painting on the floor partially obscured by the support post may well be *Supper on the Bar*, a Laurence painting of a very specific spot on the tidal bar of the Gastineau Channel, now belonging to the Juneau-Douglas City Museum.[8]

The genesis of Belle and Robert Simpson's interest in Sydney Laurence's work is still unclear. This is just one of the many questions I would ask Belle Simpson now, if I could sit with her in her apartment as I did four decades ago and talk with her about Sydney Laurence. There are several stories about how and when Belle met Sydney, and how she began selling his work. Some descendants in Belle's family have suggested that it was in the late 1920s, after she'd seen Sydney's work in Anchorage.[9] But it was certainly well before that, as we know she began showing and selling it in The Nugget Shop in 1919. Another story, told by Robert Raab in an article in *Alaskafest* magazine in 1979,[10] is that a tourist carried one of Laurence's paintings to Juneau and sold it to Belle, who displayed it in the window in her shop. According to

---

7   Robert Shalkop, *Sydney Laurence, an Alaskan Impressionist: 1865–1940* (Anchorage: Anchorage Historical and Fine Arts Museum, 1975): 36.

8   The location depicted in *Supper on the Bar* has been very clearly pinpointed by Juneau collector and historian Mike Blackwell, who once owned this painting and donated it to the Juneau-Douglas City Museum. Mike Blackwell has done a phenomenal amount of original research on the sites depicted in Laurence's Juneau paintings, and has shared that knowledge with Juneau audiences in illustrated lectures, and with me.

9   Notes from Juneau historian Mike Blackwell on an interview and email correspondence with Simpson family members in 1911.

10   Robert Rabb, "Sydney Laurence," *Alaskafest*, April 1979.

this story, so many people wanted to buy the picture that she contacted him for as many paintings as he could produce.

I don't know for certain when they first met, but it may have been much earlier. I think that almost certainly both Belle's future husband, Robert Simpson, and her own brother, Isadore Goldstein, met Sydney Laurence in Iditarod around 1911–1912. Belle, in her early twenties at the time, may even have met him there herself in 1911. She traveled by sternwheeler there with her sister Minnie in 1911 to visit her brother Isadore, who ran a store in Iditarod, and it was there and on that trip that she met her future husband, Robert, an optician and jeweler who also ran a store in the gold rush community.[11]

If Laurence met Robert Simpson, Simpson's future bride Belle, or Belle's brother Isadore in Iditarod, or if they simply learned about Laurence's artwork there, it was through their acquaintance with Cyril Percy Wood, who ran the Northern Commercial Company store in Iditarod from June 1911 through late 1917. Cyril P. Wood, known as "CP," had already befriended a down-on-his-luck Laurence at Susitna Station, thirty miles north of Cook Inlet, in 1910, providing shelter and sustenance in exchange for several of Laurence's small paintings, and he would provide longer-term housing and work space for Laurence in Iditarod, beginning no more than a year or two later.[12]

In audio recordings made by his family late in life, CP Wood's son—also named Cyril, and called "Cy"—clearly remembered Sydney Laurence working in the Northern Commercial Company storage building the store manager made available to him. Cy, who would leave Alaska along with the rest of his family in 1919 and eventually become a prolific, lifelong California artist himself, was only a young

---

11   Gerbi, "Belle Goldstein Simpson."

12   Personal communication with Cyril P. Wood's granddaughter, Karen Moran, of Topanga, California, who has gathered much documentation on her family's early days in Alaska, and who has recently (July 2017) donated a trove of that documentation to the Archives in the Elmer Rasmuson Library at the University of Alaska Fairbanks. This material includes Karen Moran's chronology and narrative summary of the Wood Family in Alaska, a 1914 Sydney Laurence letter to Cyril P. Wood, a Laurence photograph of one of his paintings given to Mrs. Cyril P. Wood, 229 Cyril P. Wood Alaska photographs, and typed and handwritten stories by Cyril P. Wood.

child at the time in Iditarod, but in the audio recordings he gives a lot of the credit for his becoming an artist to growing up with Sydney Laurence's paintings all over the walls of his father's house, and to seeing Laurence at work in the warehouse out back.[13]

Cy's father, CP, not only provided shelter and studio space for Laurence and hung his artwork on the walls of his house, but also brokered sales of the artist's paintings to others. A May 19, 1914, letter from Sydney Laurence to CP Wood in Iditarod references two sales facilitated by Wood of multiple Laurence paintings. In the letter to Wood, Laurence promises to fulfill an order for a dozen or more paintings for one client and offers to paint "just as many pictures as he may want" for another collector.[14] It seems almost certain that in a community the size of Iditarod, prominent store managers and businessmen Robert Simpson, Belle's future husband, and Isadore Goldstein, Belle's brother, would have known the Northern Commercial Company store manager Wood, and would have met Sydney Laurence and seen his paintings. We have no direct evidence that this is how Robert and Belle Simpson got to know Sydney Laurence's paintings and later seek them out, but it seems very likely.

No matter when Belle met Sydney Laurence, and how she first learned about his work, beginning in 1919 she would become the single most important influence on the artist's career, and second only to Sydney's second wife, Jeanne, whom she strongly encouraged Sydney to marry, the most important influence on his life. Belle's knowledge of the curio and art trade was honed from childhood. In 1885, long before Belle and Robert Simpson opened The Nugget Shop, Belle's father, Reuben Goldstein, had come to Juneau and established the R. Goldstein Store on South Franklin Street. Belle and her family lived on the floor above the store, and by the time Belle and Robert opened The Nugget Shop, Belle knew very well how to select and market artwork. The Nugget Shop was a success from the start.

---

13   Audio tapes of her father "Cy" Wood's recollections, belonging to Karen Moran.

14   Letter referenced in footnote 12.

By the mid-1920s, The Nugget Shop was by far the biggest outlet for Laurence's work, but beginning in 1926, there was another major source as well. Carl Block of Peoria, Illinois, began correspondence with the artist that year, arranging to sell Laurence's paintings in his Midwestern department stores. We are fortunate to have today, in the Archives at the Anchorage Museum, a trove of correspondence between Laurence and Block, and some between Block and the Simpsons at The Nugget Shop as well.[15] This extensive correspondence provides a clear window into the rise and fall of the artist's business relationship with Block, the tug-of-war between Block and the Simpsons to get Laurence's paintings for sale, and Laurence's efforts to meet those demands.

Laurence wrote to Block in early November 1926 that he was very busy with commissions—"238 to be exact," he wrote—but by the 23rd of the same month, the artist wrote to Block that he would try to send him "not less than 10 pictures by January 1, and 10 more each month." Block replied immediately, lamenting that he wouldn't have the paintings in time for Christmas, so Laurence shipped him ten 16-by-20-inch canvases on Christmas Eve.

In the middle of January 1927, Laurence promised Block not less than forty new canvases by the first of April. A March 8 letter from Block to Laurence makes it clear that not only was Block already a big buyer of Laurence's work, but that he was already in competition with the Simpsons for his paintings. After acknowledging with gratitude receipt of ten Laurence paintings, and noting that he was enclosing a check for $500 to pay for them, Block says, "I note the orders that you will have to execute for Mr. Simpson, and am wondering what further orders you could take care of for me, when your present commitments are out of the way. Will you be able to give me any pictures before you go to Anchorage, and could I count on 5 to 10 a month thereafter?"

---

15   These and the other Block letters subsequently referenced and quoted in this paper are among the extensive collection of unpublished correspondence between Laurence and Carl Block in the Archives of the Anchorage Museum.

By the fall of 1927, barely a year into his business relationship with Block, Laurence was clearly having a hard time keeping up with demands from both Block and the Simpsons for more paintings. On November 15, 1927, Block wrote to Laurence, "By the way you were to send me ten 16 × 20 pictures, per month, beginning September 1. I had hoped that these would be here on my return, and would like very much to have 25 or 30 as soon as possible."

Despite the pressure, Laurence was eager to keep both of his two major outlets satisfied. He continued to provide large numbers of paintings to The Nugget Shop, and in his correspondence with Block over the next two years, he offered different images, in different sizes, outlining the price per square inch for the canvases.[16] Block, however, was increasingly demanding, and prescriptive. In a March 12, 1930, letter he not only suggests subject matter (among the suggestions are picturesque European scenes, well-known peaks like the Matterhorn and Jungfrau, other Alpine valleys, the Grand Canal in Venice, and perhaps a painting of the ship "Old Ironsides") and references a desire for paintings based on some of the photos he's sent, but also suggests the kind of brushwork that is most popular with his clients.

This kind of pressure, on top of his commitment to the Simpsons and The Nugget Shop, made Laurence's relationship with Block more and more contentious by the end of 1930. But the Great Depression, which vitiated demand for artwork everywhere, was the killer blow in the relationship with Carl Block and his department stores. On March 4, 1931, a representative from Block's company sent a letter to Laurence acknowledging termination of the business relationship.

Interestingly, in 1936—five years after terminating the arrangement with Laurence—the same representative of Block Company wrote The Nugget Shop to say they still had Laurence paintings and would be happy for The Nugget Shop to take them. The Simpsons replied on July 22, 1936, that they had enough Laurence paintings already— several dozen—and weren't having much luck selling them either, thanks to the terrible economy, but offered to trade some non-Alaska scenes they had on hand for some Alaska subject-matter ones.

---

16   Laurence to Block, June 4, 1929.

Despite the downturn in the economy and the difficulty of selling even such popular paintings as Laurence's, the Simpsons stuck by the artist, and they helped tide him over through the tough years that artists everywhere in America were having in the early 1930s. One reason for this loyalty may have been Belle's friendship with Sydney's second wife, Jeanne. Belle was a business partner and friend, but Jeanne was his even more important life partner, from their marriage in 1928 to Sydney's death in 1940.

Sydney and Jeanne had been introduced by a mutual friend in Los Angeles in late 1926. He was in poor health, not eating right, not taking care of himself, and seeing a doctor for what was believed to be heart trouble. Jeanne Kunath Holeman, an artist herself, was much younger (he was sixty-one at the time, and she was not quite forty), French, and a great cook. Over the course of that spring, and after his return to Los Angeles from Alaska in the fall, she cooked for him, looked after him, and restored him to health. Laurence told Belle Simpson about her on his way through Juneau, headed north, and after he came back through on his way south in the fall, Belle visited Los Angeles and met Jeanne that winter. She encouraged them to get married, doing a kind of "shuttle diplomacy" between the two to suggest, and finally consummate, a proposal.[17] Belle visited them in the winter of 1927–28, and the two were wed on May 8, 1928. Following their wedding, Sydney and Jeanne traveled almost immediately to Juneau and spent some time there, staying in an apartment over The Nugget Shop provided by the Simpsons and sketching in the area every day, before heading north to Seward and on to Anchorage for the summer. They would stop in Juneau and spend up to a week with the Simpsons on every trip north and south thereafter.

Jeanne and Belle were fast friends, and The Nugget Shop continued to be the major outlet for Laurence's work in the 1930s. He sold paintings in the Anchorage Hotel in summers, out of his Los Angeles studio in winters (until he gave up his Los Angeles residence entirely in 1933), and later in the New Washington Hotel in Seattle, where he and Jeanne lived and had a studio. But despite the downturn in the fortunes

---

17   Jeanne Laurence, *My Life with Sydney Laurence*, 11–14.

of artists everywhere during the Great Depression, The Nugget Shop carried his work and sold it throughout. One of Laurence's biggest sales ever, of a large Mt. McKinley (Denali) painting to a New York financier for $10,000, was brokered by Belle Simpson through The Nugget Shop in 1931.

When Sydney and Jeanne visited Belle and Robert Simpson in Juneau together for the first time in 1928, he was just finishing a painting, *Off to the Potlatch*, which would be the prize for winning a "Capital to Capital" yacht race between Juneau, Alaska, and Olympia, Washington. It was the Simpsons who told Sydney about the yacht race and suggested he paint a canvas to offer as the prize. Both the publicity of his painting's status as the prize and the resulting contact with Adolph Schmitt proved extraordinarily fortuitous for the Laurences. The race was won by Schmitt, in his yacht *Winniepeck*, and he received Laurence's painting. Schmitt and Laurence met and became immediate friends. Schmitt would go on to acquire many of Laurence's paintings, and even more importantly, would provide the couple housing at his New Washington Hotel in Seattle in the 1930s.

The benefits of the Schmitt connection—again, thanks to the Simpsons—continued to multiply. The rights to use *Off to the Potlatch* for advertising were sold in 1932 to a cooperative venture of the Alaska Steamship Company, the Alaska Railroad, and the Northern Pacific Railroad, and magazine ads and posters featuring Laurence's work throughout the 1930s brought his imagery to nationwide attention. The *Wrangell Sentinel* newspaper reported on May 6, 1932, that "Page advertisements, mostly in the rich color of Sydney Laurence's brush, will be published in the *Atlantic Monthly*, the *National Geographic*, *Forum*, *Century*, *Harper's Magazine*, *Scribners* [...] and others designed to reach a diversified audience [...] Magazines of class and quality receive the preference." W. E. Coman, vice president of the Northern Pacific Railway, was quoted in the article as saying, "who better than Sydney Laurence can express the spirit and charm of Alaska?"[18]

---

18   *Wrangell Sentinel*, May 6, 1932. I am eternally grateful to historian and researcher Sue Burrus, formerly of Anchorage, who sleuthed out this and addi-

As I stated at the outset, it was not until I was preparing a talk last December on Sydney Laurence's Juneau images and connections that I fully realized how much of the artist's success directly and indirectly stemmed from Belle and Robert Simpson and The Nugget Shop. Their gallery was the first, and for the rest of Laurence's career most important, outlet for display and sale of his paintings. Belle encouraged—practically arranged—for him to marry the woman who would be his essential partner in art, love, and life for the rest of his years. And it was through the Simpsons and The Nugget Shop that the couple made connections like the one with Adolph Schmitt, which got them through the Depression and led to widespread dissemination of Laurence's imagery beyond Alaska and the Pacific Northwest.

Without the support at a crucial time of Belle and Robert Simpson and their Juneau Nugget Shop, Sydney Laurence may never have been able to make a living as a full-time Alaskan painter. He may not have lived and worked long enough and productively enough to leave a lasting artistic legacy of any sort. And his images may never have become so widely disseminated and known. If, as I have maintained for decades, Sydney Laurence's image of Alaska has had a profound effect not only on how Alaska is seen by those who dream of coming here to visit, but on the way many Alaskans see our own home, we may have Belle and Robert Simpson and their Juneau Nugget Shop to thank for it.

BIBLIOGRAPHY (PARTIAL)

Belmore Browne Papers, Box 2, Folder 4, Stefansson Manuscript no. 190. Dartmouth College Library, Hanover, New Hampshire.

Gerbi, Mary Lou. "Belle Goldstein Simpson: A Nugget of Old Juneau." *Alaska Southeaster*, November 2000, 18.

---

tional scores of early newspaper and other references when we were organizing the large 1990 retrospective exhibition of Laurence's work, which traveled to museums throughout Alaska and down the West Coast. Her work made possible the first detailed, credible chronology of Laurence's life and career, in my catalog for the exhibition (Woodward 1990, 123–30), and has served as an essential resource for all the other work and writing I have done on Laurence since.

Laurence, Jeanne. *My Life with Sydney Laurence*. Seattle: Salisbury Press, 1974.

Rabb, Robert. "Sydney Laurence." *Alaskafest*, April 1979, 30.

Shalkop, Robert. *Sydney Laurence, an Alaskan Impressionist: 1865–1940*. Anchorage: Anchorage Historical and Fine Arts Museum, 1975.

"Sydney Laurence, Interview with the *Los Angeles Times*." *Anchorage Times*, December 3, 1925.

Woodward, Kesler E. *Sydney Laurence, Painter of the North*. Seattle: University of Washington Press in Association with the Anchorage Museum of History and Art, 1990.

———. *Painting in the North: Alaskan Art in the Anchorage Museum of History and Art*. Seattle: Anchorage Museum of History and Art, 1993.

A Note from Chris Allan

Terrence Cole has been my friend and mentor for the past twenty-five years. When I was an undergraduate trying to find my path, he encouraged me to study history. He also helped me to land my first paying history-writing job. Later he was my advisor for a master's degree in Northern Studies, and he encouraged me to proceed to a doctoral program at Washington State University. His sense of humor and compassion have always made him one of my favorite people and a valuable guide for how to conduct myself. What I enjoy about Terrence's approach to history is the way he looks to the past for moral lessons and, at the same time, delights in humanity's foibles.

TOO GOOD TO BE TRUE

Alaska's 1867 Transfer Flag and
the Problem of Unreliable Sources

Chris Allan

Joseph Isadore Keefer is a shadowy figure. He left behind no archival collections and no autobiography or memoir, and the only known photographs of him are blotchy images in newspapers. What we know is that he was born in Washington, D.C., and in 1875 he married Cordelia Winfield, with whom he had three children. The couple divorced in 1898 after Keefer accused his wife in court of "desertion." He worked in the nation's capital as a compositor, or typesetter, and joined the Columbia Typographical Union, though he also described himself as an attorney-at-law "engaged in the patent and pension claim branch of the legal profession."[1] Little else is known about Keefer's personal life, beyond his passion for history and, in particular, George Washington and other celebrated figures of the Revolutionary War. He lectured on Washington's family history, wrote guidebooks with titles like *Some of the Homes of General Washington* (1902) and *Mt. Vernon and Its Surroundings* (1906), and claimed to be related to the nation's first president through Washington's aunt as well as to the French friend of the American rebels, the Marquis de Lafayette.[2]

---

1   "Original Alaskan's Story," *Dallas Morning News*, August 15, 1897, 12; "Decree of Divorce Granted," *Evening Star*, February 23, 1898, 2; "A Peculiar Claim," *Middleburgh Post*, May 5, 1898, 4; "Joseph Keefer's Body to Arrive in D.C. Today," *Washington Post*, June 16, 1942.
2   "Alleged False Title," *Evening Star*, March 31, 1898; "Great Grandson of George's Aunt," *Buffalo Enquirer*, June 1, 1901.

Keefer's claims to be personally connected to important historical events did not end there. In 1894, he told a *Washington Post* reporter that recent Flag Day festivities caused him to reflect on the time he raised an American flag at the 1867 ceremonial transfer of Russia's American colony to the United States.[3] According to Keefer, at the age of seventeen he was "aide-de-camp to Captain T. E. Ketchum," who, he said, was in charge of the "Seward State Department expedition to Alaska." He and Ketchum, Keefer explained, were ordered to transport the flag to Alaska, raise it at the ceremony, and then return it to the man who orchestrated the purchase of Alaska, U.S. Secretary of State William H. Seward. But this was just the first part of Keefer's revelation—he had, just days earlier, made a fascinating discovery in the basement of the State Department, adjacent to the White House at the corner of Pennsylvania Avenue and 17th Street. "Supposing this bit of historical bunting to have been lost sight of during the intervening years," explained the reporter,

> Mr. Keefer, who is the last survivor of the expedition, instituted a search last week to ascertain its fate, if possible. Greatly to his satisfaction the flag was found in a box behind the Constitution of the United States in the State Department Building. The flag is not on exhibition, which probably accounts for the fact that it had passed out of the memory of all but the man who was on the spot when its unfolding colors proclaimed the presence and domination of Uncle Sam in that far-away region.[4]

Today, the flag Keefer found resides at the Alaska State Museum in Juneau, the official repository of the state's cultural and historical

---

3   On June 14, 1894, New York Governor Roswell P. Flower decreed that the American flag be displayed on all public buildings; in Illinois, schoolchildren by the thousands celebrated the holiday under the auspices of the American Flag Day Association. Thereafter Flag Day spread across the United States.

4   "Flag First Planted in Alaska," *Washington Post*, June 18, 1894, 4; "Flag First Planted in Alaska," *Sacramento Daily Union*, July 14, 1894. During this era the State Department offices were in what was known as the State, War, and Navy Building. Completed in 1888, it was for many years the largest office building in the world. Today it is called the Eisenhower Executive Building.

treasures. Known by catalog number III-O-495, the hand-sewn flag is 57 inches tall, 107 inches long, and fashioned of a wool cloth called bunting. It features thirty-six cotton stars, arranged with eight stars on the top row and seven each in its remaining four rows. The fabric is thin and frayed in places, including a missing portion several inches long between the stars in the field of blue. Since the flag first arrived in Alaska in 1933, it has been known as the "transfer flag" or the "purchase flag," as it was believed to be the same one Secretary Seward sent to be raised over Sitka when the United States took formal possession of Alaska. However, many stories, more or less credible, have emerged about the flag in the century and a half since the transfer ceremony, and it appears that in our eagerness to believe in its authenticity we have been deceived by unreliable sources.

What we call the *historical record* is a fragile and fragmentary thing. It is fragile because people forget the order of events, documents are lost, buildings (and sometimes nations) crumble, and what is left are shards and scraps that historians reassemble and interpret—arriving, as best as they are able, at a truthful account of what was. Artifacts, including flags, are particularly prone to fragmented or enfeebled pasts, and the origins of an object—its provenance—can be devilishly difficult to prove. Such is the case with Alaska's transfer flag. In the decades after the ceremony, few Americans had more than a hazy understanding of how the United States acquired Alaska, and even less awareness of what might have become of Secretary Seward's flag. But today, important elements of the flag's history can be established as fact—the ceremony itself was witnessed by roughly four hundred people, and at least fourteen of them left written accounts. Using historical newspapers, government records, letters, and journals, we can say with confidence that the following is true.

On the morning of October 18, 1867, under clear skies, the man-of-war U.S.S. *Ossipee* anchored in front of the Russian-American capital of Sitka (or New Archangel) and set in motion a pivotal event in Alaska history and the history of the nation. The *Ossipee* carried three commissioners: Captain Alexei A. Peshchurov, representing Russia's government; Captain Theodor von Koskull, as special agent for the Russian-American Company; and American Brigadier General Lovell

George L. Rousseau, son of U.S. Commissioner Lovell H. Rousseau, raising the American flag during the October 18, 1867, Alaska transfer ceremony. The artist, Harry C. Wood, is thought to have been an eyewitness to the event. *Courtesy of Alaska State Library, Dmitrii P. Maksutov Papers.*

H. Rousseau, who had suffered terribly from seasickness on the way north, and was eager to get on with the formalities. By three P.M., Russian and American troops mustered under the flagpole outside Russian colonial governor Prince Dmitrii P. Maksutov's stately home, which perched atop the rocky knoll known today as Castle Hill. The governor and his wife, Maria, various military officers, ship captains and their wives, and a clutch of local people and American onlookers were also assembled. To explain the lack of Russian civilians, a reporter for the *Daily Alta California* noted the somber mood surrounding the proceedings: "From feelings, which Americans can well appreciate, few of the Russian people were present. Aside from the military and officials whom duty compelled to be in attendance, I do not think that twenty were witnesses of the ceremony."[5]

---

5   Del Norte, "Acquisition of Alaska," *Daily Alta California*, November 19, 1867, 1.

Six months earlier, Secretary Seward, with the support of President Andrew Johnson, had negotiated the purchase of Alaska from Czar Alexander II for $7.2 million. Both sides signed the Treaty of Cession on March 30, and now General Rousseau was carrying orders to oversee the lowering of the Russian flag, the raising of the U.S. flag, and the occupation of Sitka (and, by extension, all of Alaska) by the U.S. Army. To begin, Captain Peshchurov gave the signal to lower the Russian flag with its blue and red stripes and double-headed imperial eagle, which in turn initiated a twenty-one-gun salute from the *Ossipee* and the cannons in Sitka's shore battery. But there was a problem—the Russian flag, on its way down, caught in the halyard, and after some spirited tugging, it ripped from top to bottom but remained entangled high above the heads of the attendees. After some failed attempts to reach it, a Russian marine was hoisted aloft in a rope sling and managed to free the flag. But instead of bringing it down as he was ordered, he dropped the tattered pennant, which caught on the breeze and drifted onto the bayonets of the Russian soldiers standing at attention below.

After this embarrassing incident, Rousseau's fifteen-year-old son, George, stepped forward to hoist the United States flag, given to his father by Secretary Seward for this special occasion. As the flag reached the top of the pole, the report of the last gun of the *Ossipee* echoed from the mountainsides.

With this, Peshchurov declared, "General Rousseau, by the authority of his Majesty, the Emperor of all the Russias, I transfer to you, the agent of the United States, all the territory and dominion now possessed by his Majesty on the continent of America and in the adjacent islands, according to a treaty made between these two powers." Rousseau replied using similar phrasing that he accepted the transfer, the American civilians gave a hip-hip-hooray, and the ceremony came to an end.[6] A reporter for the *New York Herald* wrote, "The transfer was conducted in a purely diplomatic and business-like manner, neither bouquets nor speech-making following . . . and at four o'clock

---

6   Ibid.

127

The State, War, and Navy Building in Washington, D.C., where Joseph I. Keefer said he found the flag used at the 1867 Alaska transfer ceremony. In this photograph from the mid-1890s, the building is decorated for Flag Day. *Courtesy of Library of Congress.*

in the afternoon a dozen American flags float over the newly born American city of Sitka."[7]

Within days Rousseau was en route once again to Washington, D.C., and in his report to Secretary Seward he wrote, "With this report and accompanying papers I return to you the United States flag used on the occasion of the transfer of the territory."[8] Within weeks, descriptions of this ceremony appeared in newspapers across the nation, and reports from Rousseau and Alaska's new military governor, General Jefferson C. Davis, entered the Congressional Record. But few Americans had access to government records or to old newspapers,

7   Byron Adonis, "Alaska," *New York Herald,* November 13, 1867, 7.

8   General Rousseau's official report and accounts from eyewitnesses agree on this sequence of events. For fourteen accounts transcribed, see Chris Allan, ed., *As the Old Flag Came Down: Eyewitness Accounts of the October 18, 1867 Alaska Transfer Ceremony* (Fairbanks: self-published, 2018). See also David H. Miller, *The Alaska Treaty* (Kingston, ON: Limestone Press, 1981), 132–37.

and as the decades passed, the public's awareness of the Alaska transfer ceremony faded.

Joseph Keefer's claim to have been present at the flag-raising in Sitka (and then to have rediscovered the flag) emerged once again, in an embellished form, in July 1897, at a time when Americans were enthralled by stories emerging from Alaska and from Canada's Klondike gold fields. In San Francisco, the *Call Bulletin* declared that "Of all the stories told and written of Alaska since the Klondyke fever set in there is none more interesting than that of Joseph Keefer . . . who had the honor of assisting in the planting of the first American flag on Alaskan soil." In the article, Keefer explained that "according to the best records obtainable" he was the last surviving member of the American delegation to Sitka and that the only other was "Joe Rothrock, a young photographer who died about ten years ago in a Philadelphia insane asylum." Keefer recounted that Rothrock, as a result of his Alaska experiences, could never get warm and even on his deathbed was wrapped in blankets and placed by a furnace.

Keefer noted, "No explanation was ever offered for his strange condition."

In the same article, Keefer made reference to a missing piece of the flag's fabric that he said had been eaten by moths before explaining that this damaged section concealed a dark history—it had been soaked in human blood. Keefer recalled that in the period before the transfer ceremony, Sitka was plagued by "a low class of people" and "ex-convicts from Russia," who tried to sabotage the efforts of the newly arrived Americans by telling the local Tlingit Indians that the newcomers were "coming to make slaves of them." These "wild stories" led to alarm among the Tlingits, who "did everything to bother and hamper our work." As part of that work, Keefer explained, "we hoisted the Stars and Stripes in the old Custom-house at Sitka and afterword floated it to the breeze from Fort Cosmos' flagpole." At this point, the story took a macabre turn:

> When the feeling was running strong against us a native happening
> by the fort tore down the precious piece of bunting. As he was

about to stamp on it a rifle shot rang out, the native whirled about and fell across the starry field, his life-blood oozing from a wound in the temple. After this occurrence there were no more attempts at flag-destruction.[9]

Keefer's dramatic storytelling exhibited a peculiar blend of reality—Tlingits at Sitka were indeed killed by the U.S. Army in the early years of American rule—and fantasy: the ceremonial flag raising did not occur at the Custom House; no flag-related killing exists in the records of the era; Fort Cosmos was a camp built on the Kobuk River north of the Arctic Circle eighteen years after the ceremony in Sitka; and while the real Joseph Rothrock was a botanist working in Alaska between 1865 and 1867, he was not a photographer, was not in Sitka at the time of the transfer, and did not die in an insane asylum.[10]

Elsewhere, Keefer told reporters, "one peculiar thing about Alaska . . . is that the cold takes the taste away from one. We could eat soap and candles and chew leather with the same amount of satisfaction as the best prepared game." He also spoke about northern curiosities like a duck he shot that had a strange type of grain in its craw that "must surely have come from some warm climate" and the time he traded with Alaska natives for "a quantity of diamonds." He said he brought back "a bas-relief hieroglyphic of a prayer on an ivory tusk" and that it was examined by experts and found to be an "authentic and a most wonderful relic." And finally, he explained there were three classes of indigenous Alaskans: the Tlingit, the Eskimo, and what he called the "Juneman tribe" who he said "crawl around on hands and knees a greater part of the time, and act greatly like monkeys." These accounts, which ran in newspapers across the country, appear to be a pastiche of pure nonsense and scraps of

---

9   "Planted Old Glory," *San Francisco Call Bulletin*, July 27, 1897, 3.

10   Joseph Rothrock served as a botanist in Alaska with the Western Union Telegraph Expedition, and the U.S. government published his findings as *Flora of Alaska* (1867). He went on to become a celebrated forest manager and conservationist, earning him the honorific "father of Pennsylvania forestry." He died in 1922 in West Chester, Pennsylvania.

information from news stories. In style and tone they resemble Christopher Columbus's breathless descriptions of Caribbean Islands or the fake medieval travelogue *Mandeville's Travels*, with its cave-dwelling troglodytes and men with dogs' heads. With Klondike fever at a high pitch, Keefer even began advising gold-seekers heading to Alaska, offering what must have been a bewildering hash of misleading information.[11]

Joseph Keefer was not the only person claiming knowledge of Alaska and its transfer flag. In 1896 the *Seattle Post-Intelligencer* announced, "The original flag that flung to the breezes upon the transfer of Alaska to the United States has been found." This news came from "an aged widow lady" in Seattle named Caroline Hall, who had recently given a flag to Sheldon Jackson, the Presbyterian missionary and Alaska's General Agent of Education, who was building a new museum in Sitka.[12] According to Hall, an American officer took the flag with him following the transfer ceremony, and after arriving in Puget Sound, he traveled cross-country by horse and ended up on the Cowlitz River, a tributary of the Columbia. There he met the sheriff of Lewis County, Javan Hall, who was finishing work on a river steamer for transport between the Cowlitz and the city of Portland. As Hall explained, "The United States officer was favorably impressed with the pluck and push of the frontier sheriff and seeing the steamer carried no flag he presented this one, brought from Sitka, to the sheriff as a token of esteem and in order that the stars and stripes might float over the little craft." But recognizing the historical value of the flag, the sheriff thought better of "wearing it out upon his steamer" and instead gave it to his fiancée, Caroline. She explained that she kept it

---

11   "Former Alaskan Parties," *Times* [Washington, DC], July 28, 1897; "Diet of Soap in Alaska," *Wichita Daily Eagle*, July 30, 1897; "Petticoats Predominate," *Buffalo Evening News*, August 2, 1897; "Some Alaskan Experiences of Thirty Year Ago," *Wilmington Messenger*, August 7, 1897; "Bound for Alaska," *Evening Star*, December 23, 1897; "Going to the Klondike," *Times*, September 27, 1897, 15.

12   The Museum of Natural History and Ethnology in Sitka—now called Sheldon Jackson Museum—was completed in 1897 and was the first concrete structure in Alaska. The building was placed on the National Register of Historic Places in 1972.

for nearly thirty years before seeing an opportunity to return it to the people of Alaska.[13]

But there was a serious problem with this story. The flag Sheldon Jackson was given had only twenty-four stars, a configuration in use between 1822 and 1836. Even casual observers doubted that a flag at least thirty-one years out of date would have been selected for the transfer ceremony. Some newspaper readers also challenged Keefer's claims. John McKinnon, formerly of the Army's Ninth Infantry, wrote to the *Call Bulletin* from a home for aging soldiers in Los Angeles. McKinnon tried to set the record straight, and although he misspelled "Rousseau," his statements had the ring of truth:

> As I had the honor of being color bearer on that occasion, I unbent the flag from its staff and fastened it to the halliard of the flagstaff. It was then raised to its place by Lieutenant George Rossoue (son of the commissioner of the transfer) and a naval officer whose name I have forgotten. As there was a double halliard on the flagstaff at the time our flag was rising the Russian flag was lowering and both were saluted by the warships in the harbor.

McKinnon could prove that he had served in the Army unit sent to Sitka because he had to provide evidence of his military service to be allowed a bed in the National Home for Disabled Volunteer Soldiers. "On the following day the garrison flag was raised in place of the original," he concluded, "and as I was orderly for General Rossoue, I was ordered to put the original flag of the transfer in a tin case, which the Commissioner carried to Washington, D.C., to be placed in the Department of State."[14]

---

13   "A Valuable Relic," *Alaskan*, June 13, 1986, 3; "The Original Flag," *Seattle Post-Intelligencer*, June 5, 1896, 8; "A Valuable Relic," *Oregonian*, July 5, 1896, 13.

14   "Old Glory in Alaska," *San Francisco Call Bulletin*, August 5, 1897, 7. See also, from a writer calling himself Historicus who spoke with John McKinnon about his role at the ceremony, "Alaska's First American Flag," *Fairbanks Daily Times*, December 4, 1906, 2. The National Home for Disabled Volunteer Soldiers was established in 1887; its location near Los Angeles is now home to a Veterans Administration hospital.

McKinnon's testimony should have been enough to undermine Keefer's accounts, but it reached only one newspaper in California, whereas Keefer's claims circulated widely in newspapers throughout the country. Ernest Ingersoll, a writer of guide books for Rand McNally and author of *Gold Fields of the Klondike and the Wonders of Alaska* (1897), gave a lively account of the transfer ceremony and then, without questioning its content or changing a word, printed Keefer's story about the angry Tlingit being shot in the head as he tried to stomp upon the transfer flag. This no doubt pleased Keefer, who appeared to delight in seeing his name in print and who frequently contacted newspapers in Washington, D.C. By the close of 1897, newspapers in the nation's capital announced Keefer's plans to turn his Alaska experiences into a play: "Mr. Joseph I. Keefer of Seward's expedition to Alaska, who planted the first American flag in that country, is getting up a three-act drama, which he will soon put upon the stage, and is now selecting the cast from a number of Washington's young ladies and gentlemen. The play is to be called 'Alaska, 1867–1869.'"[15] The results of this casting call are unknown, and it appears this project fizzled before tickets could be sold.

Alaska's fifth civilian governor, John G. Brady, was appointed to the office in 1897, at the same time Keefer's flag-related claims were in circulation. The governor soon took an interest in the transfer flag in large part because he resented what he viewed as neglect of Alaska by the federal government and was looking for any way to draw Congress's attention northward. This included collecting objects to represent Alaska on a national stage. One of his early acquisitions was a life-size marble bust of William H. Seward, donated in 1900 to the people of Alaska by New York City banker Francis L. Loring. Around the same time, Brady wrote to the War Department in Washington, D.C., asking about the location of the American flag raised over Sitka at the transfer ceremony. Acting Secretary of War George de Rue Meiklejohn responded, "I beg to advise you that the flag in question is now in the library of the Department of State in this city."[16]

---

15   "Alaska, 1867–1869," *Evening Star*, December 30, 1897, 5.

16   "First Stars and Stripes in Alaska," *Alaskan*, May 12, 1900, 3. The bust was

Three years later both the flag and the marble bust would play an important role in Governor Brady's efforts to promote Alaska at the 1904 Louisiana Purchase Exposition in St. Louis, Missouri. The Exposition (also known as the St. Louis World's Fair) was a chance for Brady to showcase Alaska's natural and cultural resources, including an impressive collection of Tlingit and Haida totem poles that Brady positioned alongside the "Alaska Building," constructed specifically for the event. During the eight months the St. Louis World's Fair was open, the calendar included special days allocated to states and their exhibits, and Brady chose October 18 as "Alaska Day." On that day, his family and dozens of Alaskan volunteers gathered for an opening speech by former St. Louis mayor and governor of Missouri David R. Francis. Governor Brady then stepped forward to unveil the marble bust of Secretary Seward concealed beneath the thirty-six-star flag the State Department mailed to St. Louis for use at the event. After more speeches and music by a quartet of Alaska Native students from Sitka, refreshments were served. Brady would later write, "At the close of the ceremonies, the flag was carefully repacked and sent back to the State Department."[17]

By the end of the festivities in St. Louis, promoters in Seattle were planning their own fair—the Alaska-Yukon-Pacific Exposition of 1909—and not everyone was convinced that the flag Governor Brady used in St. Louis was the correct one. Because of the A-Y-P Exposition's focus on Alaska, the organizers declared that they would "dispel the prevailing ignorance in regard to all things Alaskan and give the people of the country a proper conception of the northland." This included

---

carved by the sculptor Chauncey B. Ives, and it was given to Brady at a grand dinner in the Waldorf-Astoria Hotel. The bust now resides in the Alaska State Museum. "Gift to the People of Alaska," *Boston Herald*, May 9, 1900, 2.

17   Andrew J. Patrick, *The Most Striking of Objects: The Totem Poles of Sitka National Historical Park* (Anchorage: National Park Service, 2002); "Historic Flag for World's Fair," *St. Louis Republic*, September 16, 1903, 7; "Historic Flag for Alaska Day," *St. Louis Republic*, October 18, 1904, 4; "Frances Regrets End Is So Near," *St. Louis Republic*, October 19, 1904, 2; David R. Francis, *Universal Exhibition of 1904* (St. Louis, MO: Louisiana Purchase Exhibition, 1913), 292–93; qtd. in Robert N. DeArmond, "Question of Fate of 1867 Flags Unanswered," *Daily Sitka Sentinel*, October 15, 1992, 18A.

identifying the authentic transfer flag and obtaining it for display. As early as 1904, newspaper headlines began asking, "Where is the first American flag raised in Alaska?" and Alaska's *Douglas Island News* described the early results. "No sooner had a search begun for the first American flag unfurled in the Northland," wrote one reporter, "than enquirers began to be daily informed of where the 'real first flag' was to be found." He continued, "Many and ingenious were the stories told, and bitterly did some of the contestants wage war for the legitimacy of the particular flag in which they were interested."[18]

Over the next few years, a handful of claimants emerged as the most believable. The first of these was eighty-year-old Edward Ludecke, whose story followed a complex trajectory. According to Ludecke, when American troops left San Francisco in 1867 on their way to Sitka, they stopped in the southeast Alaska town of Wrangell and informed Ludecke and the other pioneers there of the sale of Alaska to the United States. Although the transfer ceremony had not yet taken place, Ludecke hurried to raise an American flag and kept it flying in Wrangell until he learned of the admission of Nebraska to the Union, at which point he took the first flag down and raised one with thirty-seven stars. Recognizing its historical importance, he saved the original flag and in 1905 turned it over to an attorney named George E. Rodman. Rodman sent the flag for safe keeping to Seattle's Dexter Horton Bank, and now, with the prospect of the A-Y-P Exposition looming, Rodman allegedly offered to sell it to Exposition organizers for $2,500. Ludecke announced he was suing to recover the flag from the bank's vaults, but as the controversy heated up, bank officials told a deputy sheriff that the bank had no such flag.[19]

---

18   "Ten Million Dollars for Seattle," *Seattle Evening Citizen*, February 15, 1907, 2; "Where Is the First American Flag Raised in Alaska?" *Douglas Island News*, July 17, 1904, 4.

19   "Bank Denies That It Has Old Flag," *Seattle Daily Times*, August 4, 1907, 12. "Highly Historic Banner," *Albuquerque Citizen*, February 15, 1907, 2; "Find Flag First Unfurled," *St. Albans Daily Messenger*, March 1, 1907, 2; "Look for First Flag Flown," *Muskegon Chronicle*, July 13, 1907, 8; "Where Is the First Flag Raised in Alaska?" *Ft. Worth Telegraph*, July 14, 1907, 15; "Where Is the First American Flag Raised in Alaska?" *Evening Star*, July 20, 1907, 23.

Edward Ludecke of Wrangell, Alaska, who claimed to have raised the first American flag in Alaska. He was one of many who insisted they either owned the transfer flag or had special knowledge of its fate. *Courtesy of Alaska State Library, Winter and Pond Photographs (P87-2393).*

Ludecke's claims were undermined by the fact that he was talking about a personal flag raised in Wrangell, not the transfer flag raised in Sitka. In addition, none of the dates or the sequence of events in Ludecke's account made sense—the ship carrying soldiers to Sitka did not stop in Wrangell, and even if it had, Nebraska became a state on March 1, 1867, over seven months before the transfer ceremony, not after, as he suggested. Over time, Ludecke's claims would become even less credible when he abandoned his story about the flag in Wrangell and began declaring that as a soldier in the Army he had personally taken part in the flag-raising ceremony in Sitka. Not only that, he stated that while in Sitka, he happened upon a batch of seven flags at auction, noticed the transfer flag was in the pile, and "bought them for $9." Ludecke is listed in an 1870 census of Sitka as an ex-soldier and as an immigrant from Germany, but is not clear in which country he might have served, and his conflicting accounts remain perplexing.[20]

The claims did not stop here. George Simmons, president of the Simmons Fur Company of Seattle, wrote to say that he had a flag on his wall from Bertha Cohen, wife of Abraham Cohen, a well-known brewer in Sitka during the early days of American rule. Mrs. Cohen told Simmons that at the time, she was the only American woman in Alaska, and that "the flag was the product of her own effort with needle and thread, and that it was raised above the capitol building in Sitka on the day the news of the territory's purchase was officially announced." Simmons informed a newspaper reporter that this "unique historical relic" had hung on his wall since 1882, and he was considering loaning it for display at the A-Y-P Exposition. But, the reporter warned, "it will never change ownership as long as he is alive." There were holes in this story as well. Historical newspapers show that Abraham Cohen did not arrive in Sitka to establish Sitka Brewery until 1868, roughly a year after the transfer ceremony, and that his wife and children joined him some time after that.[21]

The most intriguing story of this era came from John Beighley of Columbus, Ohio, who declared that all other claims must be dismissed because the flag had long since "been blown away and destroyed by the bleak winds of that frigid latitude." According to Beighley, he was a member of "the expedition organized by order of President Grant to go to Alaska" and that as "color corporal" he had strict orders from "Colonel George K. Brady" regarding the flag. As Beighley explained,

> This flag was raised every morning and taken down every night, thus being exposed every day to the severe weather of Alaska. As the flag grew old and began to tear and fray it was reported to

---

20 "First Flag in Alaska," *Oregonian*, August 3, 1907, 6; "Bank Denies That It Has Old Flag," *Seattle Times*, August 4, 1907, 12; "Wrangell Pioneer Back to Visit," *Douglas Island News*, June 6, 1919, 1.

21 "First Alaska Flag Discovered," *Seattle Daily Times*, May 30, 1909, 10; Robert DeArmond, "Breweries Part of Sitka's Past," *Daily Sitka Sentinel*, March 14, 1986, 8. The first advertisement for Sitka Brewery appeared in *Alaska Times*, November 18, 1869, 1.

Colonel Brady, who gave orders that it was to be used until there was not a piece of it left big enough to run up. And so the flag was patched from time to time, and, finally, when there was practically nothing of it left, it was thrown away, not so much as one square inch of it being kept for a relic.[22]

Military records show that Beighley was a private in the Army's 23rd Infantry in Sitka beginning on July 5, 1869, and that he served under Captain (not Colonel) George K. Brady during Ulysses S. Grant's first term as president. If he was in charge of raising, lowering, and eventually discarding a flag in Sitka, evidence suggests these events occurred nearly two years after the transfer ceremony.

As the years passed, people declaring their personal connection to the transfer flag fell into two categories: those claiming to own the flag or know of its location, and those asserting only that they were present for the transfer ceremony or had "raised the flag at Sitka."[23] In this game, none were as detailed or as persistent as Joseph Keefer. Around 1915, Keefer circulated a letter to Washington, D.C., newspapers in which he again described his association with "Capt. T. E. Ketchum" at the flag-raising, adding that the transfer involved "Russian Governor Swineburn," who he said "was kept in charge by the United States" after the transfer. The latter half of the letter contained the kind of detail that Keefer no doubt hoped would win over any doubters:

A year or so after [the ceremony] General Rosecrans came there on a government vessel and displayed a small flag, which he

---

22   "Flag Sued for Does Not Exist," *Leavenworth Post*, September 10, 1907, 4. See also "Twenty-three Years in the Service," *Daily City News*, February 1, 1887.

23   This is a sample of claims by people saying they were present for the 1867 flag-raising: "Raised American Flag at Transfer of Alaska," *Daily Alaska Dispatch*, April 27, 1911, 3; "Alaska Transfer Seen," *Oregonian*, November 27, 1921, 9; "Alaska Purchase Witness Lives in Odd Fellows Home," *San Francisco Chronicle*, October 14, 1928, 4; "Death Claims Aged Citizen of Danville," *San Francisco Chronicle*, October 29, 1929, 3; "Seaman Recalls Day That Gave Alaska to U.S.," *Seattle Daily Times*, July 6, 1930, 14. Such claims began to appear in American newspapers in 1890 and continued until 1955.

Joseph Keefer (right) and a friend hold up the American flag he said was raised at the October 18, 1867, Alaska transfer ceremony. *From Evening Star, October 3, 1926.*

afterwards claimed was the original. Ketchum and myself stayed in that country until October 1869 when we came down to San Francisco, arriving in New York City, Sunday morning Dec. 6, and left there for Washington so as by Monday morning ten o'clock we presented the flag we had hoisted upon the custom house, to Secretary William Seward at his residence in Lafayette Square. The first 'flag day' we had in 1894 I had my flag placed behind the original Declaration of Independence in the State Department library, top floor, in Washington, D.C. The Declaration was fading; so they put that away; and my flag was becoming moth eaten; so that was packed in camphor.[24]

---

24   Qtd. in "Alaska Flag Raised by Garp," *Alaska History News* 16 (June 1985), 3. Portions of the same letter were repeated in this article describing preparations for a parade by the veterans organization Grand Army of the Republic, "Veteran Who First Placed U.S. Flag Over Alaska Will March in Parade," *Washington Herald*, August 31, 1915, 3.

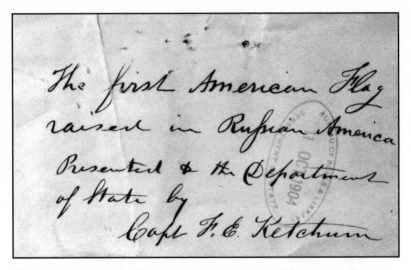

"The first American flag raised in Russian America presented to the Department of State by Capt. F. E. Ketchum." On the opposite side of this card is Department of State letterhead from the 1860s. The red stamp from 1904 was added later by library officials. *Courtesy of Alaska State Museum, Accession file, III-O-495.*

This narrative has the same shape as the one Keefer first offered over twenty years earlier, but new and perplexing details have appeared. Is Keefer referring to General William S. Rosecrans, the Civil War veteran who became U.S. Minister to Mexico in 1868? How would Secretary Seward have received the transfer flag on December 7, 1869, when he retired from his post on March 1 of that year? And is "Russian Governor Swineburn" a hybrid of Alaska's governor Alfred P. Swineford, who served from 1885 to 1889, and Elihu B. Washburne, the man who followed Seward as Secretary of State? The use of camphor for flag preservation and Keefer's precise itinerary seem designed to convince his audience, but what emerges is a bewildering muddle.

This, however, did nothing to diminish Keefer's reputation. Maude Frances, a speech teacher at Wisconsin's Marquette University, began summering in Alaska in 1926, and took an interest in the transfer flag and the stories told by Alaska pioneers. She was already a successful lecturer (one of her talks was titled "The Magic Art of Story Telling") and she became acquainted with Joseph Keefer during a visit to Washington, D.C. In an article for the *Evening Star*, Frances described the Alaska Purchase before declaring, "Few are living today who witnessed the ceremony that attended the passing of ownership to the United States. One of these few is Col. Joseph I. Keefer." Inexplicably, Keefer had acquired a military rank, and what followed was his oft-repeated account and a photograph of him holding the flag with help from a local architect named Frederick Kendall. Frances concluded by saying, "Today the flag may be seen in the library of the State Department, but one must seek to find it. Its place is not one of prominence or of dignity, but an obscure shelf where a bundle wrapped in brown paper contains this historic flag." Two years later, during a research trip to Fairbanks, Alaska, Frances told reporters that she believed "the flag should be in the land where it was first unfurled rather than in the basement of a government building in Washington."[25]

By this time some Alaskans were reading Frances's articles and beginning to agree. In Juneau, the printer Latimer "Dolly" Gray spoke to Andrew Kashevaroff, director of the Alaska Territorial Museum, and to members of Juneau's American Legion Post, suggesting they take steps to secure the flag for Alaska. The question lay dormant for a time, but in 1933 the American Legion passed a resolution echoing Frances's descriptions of the flag "laying un-noticed and forgotten in the Archives in Washington, D.C." The resolution went on to declare, "We believe the flag should be in Alaska."[26] Within days, both the American Legion and the Alaska Chamber of Commerce sent letters to Alaska Governor George A. Parks, who in turn wrote to U.S. Secretary of State Henry L. Stimson requesting the flag. Just over a month later, Secretary Stimson replied with a package containing the flag, some

---

25 "Stars and Stripes First Raised in Alaska Now Preserved Here by the Government," *Evening Star*, October 3, 1926, 94; "Flag That Marked Alaskan Sale Saved," *Washington Post*, February 28, 1926, 10; "Gathers Lecture Material Alaska," *Fairbanks Daily News*, July 11, 1928, 8.

26 "Alaska Museum Should Have First Flag," *Stroller's Weekly* [Juneau, AK], October 7, 1932, 12; American Legion Post Commander John M. Clark to Alaska Governor George A. Parks, January 27, 1933, III-O-495 documentation, Alaska State Museum; "Legion Asks for Flag Raised at Transfer of Ty.," *Stroller's Weekly*, January 27, 1933, 1.

flag-related documentation, and a letter agreeing that Alaska's territorial museum was "a most suitable depository."[27]

Juneau residents were delighted, and on March 20, 1933, townspeople packed the gallery of the House of Representatives in the territorial capitol building to celebrate the flag's return to Alaska.

High school students from an American history class were also present as legislators Alfred Lomen and Joseph Kehoe, acting as an impromptu color guard, carried the flag to the House Speaker's office and, as a reporter explained, "all present stood at attention, and joined in the salute given when it was placed across the desk." Kashevaroff, who was a four-year-old boy in Sitka when the transfer took place, then delivered a "dramatic and graphic recital" of the story of the 1867 flag-raising. The reporter noted, "A worn and tattered flag, with only thirty-six stars on its field of blue served to roll back the curtains of history for more than sixty-six years in the ceremony held in the hall of the House of Representatives . . . a ceremony unmatched for interest and impressiveness in recent years in Juneau." After the event, the crowd saluted the flag once again as it left the building on its way to the territory's museum collections, and newspapers around the country announced that the flag was back in Alaska.[28]

But did this flag represent historical fact or a well-worn fiction? The only person to claim firsthand knowledge of it was Joseph Keefer. And who was this man? Most of what we know today comes from

---

27 M. S. Whittier of Alaska Territorial Chamber of Commerce to Alaska Governor George A. Parks, January 28, 1933, Alaska State Museum; Department Adjutant J. T. Petrich to Alaska Governor George A. Parks, January 28, 1933, Alaska State Museum; Alaska Governor George A. Parks to Secretary of State Henry L. Stimson, January 31, 1933, Alaska State Museum [all from III-O-495 documentation]; "Support Given by All-Alaska Chamber Board," *Daily Alaska Empire*, January 31, 1933, 5; "Seeking First U.S. Flag Raised in Alaska," *Fairbanks Daily News*, February 20, 1933, 5; "Report Done by Alaska Chamber," *Fairbanks Daily News*, March 17, 1933, 4.

28 "Historic Flag Recital Given by Kashevaroff," *Juneau Empire*, March 20, 1933, 1; "Original Flag Restored to Alaska Museum," *Alaska Press*, March 24, 1933, 2. The following is a sample of the newspapers that carried the story: "Alaska Given Historic Flag," *Healdsburg Tribune*, April 21, 1933; "Historic U.S. Flag Goes to Alaska," *Trenton Evening Times*, June 3, 1933; "Flag of Castle Hill Presented to Alaska," *Daily Advocate* [Stamford, CT], June 2, 1933 "Alaska's First Flag Back Home," *Dallas Morning News*, April 27, 1933.

articles in Washington, D.C., newspapers, in which Keefer offers ideas to alter the city's urban landscape. These include requests to improve traffic flow by rerouting streets, to widen the front gates of the White House, and to dedicate a fountain to Robert Fulton, who built the first commercially successful steamboat in the early 1800s. On one occasion, Keefer described being hit by lightning in a city park—the bolt struck his umbrella; he was "stunned but not injured"—and on another he wrote complaining about "embers being left on the streets" by coal-powered fire engines.[29] Keefer made a splash in 1901 when he proposed joining the American and Canadian cascades of Niagara Falls into "one grand torrent of water." As he explained, "My idea is to build a great giant wall or abutment with a stone top or coping that cannot be washed away, and let the water from both sides of Goat Island gracefully glide over the dam or stone esplanade thus making one continuous stream of pure white water from the jut of one shore to the jut of the other." As with so many newspaper stories about him, this article ended by stating, "Mr. Keefer already enjoys distinction of being the man who raised the first American flag in Alaska. He is also a cousin of General George Washington."[30]

Keefer belonged to a number of fraternal organizations with a historical focus, including the Sons of the American Revolution and Washington, D.C.'s Oldest Inhabitants Association, and he portrayed himself as a sleuth who found historical objects with startling frequency. Here is a partial list of such items: a wooden box owned by George Washington's mother (1901), Washington's cradle (1904), a mantelpiece from a home built by Washington for his brother Samuel (1905), an engraving of King Louis XVI of France given to Washington (1905), a volume of Shakespeare with marginal notes by Washington

---

29   "A Suggested Improvement," *Evening Times*, October 27, 1900; "Petition to Congress for Improvement," *Evening Star*, October 29, 1900; *Washington Times*, November 7, 1901; "Wants a Fountain," *Evening Star*, November 9, 1901; "Referred to Col. Bingham," *Evening Star*, September 24, 1901; "Lightning Hits Umbrella," *Evening Star*, June 9, 1914; "Asks for Names of Offenders," *Evening Star*, October 21, 1901.

30   "He'd Change Niagara," *Beaumont Enterprise*, June 20, 1901; "Would Alter Niagara," *Daily Illinois State Journal*, June 22, 1901; "He Would Change Niagara," *Kalamazoo Gazette*, June 30, 1901.

(1906), a locket containing a portrait of Martha Washington (1906), the grave of Declaration of Independence signer Benjamin Harrison (1907), a signet ring owned by Washington (1916), an American flag from a ship commanded by John Paul Jones (1922), and the burial place of John Wilkes Booth (1923). What all of these alleged discoveries have in common is that in each case, Keefer offered scant evidence, and in most cases the objects or grave sites carried no defining marks, making his claims difficult to disprove.[31]

Joseph Keefer died on June 14, 1942, after being struck by a bus in New York City, and his body was transported to Washington, D.C., for burial. Yet even in death he could deceive. The obituary in the *Washington Post* indicated he was ninety-two years old, which fit with his longtime assertion that he was born in 1850 and was therefore seventeen years old at the Alaska transfer ceremony. But census records from 1860 and 1870 indicate he was younger and give his birth date as 1857 (which would make him a boy of ten when the transfer occurred).[32] Whatever his sins, the myth that Keefer created surrounding the transfer flag endured. Two years after his death, when a researcher inquired about the location of the Alaska transfer flag, a curator at the Alaska Territorial Museum replied,

> You have been correctly informed that we have the actual flag which was used in the ceremony of transfer of Alaska at Sitka,

---

31   "Memento of Washington's Mother," *Evening Star*, February 18, 1901; "George Washington's Cradle," *Pittsburgh Press*, December 30, 1904; "Historical Discovery," *Evening Star*, March 24, 1905; "Rare Portrait of Louis XVI," *Washington Post*, September 9, 1905; "Finds Washington Locket," *Washington Post*, February 22, 1906; "Book Owned by George Washington," *Evening Star*, April 27, 1906; "Makes a Discovery," *Evening Star*, April 25, 1907; "Historic Relic Identified," *Evening Star*, November 14, 1916; "Locate Old U.S. Flag," *Evening Star*, December 29, 1922; "Body of Booth Under Arsenal, Says Historian," *Richwood Gazette*, August 2, 1923. In *Mt. Vernon and Its Surroundings* (1906), 53–54, Keefer includes a section called "Recent Discoveries" with details about some of these Washington-related discoveries.

32   "Joseph I. Keefer, 92, Critically Injured," *Evening Star*, June 12, 1942; "Joseph Keefer's Body to Arrive in D.C. Today," *Washington Post*, June 16, 1942. Keefer was inconstant regarding his birthdate at various points in his life—in an application to join the Sons of the American Revolution he wrote 1852, and in the 1880 U.S. Census it is listed as 1854.

October 17 [sic], 1867. This flag was taken down immediately after the ceremony by Col. Keefer who delivered it two years later to Secretary of State Seward. It was subsequently lost, but after a long search, Col. Keefer found it in the basement of the State Department in 1894.

A researcher in the 1950s received a similar explanation of the flag's origins, and into the 1960s Alaskan newspapers reprinted Keefer's account, describing a shooting in Sitka as the reason why the flag's "blue field had been destroyed by moths and a portion of it was caked with blood."[33]

In 1967 Alaskans marked the centennial of the purchase of Alaska with statewide celebrations and a building spree that included museums, libraries, and other venues to protect Alaska's cultural heritage. In Fairbanks, organizers held their centennial exposition in a newly constructed fairgrounds they called Alaskaland, complete with a village of historic log cabins and a paddle-wheel steamboat from the 1930s. For the opening ceremonies, Don Dickey of the Alaska State Chamber of Commerce requested the transfer flag be sent from Juneau to be displayed at Alaskaland. After it arrived, Dickey added a peculiar twist to the flag's story when he told a reporter, "Seward apparently wadded the flag into a large bottle and stored it in a closet, where it remained for many years and [was] finally lost." When the Fairbanksans were done with it, the flag traveled to Sitka for that city's "Alaska Day" celebrations, which included locals in period costumes reenacting the 1867 transfer ceremony atop Castle Hill. This event was made even more authentic with a black-powder blast from a nineteenth-century Russian cannon. The flag then returned to Juneau for the

---

33   Edward L. Keithahn of Alaska Territorial Library & Museum to Hazel G. Kinscella of University of Washington, August 12, 1944, Alaska State Museum; Valerie K. Stubbs to Alaska Territorial Museum, February 26, 1956, Alaska State Museum; Rosemary A. Allen of Alaska Territorial Museum to Valerie K. Stubbs, February 29, 1956, Alaska State Museum [all from III-O-495 documentation]; "Blood Marked First Raising of American Flag in Alaska," *Fairbanks Daily News-Miner*, July 18, 1958, 59; "Old Glory Raised with a Shot," *Fairbanks Daily News-Miner*, July 18, 1963, 2.

capital's own centennial celebrations at the grand opening of a new building for the Alaska State Museum.[34]

At that time, few Alaskans had any doubts about the flag's origins or its importance as a symbol of Alaska's transformation from Russian colony to American territory. However, we can now see that the historical record has been tampered with over the years by people making dubious claims about the transfer flag. Joseph Keefer's storytelling related to the flag lasted all of his adult life, and it appears he chose the setting for these heroic fictions with care. To most Americans in the 1890s, when he began telling flag-related tales, Alaska seemed a distant, mysterious land, and the transfer ceremony was an important but thinly documented event. In the absence of reliable sources, Keefer's outlandish stories and counterfeit biography, repeated often enough, gradually achieved the appearance of truth.

Few of us are comfortable with an unsolved mystery. And clues exist that offer a possible provenance for III-O-495. In 1933, when Secretary of State Stimson sent the flag to Juneau, he included several documents, one of which was a card with Department of State letterhead from the 1860s and the following words in flowing cursive: "The first American flag raised in Russian America presented to the Department of State by Capt. F. E. Ketchum." Captain Frank E. Ketchum was a Canadian explorer who, beginning in 1865, served with the Western Union Telegraph Expedition on a mission to link North America and Asia with telegraph cable across Alaska and the Bering Strait. This effort was abandoned two years later, when a submarine cable was installed between Ireland and Newfoundland, Canada, but while members of the expedition were in Alaska, several described raising American flags at their field camps and at locations along the Yukon River.[35]

---

34 "Century-Old Sitka Flag Will Be at A-67 on Sunday," *Fairbanks Daily News-Miner*, May 26, 1967, 8; "Alaska's 1st Flag Show at A-67," *Fairbanks Daily News-Miner*, May 29, 1967, 9. Alaskaland was renamed Pioneer Park in 2001.

35 For more about the Western Union Telegraph Expedition and examples of American flag-raising in Russian America, see Rosemary Neering, *Continental Dash: The Russian-American Telegraph* (Ganges, BC: Horsdal & Schubart Publishers, 1989), 199; and George R. Adams, *Life on the Yukon, 1865–1867*, ed. Richard A. Pierce (Kingston, ON: Limestone Press, 1982), 55.

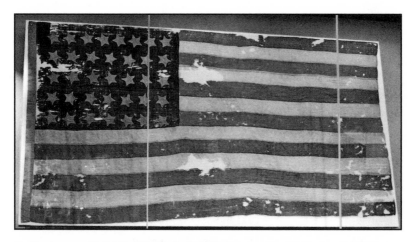

The flag known as III-O-495 at the Alaska State Museum was identified by Joseph I. Keefer as the one he raised over Sitka during the October 18, 1867, Alaska transfer ceremony, and then rediscovered twenty-seven years later in the basement of the State Department. *Courtesy of Steve Henrikson, Alaska State Museum.*

These flag-raisings took place in what was still Russian America, and it seems plausible that Joseph Keefer came upon a flag labeled with this card and mistook "F. E. Ketchum" for "T. E. Ketchum." In 1897, Keefer spoke to a *Washington Times* reporter and appeared to be mingling the story of one "lost flag" with another:

> I want to mention that in the summer of 1894, in hunting for our flag, which is unquestionably the one entitled to the honor of being first, curiously enough I came across the Western Union flag in the Smithsonian. I suppose the fact is unknown to the people who were with the Western Union party. Our flag—the Seward flag—is behind the framed copy of the original Declaration of Independence.[36]

Although it is difficult to untangle Keefer's many baffling statements, evidence suggests that he may have discovered a flag from

---

36   "Former Alaskan Parties," *Washington Times*, July 28, 1897.

the Western Union Telegraph Expedition (at the State Department? at the Smithsonian Institution?) and used it as the basis for his heroic fictions regarding the Alaska transfer ceremony and his role in it. This would also account for the number of stars on III-O-495—the Western Union Telegraph Expedition was launched shortly after Nevada gained statehood and added the thirty-sixth.

BIBLIOGRAPHY (PARTIAL)

Allen, Rosemary A. (Alaska Territorial Museum) to Valerie K. Stubbs, February 29, 1956, Alaska State Museum.

Clark, John M. (American Legion Post Commander) to Alaska Governor George A. Parks, January 27, 1933, III-O-495 documentation, Alaska State Museum.

Francis, David R. *Universal Exhibition of 1904* (St. Louis, MO: Louisiana Purchase Exhibition, 1913), 292–93; qtd. in Robert N. DeArmond, "Question of Fate of 1867 Flags Unanswered," *Daily Sitka Sentinel*, October 15, 1992, 18A.

Keitahn, Edward L. (Alaska Territorial Library & Museum) to Hazel G. Kinscella of University of Washington, August 12, 1944, Alaska State Museum.

Parks, George A. (Alaska Governor) to Secretary of State Henry L. Stimson, January 31, 1933, Alaska State Museum.

Patrick, Andrew J. *The Most Striking of Objects: The Totem Poles of Sitka National Historical Park*. Anchorage: National Park Service, 2002.

Petrich, J. T. (Department Adjutant) to Alaska Governor George A. Parks, January 28, 1933, Alaska State Museum.

Stubbs, Valerie K. to Alaska Territorial Museum, February 26, 1956, Alaska State Museum.

Whittier, M.S. (Alaska Territorial Chamber of Commerce) to Alaska Governor George A. Parks, January 28, 1933, Alaska State Museum.

A Note from Ross Coen

It was at a 2002 orientation for new graduate students, of which I was one, where I gained a mentor, colleague, and friend. I had met Terrence Cole a time or two before that gathering, but that's really when it started. For a minute or two, I explained to the assembled faculty my very undeveloped idea for a thesis project. Terrence, seated across the table from me, began talking and gesticulating in that animated way familiar to anyone who knows him. By the time I left the room, I had a thesis advisor, an approved topic, and instructions to march over to the library and get these dozen books. There is a direct line from that seminar room to the scholar I am today. I submit this article in honor of Terrence because it embodies so much of the detective-like approach he taught me: do not merely read your sources, but question, critique, and contextualize them, always probing their depths for the real story.

"NO DOGS OR NATIVES ALLOWED"

Myth, Memory, and the History
of a Sign that Did Not Exist

Ross Coen

Eight members of the Crow and Northern Cheyenne tribes of Big Horn County, Montana, brought a voting rights lawsuit against the county in 1983.[1] The complaint alleged that the at-large elections for county commission and school board effectively enabled the majority-white population to control both bodies. No Indian had ever held elected office in Big Horn County, the plaintiffs noted, despite Native Americans accounting for 41 percent of the county's population. In the trial held in federal court, Joe Medicine Crow, an author, historian, and World War II veteran who years later at age ninety-six would receive the Presidential Medal of Freedom from Barack Obama, took the stand and testified about the discrimination his people faced in the 1940s: "When you would go into a restaurant the proprietor would shake his head. That means get out of here. And after being given that treatment for a while, you know where to go or where not to go." Medicine Crow continued, "In those days there were signs on restaurant doors, 'No Indians Allowed'. Or sometimes 'No Dogs or Indians Allowed'. It was harsh, very harsh, crude."[2]

No one conversant in the rhetoric of the Red Power movement, or even only casually aware of the issue of Native rights at the time,

---

1   *Windy Boy v. County of Big Horn*, 647 F. Supp. 1002 (D. Mont. 1986).

2   Quoted in Laughlin McDonald, *American Indians and the Fight for Equal Voting Rights* (Norman: University of Oklahoma Press, 2010), 64.

would blink an eye at Medicine Crow's statement about discriminatory signs. It was widely accepted that signs equating Indians and
dogs, and prohibiting both from entering shops, restaurants, and
other public places, were commonplace in bygone, less enlightened
eras. During the 1940s through the 1960s, the period of the national
civil rights movement in general and just before the Red Power movement in particular, seems to have been the heyday of "No Dogs or
Indians Allowed." Indeed, there are numerous testimonies of the type
offered by Medicine Crow: personal recollections of having seen such
signs many years before. Stories have popped up in New Mexico,
Idaho, Wyoming, Iowa, California, Montana, and other locations
across the country.[3] Native Americans were not the only ones who
shared memories of the signs; versions of the story have turned up
in Great Britain, Ireland, Canada, Cuba, Algeria, Australia, China, and
India. Even punk rocker Johnny Rotten got into the act, titling his
1994 memoir *No Irish, No Blacks, No Dogs*.

And then there is Alaska. It is widely believed that signs equating
Natives with dogs were commonplace in the territory prior to 1945,
the year an equal rights bill was passed that prohibited race-based
exclusion in public places. In recent decades, stories of the hateful
signs have become a sort of common currency used by Native elders,
non-Native Alaskans, journalists, politicians, authors, educators,
and really anyone who wishes to comment on the evils of racism.
The instances are almost too numerous to cite, but suffice it to say

---

3   Karren Baird-Olson, "Reflections of an AIM Activist: Has It All Been
Worth It?" in Troy Johnson, Joane Nagel, and Duane Champage, eds., *American
Indian Activism: Alcatraz to the Longest Walk* (Urbana: University of Illinois Press,
1997), 234; Kathleen Dean Moore, Kurt Peters, Ted Jojola, and Amber Lacy, eds.,
How It Is: The Native American Philosophy of V. F. Cordova (Tucson: University
of Arizona Press, 2007), 193; LaNada Boyer, "Reflections of Alcatraz," in Troy
Johnson, Joane Nagel, and Duane Champage, eds., *American Indian Activism:
Alcatraz to the Longest Walk* (Urbana: University of Illinois Press, 1997), 88; Joyce
Hollyday, *Clothed With the Sun: Biblical Women, Social Justice, and Us* (Louisville,
KY: Westminster John Knox Press, 1994), 52; Kathleen J. Fitzgerald, *Beyond White
Ethnicity: Developing a Sociological Understanding of Native American Identity
Reclamation* (Lanham, MD: Lexington Books, 2007), 35; Peter B. Dedek, *Hip to
the Trip: A Cultural History of Route 66* (Albuquerque: University of New Mexico
Press, 2007), 80.

that one may select at random any newspaper article about discrimination published in the last thirty years, and the words "No Dogs" will appear no lower than the third paragraph.[4] The phrase has so thoroughly pervaded the public discourse on discrimination in Alaska that it has become shorthand for that very discrimination. A speaker or writer need only invoke "No Dogs or Natives Allowed" and the entire pre-1945 history of racial exclusion is made manifest. The words conjure an image that is visually arresting and requires no elaboration, much the way a photograph of white-hooded figures burning a cross in a clearing in the woods is not merely self-explanatory but actually explains a great deal more than what is observable in the photograph itself.

But there is a catch. "No Dogs or Natives Allowed" is a myth. The signs never existed in Alaska. There is no contemporaneous evidence for them, and a close review of the public record reveals the phrase was first used in 1971, some three decades *after* the signs were supposedly on display. Apocryphal stories of "No Dogs or _____ Allowed" were in wide circulation around the world in the 1970s, and it appears the Alaska version of the story is a form of mimesis—the purposeful imitation of one group's speech by another as a factor in social change. In effect, the trope of discriminatory signs comparing Natives to dogs is a collective false memory—but one whose usefulness in condemning the evils of the past ensures its continued employ.

---

4   For a selection of books and articles that include mention of "No Dogs" signs, see Janie Leask, "The Alaska natives special blessings," *Anchorage Daily Times*, 11/29/1987; Carolyn Brown, "Elizabeth Peratrovich, one powerful woman," *Juneau Empire*, 2/14/2011; James Mason, "Elizabeth Peratrovich, bringing light to all people," *The Arctic Sounder*, 7/4/2011; William L. Iggiagruk Hensley, "Russia gave up Alaska. Why?" *Alaska Dispatch News*, 4/2/2017; Nick Bowman, "Ketchikan theater named for Elizabeth Peratrovich," *Ketchikan Daily News*, 2/17/2017; Shannyn Moore, "First People still feel brunt of racism, subtle and overt," *Alaska Dispatch News*, 11/6/2016; Donald Craig Mitchell, *Sold American: The Story of Alaska Natives and Their Land, 1867–1959* (Hanover: University Press of New England, 1997), 332–33; Claus-M. Naske, *Ernest Gruening: Alaska's Greatest Governor* (Fairbanks: University of Alaska Press, 2004), xx; Phyllis A. Fast, "Alaska at 50: Language, Tradition, and Art," in G. W. Kimura, ed., *Alaska at 50: The Past, Present, and Future of Alaska Statehood* (Fairbanks: University of Alaska Press, 2009), 77.

This article examines the tangled history of "No Dogs or Natives Allowed," finding no historical basis for the claims such signs were, as one present-day discussant put it, "common in public businesses in territorial Alaska."[5] Simply poking holes in bad history, however, as though the exercise were nothing more than a sorting game where one separates true statements from false, is not the point. "No Dogs" is more than just a harmless embellishment; the story embeds racism in this menacing, loutish form, and because the signs have all been eradicated from polite society, we are lulled into the misconception that discrimination has withered as well. The signs also direct our attention to acts of individual discrimination, where the problem can be reduced to a bigoted bar owner, for example, leaving unexamined the institutional discrimination that dehumanized Alaska Natives in ways that were simultaneously subtler and yet more powerful.

As Carol Anderson notes in her book *White Rage*, when racism in the American South came to be associated solely with the KKK, belligerent sheriffs, bus seats, and "Colored Only" water fountains, it "helped to designate racism as an individual aberration rather than something systemic, institutional, and pervasive."[6] The misplaced focus on symbols created breathing space for liberal, well-meaning whites to renounce jackbooted thugs and their overt displays of bigotry, while still benefiting from the unequal distribution of capital that was the central feature of such systems. In Anderson's view, the oppression of African Americans by Congress, the courts, school boards, housing authorities, city councils, and other institutions of the state goes unchecked when we cannot turn our eyes away from Bull Connor and his attack dogs and fire hoses. In the case of Alaska's oft-cited but nonexistent "No Dogs" signs, reducing the complex nature of discrimination to an oversimplified trope precludes an honest public discussion of the systematic degradation of Alaska

---

5   Heather Kendall-Miller, "A Legacy to Aspire to," *The Arctic Sounder*, 7/4/2011, p. 7.
6   Carol Anderson, *White Rage: The Unspoken Truth of Our Racial Divide* (New York: Bloomsbury, 2016), 100.

Natives that did not stop, or even slow down much, when the equal rights bill was passed in 1945.

On December 10, 1971, Roy Peratrovich wrote a letter to the editor of the *Anchorage Daily News*. A week earlier, the paper had run an article about the Alaska Native Brotherhood (ANB), to which it referred as a "social organization." Peratrovich, the ANB president from 1940 to 1945, and a man who by his own admission was eager, electrified even, to set the record straight on all things Native, responded with a missive that cited the group's many political accomplishments over the years. In discussing the equal rights bill, he asserted that in Juneau in the 1940s, "Signs were placed...on business establishments saying, 'No Indians Allowed' or 'We cater to white trade only' and some went so far as saying, 'No Indians or dogs allowed here.'"[7]

Peratrovich's letter was the first ever public mention of "No Dogs" in Alaska. Any attempt to validate his claim requires a careful examination of the public record in the years before and after 1945. If the signs had indeed been displayed in the territory in that era, one would expect to find mention in contemporaneous records—such as letters, newspaper editorials, or the minutes of ANB conventions. But the records of the time, today preserved in libraries, museums, and archives in Alaska and around the country, contain not a single mention of "No Dogs." Although the ANB lobbied for the equal rights bill from 1941 to 1945, the phrase appears in none of its testimonies, letters, press releases, resolutions, newsletters, or legislative bulletins. Upon review of the collected letters of Roy Peratrovich, Walter Soboleff, Louis Shotridge, Frank Johnson, Andrew Hope, Cyrus Peck, Amy Hallingstad, William L. Paul, and other Native leaders of the time, none mention "No Dogs." The same goes for the correspondence of territorial officials, including Ernest Gruening, Anthony Dimond, and Bob Bartlett. Ruth Gruber, a special assistant to Interior Secretary Harold Ickes, reported on discrimination in Alaska in the 1940s without once citing "No Dogs" signs. Neither does the phrase appear in

---

7   Roy Peratrovich, "A Close Look at the ANB," *Anchorage Daily News*, 12/10/1971.

newspapers of the era. No photograph has been located, despite extensive searching by this writer and other scholars.

One can never prove a negative, of course, and therefore it remains possible that such a document or photograph rests heretofore unexamined in a shoebox in someone's attic. There is no way to definitively prove otherwise. The point, however, is that the sheer abundance of stories, which has led Alaskans to believe that "No Dogs" signs were displayed in every public space from Ketchikan to Nome, are simply not sustainable for the complete lack of evidence.

Signs with other offensive language *were* once displayed in Alaska. Extant records of the era prove it. Most famous is a letter Peratrovich sent to Ernest Gruening, the territory's governor, on December 30, 1941, an eloquent plea that marked the start of the campaign to pass an equal rights bill: "My attention has been called to a business establishment in Douglas, namely, 'Douglas Inn,' which has a sign on the door which reads, 'No Natives Allowed.'"[8] Over the next four years, Peratrovich cited this case repeatedly, speaking about the sign in testimony before the territorial legislature and writing about it in letters to public officials and newspaper editors.[9] At no time between 1941 and 1945, however, did he claim to have observed "No Dogs," despite the fact that such a sign would have been the most hateful example of bigotry in the territory and therefore a powerful lobbying tool.

For his part, Gruening spoke often about the sign in the Douglas Inn and another he personally observed in an Anchorage restaurant, but he too failed to utter a single word about the eventually supposedly pervasive "No Dogs."[10] In his address to the ANB convention in November 1944, for example, the governor spoke at length about the

---

8   Roy Peratrovich to Ernest Gruening, 12/30/1941, Peratrovich Family Papers, MS 129, Alaska State Library Historical Collections, Juneau.

9   Roy Peratrovich, letter in *Alaska Fishing News* (Ketchikan), 3/12/43; "Packed House Hears Debate Equal Rights," *Juneau Empire*, 1/31/1945, 8; Roy Peratrovich to Anthony Dimond, 4/28/1943, Peratrovich Family Papers, MS 129, Alaska State Library Historical Collections, Juneau.

10   Ernest Gruening, *The State of Alaska* (New York: Random House, 1954), 377; Ernest Gruening, *Many Battles: The Autobiography of Ernest Gruening* (New York: Liveright, 1973), 318–19.

issue of discrimination, noting that "the signs which I had occasionally encountered in Alaska restaurants and other establishments saying 'no natives allowed' or 'we do not cater to native trade' were profoundly offensive not merely in themselves but for the discriminatory practice which they disclosed."[11] Gruening cited these examples at the very convention where the ANB was solidifying its lobbying campaign for the upcoming legislative session, at which the equal rights bill would pass. As with Roy and the other delegates, however, he made no mention of "No Dogs."

The questions must therefore be asked: If the signs were commonplace in Alaska prior to 1945, how do we explain the fact that no mention of them appears in records of the era? And how do we explain that mention suddenly abounds decades later, once Peratrovich began speaking and writing about them? Most importantly, why do so many people believe something that never happened?

In many ways the truthfulness of the claim is of secondary concern. The later testimonies of Peratrovich, as well as those of other Native elders who picked up on the theme, have value simply for having been shared. It does not matter whether they are "true" in the sense of being historically accurate, because that is not the point. In a phenomenon widely observed first among Holocaust survivors, personal accounts of suffering become elevated in importance precisely because the associated trauma is real for the group irrespective of the veracity of individual experience. Thus, when Alaska Natives testify to their memories of "No Dogs" signs, their statements transcend basic categories of true/false and are accepted at face value for the firsthand knowledge of the pain of discrimination they impart.

In The Postmodern Condition, Jean-François Lyotard argues that knowledge is legitimized (or not) according to the power relationships of those doing the communicating, and the statements we make are like moves in a game. Building off Ludwig Wittgenstein's theory of "language games," Lyotard observes that the words we speak can be

---

11   Ernest Gruening, "Message to the Thirty-First Annual Convention of the Alaska Native Brotherhood," November 1944, Box 12, Ms 009, Alaska Packers Association Records, Alaska State Library, Juneau.

categorized "in exactly the same way as the game of chess is defined by a set of rules determining the properties of each piece, in other words, the proper way to move."[12] For Lyotard, knowledge and power are connected. Those in the elevated position of saying what the rules are—i.e., legislators who make bigoted statements about Alaska Natives and who may or may not then extend to them the privilege of testifying—exert tremendous influence over the communication that follows.

Among the seemingly infinite points of data floating in the discursive ether, those transformed into "knowledge" do so only in the course of the "game" where those players with power agree (or are forced) to recognize them as such. To extend Lyotard's chess metaphor, a common pawn has within itself the ability to defeat every other piece on the board, even the king and queen, but it gets that chance— that is, its ability to act, to communicate its message—only in the rarest of circumstances when power relationships align just so.

In the 1940s, Alaska Native testimonies about discriminatory signs were accepted by some and rejected by others, the difference having to do with the political context in which the conversation took place. Upon the passage of the equal rights bill, the existence of discrimination against Natives became "knowledge" in the Lyotardian sense, particularly as it gave voice to previously marginalized peoples. In the decades that followed, the language of discriminatory signs came to represent discrimination itself, and thus the language was legitimized by association.

Alaskans born after 1945 unhesitatingly believed in the existence of "No Dogs" signs, an impulse that derived not merely from the understandable desire to validate elders' testimonies, but also because the rules of the rhetorical playfield had been altered to a degree where dissenting from the claim was simply not possible without causing offense. When Roy Peratrovich first inserted "No Dogs" into public

---

12   Jean-François Lyotard, *The Postmodern Condition: A Report on Knowledge*, Geoff Bennington and Brian Massumi, trans. (Minneapolis: University of Minnesota Press, 1984), 10. See also Ulrich Baer, "What 'Snowflakes' Get Right About Free Speech," *New York Times*, 4/24/2017.

discourse in 1971, his statement was basically a rhetorical thrust in the language games, the sort of move Lyotard may have had in mind when he wrote that "to speak is to fight, in the sense of playing [the game]."[13] This claim, which in 1945 would have been dismissed out of hand for its untrue and hyperbolic nature, received instant and unquestioning validation in the 1970s for a number of reasons: abhorrence of racist language in the era of civil rights, the Alaska Native land claims movement of the era that authenticated both Native testimonies and their participation in public affairs, and, most importantly, Peratrovich's status as elder, sponsor of the equal rights bill, and last surviving witness to the events in question. Who was going to suggest he might be inaccurate?

Deconstructing his statements is nevertheless a useful exercise. In his every written and spoken mention of "No Dogs," Peratrovich deployed what linguists refer to as *hedges*—mitigating words and vague sentence constructions that make a statement less forceful (not to mention less believable) by creating distance between it and both the addresser and addressee.[14] In his letter to the *Anchorage Daily News* on December 10, 1971, Peratrovich wrote (emphasis added), "Signs were placed . . . on business establishments saying, 'No Indians Allowed' or 'We cater to white trade only' and *some went so far as saying*, 'No Indians or dogs allowed here.'" And this from a letter Peratrovich wrote to the *Anchorage Daily Times* on January 27, 1977: "Signs appeared . . . saying, 'No Natives Allowed' or 'We Cater to White Trade Only,' *or even this in some cases*, 'No Natives or Dogs Allowed.'" Note the prevarication in the last instances in both letters. Although signs equating Natives and dogs would have been the most egregious example of the racism faced by Natives, Peratrovich not only mentions them last but does so with qualifiers signaling a lack of confidence in the claim.

The pattern is repeated in his keynote address to the ANB convention in Hydaburg in November 1977: "When I first arrived in Juneau,

13   Lyotard, *The Postmodern Condition*, 10.
14   George Lakoff, "Hedges: A study in meaning criteria and the logic of fuzzy concepts," *Journal of Philosophical Logic* 2, no. 4 (1973), 458–508.

I was shocked to see signs in front of business houses stating, 'We Cater to White Trade Only.' In another place, 'No Natives Allowed,' and *some even went further and became more insulting with* 'No Dogs or Indians Allowed.'"[15] The equivocation with which he cites "No Dogs" is again telling. His first two examples of discriminatory language are cited without hesitancy, likely because both are historically valid. But the last example Peratrovich prefaces with "some even went further and became more insulting with," a hedge that both belies an apparent certainty of the claim and softens the impact of what should be the most potent symbol of bigotry in evidence.

Despite its markers of uncertainty, "No Dogs" proved so vivid an image, so encapsulating of the experience, that Alaskans quickly accepted it as true. The hedges used by Peratrovich actually may have helped. Research into language and cognition shows that hedges cause people to think more about the information being hedged than they might if it was presented directly. Their attention lingers on the qualifiers, and their brains work a little harder to comprehend the speaker's timidity. As explained by Art Markman, cognitive scientist at the University of Texas, "The more work you put into something, the more likely you are to remember it later."[16]

Within a few years of Peratrovich's linguistic chess move, many Alaskans, who in over thirty years had never said a public word about "No Dogs" signs, suddenly began remembering having seen them years before. George Rogers, professor and longtime state economist, was one such respondent, claiming in a 2008 interview to have seen the signs in Anchorage, Fairbanks, and Nome.[17] One Native elder born in Sitka in 1932 relayed in a 2008 interview her

---

15   Roy Peratrovich, "Keynote Address," Minutes of the Proceedings of the 65th Annual Convention, Mss. 7, Series 2, Box 6, Walter A. Soboleff Papers, Sealaska Heritage Institute Archives, Juneau (emphasis added).

16   Art Markman, "What Do (Linguistic) Hedges Do?" *Psychology Today*, psychologytoday.com/blog/ulterior-motives [accessed 9/7/2017]; Kris Liu and Jean E. Fox Tree, "Hedges Enhance Memory but Inhibit Retelling," *Psychonomic Bulletin and Review* 19, no. 5 (October 2012).

17   George Rogers interviewed by Michael Letzring, 4/8/2008, Interview #2008-26, Alaska and Polar Regions Collections, Elmer E. Rasmuson Library, University of Alaska Fairbanks.

memory of signs reading, "No Colored, No dogs, No Natives," a most curious phrasing when one considers the population of blacks in Alaska, even in urban centers, was negligible at the time. Another elder remembered as a child seeing signs on Fourth Avenue in Anchorage even into the 1950s.[18]

A particularly noteworthy example is found in two interviews, nearly two decades apart, with Cecilia Koontz, a Tlingit woman from Juneau. In the first interview, conducted for a public radio program in 1974, Koontz remarked, "They had signs at certain places saying 'No Indians Allowed Here' and 'We Cater to Whites Only.'"[19] Koontz also told the story of how she and a few other Alaska Native Sisterhood members marched downtown to the military recruitment office and insisted they post a "No Indians Allowed" sign in the window. In the second interview, this one conducted in 1992, Koontz told the same story again—but this time she reported the sign read "No Natives, No Dogs Allowed."[20] The fact that Koontz made no reference to "No Dogs" in the first interview but did in the second may be evidence of nothing more than involuntary word choices on those particular days. It may also be evidence that in 1974, she hadn't yet heard or internalized the nascent but burgeoning "No Dogs" trope—but that by 1992, she had.

Koontz is by no means alone in exhibiting this type of faulty recall. Research into cognitive psychology has consistently shown that memory does not work like a video recorder, where a person's experience is captured on tape and can be unerringly played back at a later time. Instead, memories, at the moment of their retrieval, are reconstructed according to the individual's knowledge, beliefs, and goals, oftentimes in order to conform to social imperatives at the time of retrieval. As early as the 1930s, cognitive scientists recognized that individuals regularly and subconsciously supplant their memories

---

18   Holly Miowak Guise, "Alaskan Segregation and the Paradox of Exclusion, Separation, and Integration," in *Transforming the University: Alaska Native Studies in the 21st Century*, conference proceedings (2014), 280.

19   Cecilia Koontz interviewed by Walter Johns, 1974, Interview #88-49-13, Alaska and Polar Regions Collections, Elmer E. Rasmuson Library, University of Alaska Fairbanks.

20   Diane E. Benson, "Being Elizabeth," *The Arctic Sounder*, 7/4/2011, p. 6.

with false data, bits of information culled from lived experience and retained precisely because they buttress the interpretation the memory is meant to convey. In other words, according to Henry L. Roediger III and Kurt A. DeSoto, "A person's present knowledge and goals may shape and determine how he or she remembers the past."[21] In the case of "No Dogs," respondents who claim to remember seeing the signs in Alaska in the 1940s represent a textbook example of reconstructive memory: having heard the stories of the signs and intuitively recognizing that the image both aligns with their experience and intensifies the message they wish to impart, they integrate the detail into their own memory so vividly that they "remember" the experience.

Tales of the signs were repeated throughout the world in much the same way. In effect, the Alaska case is a microcosm of what happened internationally. The sheer profusion of "No Dogs" stories in places as varied as a diner in Iowa, a hotel in London, and beaches in Algiers (where French colonists reportedly proclaimed, *"Interdit aux chiens et aux indigènes"*[22]) suggests one of two things. Either it's a coincidence on an astonishing scale, evidence that bigots around the world were somehow of a single mind in their choice of language that not only segregated minorities but also demeaned them—or "No Dogs" is indeed mimetic in nature, a trope that originated in a particular time and place where the first such sign may have been displayed and, as the story was told over and over again across the globe, came to be integrated into the constructed memories of individuals eager to underscore the pain of discrimination they once faced.

Not to belabor the point, but it is important to note that in every example cited in this paper, what is being spoken and written down is not contemporaneous evidence of "No Dogs" signs, but rather the *memory* of having seen such signs long ago, in some cases more than seventy years after the supposed fact. This delay in reporting, along with the near total lack of primary evidence and the human mind's

---

21   Henry L. Roediger III and Kurt A. DeSoto, "Psychology of Reconstructive Memory," in James D. Wright, ed., *International Encyclopedia of the Social and Behavioral Sciences*, 2nd ed. (Amsterdam: Elsevier, 2015), 54.

22   Cassia Meare, *The World and I*, Vol. 1 (e-book, 2017, not paginated).

capacity for creating false memories, further suggests the signs either were not as prevalent as many believe or did not exist in the first place.

It may be a collective false memory that spans several cultures, but that doesn't mean "No Dogs or _____ Allowed" was invented from whole cloth, either. There is credible historical evidence the sign, or some version of it, was displayed in parts of the United States as late as the 1950s. Cynthia E. Orozco has found that in the 1930s and 1940s, signs excluding Mexicans and dogs (as well as "negroes," for that matter) were posted in restaurants in Texas.[23] And a 1960 congressional report on Native Americans observed that "'No dogs, no Indians' signs have disappeared only recently in Montana and North and South Dakota border areas."[24] The claim is credible for its contemporaneous timing.

These isolated incidents do not explain the ubiquity of later claims, however. Amazingly, it was a 1972 Bruce Lee movie that brought the trope of discriminatory signs to a worldwide audience. *Fist of Fury* stars Lee as Chen Zhen, a martial arts student who seeks retribution against those who caused his master's death. At one point in the film, Chen attempts to enter a public park but is stopped by an attendant who points to a sign reading, "No Dogs and Chinese Allowed." A group of Japanese men jeer at Chen, saying they will allow him to enter if he barks like a dog. After besting his tormenters with a series of powerful blows, Chen knocks the sign from its post and shatters it to pieces with a perfectly timed jump-kick.

According to one critic, *Fist of Fury* was "the most politically and historically charged" of Lee's many films.[25] Set during the Japanese occupation of Shanghai, the film shows Lee engaged in acts of personal resistance set within the broader context of colonial oppression. As for the famous "No Dogs and Chinese Allowed" scene, it was loosely

---

23 Cynthia E. Orozco, *No Mexicans, Women, or Dogs Allowed: The Rise of the Mexican American Civil Rights Movement* (Austin: University of Texas Press, 2009).

24 "Problems of the 'First Americans,'" *Congressional Quarterly Weekly Report* 18, no. 3 (January 15, 1960), 75.

25 Dwayne Wong, "'No Dogs and No Chinese Allowed': The Historical Significance of Bruce Lee's Fist of Fury," www.huffingtonpost.com/dwayne-wong-omowale/no-dogs-and-no-chinese-al_b_9455424.html [accessed 1/2/2018].

based on the administration of Shanghai's Huangpu Park in an era when Western business interests exerted tremendous control over the city's politics and society. But here, too, the history of the sign posted at the park's gate is shrouded in myth, and scholars who investigated the issue have concluded that no sign equating Chinese and dogs ever existed.

Built in 1868 next to the British consulate, Huangpu Park was closed to Chinese except for "respectable and well-dressed" city employees and servants of Westerners. Often left to the discretion of police, the ban was enforced sporadically over the new few decades. In 1894, it was codified with a posted sign ordering, "No Chinese shall be admitted." The text of the sign was revised at least three times over the next few decades, with park administrators adding several new rules as perceived needs arose. At one point, the sign's first rule ordered "No dogs or bicycles are admitted," while the ban on Chinese was bumped to the fifth rule on the list. A later version of the sign proclaimed "The Gardens are reserved for the foreign community" as the first rule, while the prohibition on dogs and bicycles was moved down to number four. According to Robert A. Bickers and Jeffrey N. Wasserstrom, "[I]t is quite apparent that the phrase 'Chinese and Dogs Not Admitted' did not appear on any officially sanctioned sign," but that over time, as stories of the demeaning signs were told and retold, the two separate rules came to be conflated into one.[26] Although untrue, the mental image of a sign that explicitly compared the Chinese to dogs proved such a powerful symbol of the indignities of the colonial period that the story was universally accepted as fact. *Fist of Fury* was wildly popular in China upon its release, with audiences reportedly standing and cheering when Bruce Lee smashes the "No Dogs and Chinese Allowed" sign to bits.

The Huangpu Park sign is the most well-known and the only "No Dogs" claim with extensive, albeit inconsistent, historical evidence behind it. Upon the release of *Fist of Fury*, the trope of discriminatory

---

26 Robert A. Bickers and Jeffrey N. Wasserstrom, "Shanghai's 'Dogs and Chinese Not Admitted' Sign: Legend, History and Contemporary Symbol," *The China Quarterly* no. 142 (June 1995), 446.

signs gained an ever-wider audience as countless people around the world encountered it for the first time. The film doubtlessly influenced reports of discrimination by other minority groups. For his part, Roy Peratrovich first wrote about "No Dogs" in December 1971, three months *before* the film was released in the United States. Where Peratrovich first heard the story cannot be known, but in the 1950s, once he moved to the Lower 48 and became active in the National Congress of American Indians (NCAI), he almost certainly learned of the signs in Montana and the Dakotas from people who experienced them firsthand. Helen Peterson, an Oglala Dakota (Sioux) from Pine Ridge, South Dakota, who certainly would have known about the signs, served as NCAI director from 1953 to 1961, and developed a close friendship with the Peratrovich family.[27] Whatever the source, Peratrovich transposed the history to Alaska and mentioned the signs in letters, speeches, and interviews throughout the 1970s. Others picked up on the theme, and today it is nearly impossible to imagine an article about discrimination that does not include the phrase.

Like the Chinese moviegoers who thrilled at the sight of Bruce Lee smashing a sign in Huangpu Park, Alaskans today exult in the belief that the ANB and the equal rights bill vanquished "No Dogs" signs from Ketchikan to Nome. In both cases, however, those who applaud are cheering for something that never actually existed.

BIBLIOGRAPHY (PARTIAL)

Anderson, Carol. *White Rage: The Unspoken Truth of Our Racial Divide*. New York: Bloomsbury, 2016.

Baird-Olson, Karren. "Reflections of an AIM Activist: Has It All Been Worth It?" in Troy Johnson, Joane Nagel, and Duane Champage, eds., *American Indian Activism: Alcatraz to the Longest Walk*. Urbana: University of Illinois Press, 1997.

Benson, Diane E., "Being Elizabeth," *The Arctic Sounder*, 7/4/2011, p. 6.

---

27 Peter Metcalfe, *A Dangerous Idea: The Alaska Native Brotherhood and the Struggle for Indigenous Rights* (Fairbanks: University of Alaska Press, 2014), 80–82, 117n173.

Bickers, Robert A. and Wasserstrom, J. N. "Shanghai's 'Dogs and Chinese Not Admitted' Sign: Legend, History and Contemporary Symbol," *The China Quarterly* no. 142 (June 1995), 446.

Boyer, LaNada. "Reflections of Alcatraz," in Troy Johnson, Joane Nagel, and Duane Champage, eds., *American Indian Activism: Alcatraz to the Longest Walk*. Urbana: University of Illinois Press, 1997.

Dedek, Peter B. *Hip to the Trip: A Cultural History of Route 66*. Albuquerque: University of New Mexico Press, 2007.

Fitzgerald, Kathleen J. *Beyond White Ethnicity: Developing a Sociological Understanding of Native American Identity Reclamation*. Lanham, MD: Lexington Books, 2007.

Gruening, Ernest. *The State of Alaska*. New York: Random House, 1954.

———. *Many Battles: The Autobiography of Ernest Gruening*. New York: Liveright, 1973.

———. "Message to the Thirty-First Annual Convention of the Alaska Native Brotherhood," Box 12, Ms. 009, Alaska Packers Association Records, Alaska State Library, Juneau. November 1944

Guise, Holly Miowak. "Alaskan Segregation and the Paradox of Exclusion, Separation, and Integration," in *Transforming the University: Alaska Native Studies in the 21st Century*, conference proceedings (2014).

Hollyday, Joyce. *Clothed With the Sun: Biblical Women, Social Justice, and Us*. Louisville, KY: Westminster John Knox Press, 1994.

Kendall-Miller, Heather. "A Legacy to Aspire to," *The Arctic Sounder*, 7/4/2011, p. 7.

Koontz, Cecilia, interviewed by Walter Johns, 1974, Interview #88-49-13, Alaska and Polar Regions Collections, Elmer E. Rasmuson Library, University of Alaska Fairbanks.

Lakoff, George. "Hedges: A study in meaning criteria and the logic of fuzzy concepts," *Journal of Philosophical Logic* 2, no. 4 (1973), 458–508.

Liu, Kris, and Fox Tree, J. E. "Hedges Enhance Memory but Inhibit Retelling," *Psychonomic Bulletin and Review* 19, no. 5 (October 2012).

Lyotard, Jean-François. *The Postmodern Condition: A Report on Knowledge*, Geoff Bennington and Brian Massumi, trans. Minneapolis: University of Minnesota Press, 1984.

Markman, Art. "What Do (Linguistic) Hedges Do?" *Psychology Today*, psychologytoday.com/blog/ulterior-motives [accessed 9/7/2017].

McDonald, Laughlin. *American Indians and the Fight for Equal Voting Rights*. Norman: University of Oklahoma Press, 2010.

Meare, Cassia. *The World and I, Vol. 1* e-book. 2017.

Metcalfe, Peter. *A Dangerous Idea: The Alaska Native Brotherhood and the Struggle for Indigenous Rights*. Fairbanks: University of Alaska Press, 2014.

Moore, K. D., K. Peters, T. Jojola, and A. Lacy, eds., *How It Is: The Native American Philosophy of V. F. Cordova*. Tucson: University of Arizona Press, 2007.

Orozco, Cynthia E. *No Mexicans, Women, or Dogs Allowed: The Rise of the Mexican American Civil Rights Movement*. Austin: University of Texas Press, 2009.

Peratrovich, Roy. "A Close Look at the ANB." *Anchorage Daily News*, 12/10/1971.

———. "Keynote Address," *Minutes of the Proceedings of the 65th Annual Convention*, Mss 7, Series 2, Box 6, Walter A. Soboleff Papers, Sealaska Heritage Institute Archives, Juneau.

Peratrovich, Roy, to Ernest Gruening, 12/30/1941, Peratrovich Family Papers, MS 129, Alaska State Library Historical Collections, Juneau.

"Problems of the 'First Americans,'" *Congressional Quarterly Weekly Report* 18, no. 3 (January 15, 1960), 75.

Roediger, Henry L. III, and K. A. DeSoto. "Psychology of Reconstructive Memory," in James D. Wright, ed., *International Encyclopedia of the Social and Behavioral Sciences*, 2nd ed. Amsterdam: Elsevier, 2015.

Rogers, George, interviewed by Michael Letzring, 4/8/2008. Interview #2008-26, Alaska and Polar Regions Collections, Elmer E. Rasmuson Library, University of Alaska Fairbanks.

Windy Boy v. County of Big Horn, 647 F. Supp. 1002 (D. Mont. 1986).

Wong, Dwayne. "'No Dogs and No Chinese Allowed': The Historical Significance of Bruce Lee's *Fist of Fury*," www.huffingtonpost.com/dwayne-wong-omowale/no-dogs-and-no-chinese-al_b_9455424.html [accessed 1/2/2018].

A Note from Stephen Haycox

When Terrence was completing his doctoral work at the University of Washington, I was chair of the history department at UAA, and we had a new position available. Terrence applied for the position, and I was anxious that he get it. But he had not quite finished his PhD, and the Provost's Office would not allow me to hire anyone who did not have their degree in hand. There was nothing I could do, and I'm not sure my assurances to Terrence that the technicality was the only reason he didn't get the position carried the degree of credibility I sought.

Terrence worked in Seattle for a time, and then a position opened at UAF, created, I believe, by Claus Naske. I was very pleased Terrence could get on at UAF, for his background, for his friendship with Claus, and for what he would bring to the department there. I still am. But it would have been the greatest delight if we could have had his talent, his dedication, his marvelous wit, at UAA.

Such are the vicissitudes of academia.

CONTINGENCY AND ALASKA HISTORY

How Congress's 1871 Cessation of
Treaty-Making Helped Create ANCSA
a Hundred Years Later

Stephen Haycox

This essay addresses a relationship between the Alaska Purchase and Alaska's modern Native land claims history of which few people are likely aware. The critical point: there were no traditional Indian treaties with Alaska Natives, and because there were not, at the time of the Alaska Native Claims Settlement Act (ANCSA) in 1971 much of Alaska land was potentially subject to Native title, a circumstance quite different from the history of Native title in the contiguous states, and one that worked to the great advantage of Alaska Natives.

Indian law is complex, often controversial, and in some respects, ever changing. There are significant debates of various legal elements—for example, the history of Native sovereignty.[1] But the central points in this paper seem to be accepted by most.

The context for the story in this essay begins in late November 1864. Colonel John Chivington led a regiment of Colorado militia volunteers, 675 men strong, in the massacre and mutilation of between 70 and 163 Cheyenne and Arapaho Indians, mostly women and

---

1 David S. Case and David A. Voluck, *Alaska Natives and American Laws*, 3rd ed. (Fairbanks: University of Alaska Press, 2012); Donald Craig Mitchell, *Sold American: The Story of Alaska Natives and Their Land, 1867–1959* (Fairbanks: University of Alaska Press, 2003), *Take My Land, Take My Life: The Story of Congress's Historic Settlement of Alaska Native Land Claims, 1960–1971* (Fairbanks: University of Alaska Press, 2001).

children, camped along the banks of Sand Creek in eastern Colorado.[2] Far from indifferent to the atrocity, public figures and Congressional leaders condemned it, and Congress launched a two-year investigation, headed by Senator James Doolittle of Wisconsin. While discussing Doolittle's report in 1867, Congress learned of another massacre, this by General Winfield Hancock, of a combined Sioux and Cheyenne village, this in retaliation for the Indian destruction of Lieutenant William Fetterman's command near Fort Phil Kearny in northeast Wyoming. This, along with other considerations, led Congress to create a seven-man Indian Peace Commission to confer with the Indians and recommend to Congress a long-term policy that would bring peace to the plains and ensure the safety of miners and settlers moving west.[3] The Commission initiated new treaties with several Indian groups, and made a comprehensive report in 1868. The policies that proceeded from the report, which included concentration, education, and civilization, we label today as failures, both in bringing peace and in their disregard of Indian history, rights, and dignity.

One recommendation of the Commission, though, is relevant to the history of Alaska Natives. Their treaties, the 1868 Commissioners urged, should be the last treaties the U.S. should make with Indians; no further treaties should be necessary.[4] Congress implemented this recommendation in 1871, in the Indian Appropriation Act of that year.[5] That act directed that all Indians should henceforth be treated as individuals and legally designated "wards" of the federal government, and further declared that "no Indian nation or tribe would be recognized as an independent nation, tribe or power with which the United States may contract by treaty." By that act, then, treaty-making

---

2   Gregory F. Michno, *The Three Battles of Sand Creek: In Blood, In Court, and As the End of History* (Eldorado Hills, CA: Savas Beatie, 2017).

3   Kerry R. Oman, "The Beginning of the End: The Indian Peace Commission of 1867–1868," *Great Plains Quarterly* 22 (2002): 35–51.

4   Report to the President of the Indian Peace Commission, January 7, 1868, point 10, http://history.furman.edu/~benson/docs/peace.htm, accessed 24 February 2018.

5   25 U. S. C. 71, http://digitalexhibits.libraries.wsu.edu/files/original/3e5f 6367dcd8f5f4a40b41ea429e69c2.PNG, accessed 24 February 2018

with Indigenous people in the U.S. came to an end. This development occurred virtually coincident with the purchase of Alaska, in 1867.

What, then, is the significance of the absence of treaties for Alaska? It is useful here to remember that all of the land in the United States was at one time federal land, with the exception of the thirteen original colonies. By means fair or foul, by purchase or conquest, the federal government, acting in the name of the people of the U.S., acquired all the lands now possessed by the country. Article IV, Section 3, of the U.S. Constitution gives Congress the authority to designate the use of its land—all of its land. "The Congress shall have the power," the section reads, "to dispose of and make all needful rules and regulations respecting the territory or other property belonging to the United States." Treaties were one way of designating land use. Article IV gives Congress the authority to create states, another way to marshal the country's land.[6] Beginning near the end of the nineteenth century, the establishment of national forests, parks, fish and wildlife refuges, and other conservation withdrawals became another form of land designation.[7] The establishment of military reservations is yet another. The salient point here is the Congress decides how the territory under U.S. sovereignty shall be disposed of, or designated. Congress's authority applies equally to Native land. The U.S. Supreme Court confirmed that authority in the case *Lone Wolf v. Hitchcock* in 1903, finding that Congress's power over Native land is absolute.[8]

Most students of Alaska history know that the territory's purchase treaty provided that the "uncivilized tribes" would be subject to such laws and regulations as Congress might make.[9] Further, the 1884 Civil

---

6   Gary Lawson and Guy Seidman, *The Constitution of Empire: Territorial Expansion and American Legal History* (New Haven: Yale University Press, 2004), 72ff.

7   Douglas Brinkley, *The Wilderness Warrior: Theodore Roosevelt and the Crusade for America* (New York: Harper, 2009); David Harmon, Francis McManamon, and Dwight Pitcaithley, eds., *The Antiquities Act: A Century of Archaeology, Historic Preservation and Nature Conservation* (Tucson: University of Arizona Press), 2006.

8   187 U.S. 553 (1903); Blue Clark, *Lone Wolf v. Hitchcock: Treaty Rights and Indian Law at the End of the Nineteenth Century* (Lincoln: University of Nebraska Press, 1994).

9   Case and Voluck, *Alaska Natives and American Law*, 67.

Government Act provides that Natives should not be disturbed in their occupation and utilization of their lands, whichever lands those may be.[10] There was no determination at the time as to what those lands were, and Congress was laggard in disposing of Alaska land— that is, how the various lands in Alaska should be designated. This was mostly because Alaska was vast and remote, and largely unsettled, at least in western cultural terms. David Case and Don Mitchell have written important books on the history of Alaska Native land claims, and while their conclusions are different, the history they recount and the facts on which they base their conclusions are essentially the same: though there were various court and executive actions during the first half of the twentieth century, there was no finality on the issue of Alaska Native land claims. Perhaps the most important development of those years was the Tlingit Haida Jurisdictional Act of 1935.[11] After the cessation of treaty-making, Congress on occasion passed acts authorizing the courts to take jurisdiction over specific Indian land claims.[12] The Tlingit Haida act was one such action by the Congress.

Then, in a wholly unprecedented and unexpected action, in a 1941 case put together by so-called founder of modern Indian law, Felix Cohen, involving Arizona Indians and the Santa Fe Railroad, the U.S. Supreme Court found in *United States v. Santa Fe Railroad* for the validity of aboriginal title.[13] This case is generally known as the *Hualapai* case, for the Arizona Indians whose land was coveted by the railroad. What is aboriginal title?[14] It is Native title to any land Natives have ever utilized or occupied, whether they continue to utilize and occupy it

---

10   Mitchell, *Sold American*, 91–99.

11   49 Stat 388.

12   U.S. Department of Justice, "Lead Up to the Indian Claims Commission Act of 1946," https://www.justice.gov/enrd/lead-indian-claims-commission-act-1946, accessed 24 February 2018; Nancy Oestreich Lurie, "The Indian Claims Commission Act," *Annals of the American Academy of Political and Social Science* 436 (1978): 97–110.

13   Stephen Haycox, "Felix Cohen and the Indian Legacy of the New Deal," *Yale University Library Gazette* 64 (1994): 135–56.

14   Felix S. Cohen, "Original Indian Title," *Minnesota Law Review* 28 (1947): 64–96.

or not, unless that title has been formally extinguished by Congress. This was a remarkable about-face for U.S. courts dealing with Native land claims. In the contiguous states, virtually all such title had been extinguished, mostly by treaty. But in Alaska, because Congress had been laggard in disposing of the territorial land, potentially most of Alaska might be subject to Native title. This was the circumstance after the *Hualapai* finding.[15]

In 1947, pursuant to the jurisdictional act, the Tlingit Haida Central Council filed suit in what became the U.S. Court of Federal Claims, claiming ownership of all 18 million acres of the Alexander Archipelago from 1867. The case would be settled by that court in 1959,[16] when it found that, based on their concept of property ownership, the Tlingit and Haida Indians of Alaska had in fact owned the land in the Alexander Archipelago in 1867, nearly 18 million acres, and that except for some specific, small tracts, the Russians had never acquired title to the land at all.[17] The United States had taken most of that land for the Tongass National Forest in 1905 and 1908, effectively extinguishing any existing aboriginal title. The court's finding shocked most Alaskans, and indeed was seen as revolutionary in a broader context because of the vast acreage involved.[18] In 1968 the court approved a compensatory award for the taking.

But what brought Alaska Native claims to a head was Alaska statehood. Though Congress had designated 54 million acres of Alaska's 375 million total acres prior to 1958, the Alaska statehood act of that year initiated a twelve-year saga that would see Congressional disposal of all but about 70 million acres of the state. In section six of the statehood act, Congress provided for state title to 104 million acres. But in section four of the same act, Alaskans disclaimed any right or

---

15 Christian McMillen, *Making Indian Law: The Hualapai Land Case and the Birth of Ethnohistory* (New Haven: Yale University Press, 2007).

16 77 F. Supp. 172 (1959).

17 Mitchell, *Sold American*, 361–63, 434–36.

18 "Vast Wealth Could Await State Tribes," *Anchorage Daily Times*, October 14, 1966; "Native Group Enters Claim to Big Tracts," *Anchorage Daily Times*, January 17, 1967.

title to any land that might be subject to Native title.[19] By the *Hualapai* doctrine of aboriginal title, that may have included virtually all the land in Alaska, or any land Natives could demonstrate they had ever utilized or occupied. In January 1959, officials of the State of Alaska began to select the land the state wanted title to under its section six entitlement. Within months, Natives began to protest some of the proposed selections. A chess match of selection and protest proceeded over the next eight years, resulting in the federal government trans-ferring title to about 12 million of the 104 million acre entitlement to the state.[20] But by 1966, the state was blanketed with proposed state selections and millions of acres of Native protests. In that year, Secretary of the Interior Stewart Udall took the first of several actions which led to federal freeze on any further transfers of title to the state, until such time as Congress should have settled Alaska Native land claims.[21] This meant that there could be no further economic devel-opment in Alaska involving resources on the land, because no one would invest in land with clouded titles. It is important to note that this freeze was implemented before the great Prudhoe Bay oil discovery in 1968. Oil discovery did not generate a solution to the Native land claims challenge; it only exacerbated what was already there. There would have had to be a settlement with or without Prudhoe Bay.

The Alaska Native Claims Settlement Act (ANCSA), then, was a direct outcome of the statehood act. What it did, in addition to titling 44 million acres of Alaska to Native corporations, was to extinguish all other Native or aboriginal title in Alaska.[22] It also established the process that would produce the Alaska National Interest Lands Conservation Act (ANILCA) in 1980, and the disposal of 104 million additional acres in new federal conservation units. Doing the math, out of Alaska's 375 million acres, about 70 million are still not desig-nated by Congress for specific uses, and haven't been disposed of in

---

19   72 Stat. 339 (1958).

20   John Boyce and Mats Nilsson, "Interest Group Competition and the Alaska Native Claims Settlement Act," *Natural Resources Journal* 39 (1999), 755–98.

21   Mitchell, *Take My Land, Take My Life*, 131–32, 144, 185–86 and *passim*.

22   43 U.S.C. 1601 *et seq.*

that sense. These lands are administered by the Bureau of Land Management.[23]

We should imagine, then, what Alaska would have looked like at statehood, or in 1971, and in what circumstances Alaska Natives might have been, had the Congress not ceased treaty-making coincident with the Alaska Purchase. There may well have been treaties with Alaska Natives, and the establishment of traditional Indian reservations. Or, following the model of the Dawes Severalty Act, or the General Allotment Act, of 1887, Natives would have been granted citizenship in return for severing whatever tribal relationship they may have had, and given individual allotments.[24] They would have been fragmented, however, and the challenges of gaining land title, recognition, and legitimacy in the eyes of the dominant culture (all of which ANCSA has brought) would have been far more difficult, if achievable at all. Would the *Hualapai* decision have had the same effect on Alaska if there had already been treaties and allotments? No, because Native land title would have been extinguished piecemeal over the years of the last part of the nineteenth century and the first half of the twentieth, and there'd have been far fewer Natives to challenge the state selections beginning in 1959. Congress would have adjusted the treaty lands, and would have bought out the allotments to make way for the oil pipeline. The circumstances of Alaska Natives collectively would have been far less advantageous than they are today.

History is filled with contingencies; because this happened, that was possible; because that didn't happen, this was or was not possible. In our work as historians, we pay attention not only to what happened, but how and why, and those contingencies are as important a part of the story as the other realities we record and remember. It is surely incumbent on those of us who would purport to inform about Alaska history to remember and elucidate those contingencies, as attempted in this paper.

---

23   Daniel Nelson, *Northern Landscapes: The Struggle for Wilderness Alaska* (Washington, D.C.: Resources for the Future, 2004).

24   Janet A. McDonnell, *The Dispossession of the American Indian, 1887–1934* (Bloomington: Indiana University Press, 1991).

A note on the Tlingit Haida land suit, filed in 1947. The Fifth Amendment of the U.S. Constitution provides that compensation be paid for federal land takings by eminent domain, or by other means. In 1955, in a case brought by William Paul, *Tee-Hit Ton Indians v. U.S.*, the Supreme Court found that the extinguishment of Native title (in this case, to timber taken from the forest) is not compensable under the Fifth Amendment.[25] In 1968, however, the Court approved the compensatory award to the Central Council of Tlingit and Haida Indians of Alaska on the grounds that, though not constitutionally required, compensation should be paid on moral grounds. The award was $7.5 million, the appraised value of the timber in the Tongass Forest at the time of the taking.[26] The parsimonious nature of the award helped persuade the Tlingit and Haida leadership to join in the ANCSA settlement.

In summary, the absence of treaties with Alaska Native people, which dates from the period of the Alaska Purchase Treaty and which might well have been a part of the Alaska Purchase Treaty had Congress not ceased making treaties with Indians at that time, created, following on the 1941 *Hualapai* decision upholding the validity of aboriginal title, a circumstance highly favorable to Alaska Native land claims when Congress finally addressed those claims in 1971. But for that contingency, Alaska history might read quite differently today.

BIBLIOGRAPHY (PARTIAL)

Boyce, John, and Nilsson, M. "Interest Group Competition and the Alaska Native Claims Settlement Act," *Natural Resources Journal* 39 (1999), 755–98.

Brinkley, Douglas. *The Wilderness Warrior: Theodore Roosevelt and the Crusade for America*. New York: Harper, 2009.

---

25   348 U. S. 272 (1955); Case and Voluck, *Alaska Natives*, 71ff.; "Tee-Hit Ton and Alaska Native Rights," in *Law for the Elephant, Law for the Beaver: Essays in the Legal History of the North American West*, eds. John McLaren, Hamar Foster, and Chet Orloff (Regina: Canadian Plains Research Center, Univ. of Regina; Pasadena: Ninth Judicial Circuit Historical Society, 1992), 125–45.

26   Mitchell, *Take My Land, Take My Life*, 485.

Case, David S., and Voluck, D. A., *Alaska Natives and American Laws*, 3rd ed. Fairbanks: University of Alaska Press, 2012.

Clark, Blue. *Lone Wolf v. Hitchcock: Treaty Rights and Indian Law at the End of the Nineteenth Century*. Lincoln: University of Nebraska Press, 1994.

Cohen, Felix S. "Original Indian Title," *Minnesota Law Review* 28 (1947), 64–96.

Harmon, David, McManamon, F., and Pitchaithley, D., eds. *The Antiquities Act: A Century of Archaeology, Historic Preservation and Nature Conservation*. Tucson: University of Arizona Press, 2006.

Haycox, Stephen. "Tee-Hit-Ton and Alaska Native Rights," in *Law for the Elephant, Law for the Beaver: Essays in the Legal History of the North American West*, eds. John McLaren, Hamar Foster and Chet Orloff. Regina: Canadian Plains Research Center, Univ. of Regina; Pasadena: Ninth Judicial Circuit Historical Society, 1992, 125–45.

———. "Felix Cohen and the Indian Legacy of the New Deal," *Yale University Library Gazette* 64 (1994), 135–56.

Lawson, Gary, and Seidman, G. *The Constitution of Empire: Territorial Expansion and American Legal History*. New Haven: Yale University Press, 2004.

Lurie, Nancy O. "The Indian Claims Commission Act," *Annals of the American Academy of Political and Social Science* 436 (1978): 97–110.

McDonnell, Janet A. *The Dispossession of the American Indian, 1887–1934*. Bloomington: Indiana University Press, 1991.

McMillen, Christian. *Making Indian Law: The Hualapai Land Case and the Birth of Ethnohistory*. New Haven: Yale University Press, 2007.

Michno, Gregory F. *The Three Battles of Sand Creek: In Blood, In Court, and As the End of History*. Savas Beatie: Eldorado Hills, CA, 2017.

Mitchell, Donald Craig. *Sold American: The Story of Alaska Natives and Their Land, 1867–1959*. Fairbanks: University of Alaska Press, 2003.

———. *Take My Land, Take My Life: The Story of Congress's Historic Settlement of Alaska Native Land Claims, 1960–1971*. Fairbanks: University of Alaska Press, 2001.

Nelson, Daniel. *Northern Landscapes: The Struggle for Wilderness Alaska*. Washington, D.C.: Resources for the Future, 2004.

Oman, Kerry R. "The Beginning of the End: The Indian Peace Commission of 1867–1868," *Great Plains Quarterly* 22 (2002): 35–51.n

A Note from Lee Huskey

Terrence and I have been friends since the Western Regional Science annual meetings in 1995. A mutual affection for baseball (as fans of the Phillies and the Cardinals we share the bond of the season of '64) was the beginning. Over the years we shared interests in the history and the future of Alaska's economy. I'm sure we hold the world record for projects on Alaska economic history started but never finished. I've been thankful for his kind silence about my attempts to be a historian and impressed by his economic insights about Alaska. Our long discussions about teaching have been both helpful and cathartic, though I'm still a bit steamed that the students in my spring teachers class continually rated Terrence a better speaker than me. In addition to Alaska's significant history, Terrence introduced me to his unique taste in movies. I can't pass a Waffle House without thinking of Terrence.

BOOM, BUST, AND BUILD

An Economic Lesson from Alaska History

Lee Huskey

INTRODUCTION

Alaska, today, is experiencing a season of economic anxiety. Anxiety is not uncommon for people living and working on resource frontiers. The exuberant times of resource discovery, production, and settlement are often followed by anxious times of decline. Economic anxiety accompanies a narrow economic base, built on a few resources with limits to their economic life. With few other places to turn, the possibility that economic decline will follow a boom generally haunts resource economies.

The reversal of fortune that comes with the boom-bust cycle in an economy is familiar in Alaska history. Gold in Nome, copper at Kennecott, and king crab in Kodiak illustrate the ups and downs of a resource economy. Nature, markets, and policy have all been responsible for declines. The current season of anxiety reflects an economy built around oil as Alaska's main natural resource, and the effect has been magnified by the state's reliance on oil as its primary public revenue source. This decline should not have surprised anyone. Alaska's oil production peaked in the late 1980s, and decline in the role of oil in the Alaska economy seems inescapable.

What would a future with limited oil production look like? Will the bust parallel the boom? These are the questions that the other participants in the economy ask. Alaska's boom-bust history certainly would make bankers and store owners and transport firms nervous about their businesses. Most simple economic models of regional growth contribute to this unease by identifying the region's exports as the drivers of economic growth. The rest of the economy—those businesses that support the resource sector and the population working in it—is driven by growth in resource production. This economics says that the Alaska economy will follow a decline in the oil industry back toward where it started.

But this is also where economic history may ease some anxiety by telling a longer and richer story. A long look at the economy lets us see the building stage of economic change. The economic environment can be changed during boom years. As a result, the economy may be better off after the bust than it was before the boom. This chapter looks at lessons from boom-bust cycles in Alaska's history. After looking at these cycles from the viewpoint of an economist studying history and a historian studying the economy, the text examines one lesson from history in more detail—the Jack London Hypothesis that Professor Terrence Cole and I first wrote about in a 1997 paper, explaining why there is some build that goes along with the boom and the bust. London's hypothesis reflects the economist's story of structural change and suggests connections between resource booms not imagined in the boom-bust story.[1]

THE HISTORY OF ECONOMICS, AND THE ECONOMICS OF HISTORY

According to Cole, "In uncertain climate it is too easy to be swayed by the passions of the moment, to be continually distracted by shifting wind. For that reason history is a useful corrective."[2] This section looks at what two keen observers of Alaska history have said about the boom-bust cycle in Alaska's past. George Rogers was an Alaskan economist who used history to identify the general principles at work in the Alaska economy. Terrence Cole is an Alaskan historian

---

1   Lee Huskey and Terrence Cole, "Searching for Bonanza: Economics and Alaska History," presented at the Western Regional Science Annual Meetings (1997, Hawaii).

2   Terrence Cole and Elmer Rasmuson, *Banking on Alaska, A History of NBA* (Vol. 1) (Anchorage: Rasmuson Foundation, 2000), 446.

with an interest in and a keen eye for the economic particulars of Alaska's history.

History teaches the economist that the economy has a long past. Economic results are not simply the effects of immediate changes in markets and government policy. Over time, we can see how a shift in institutions and economic environment will change the economy's response to markets and policy. While Alaska's history is told mostly as a story of politics and government decision-making, economic enterprise is common to the history of western settlement in North America. By overlooking the economics of our history, we may misinterpret history and miss important drivers of change. According to Rogers, as a result of their territorial experience, Alaskans "looked upon economic development as essentially political in nature requiring only changes and manipulations in the forms of institutions."[3] Our reactions to economic problems depend on the stories we have developed about the past. Studying the economics of history provides economic facts that allow us to separate the good stories from the bad.

While George Rogers wrote about Alaska's history, the real purpose of his work was public policy. He felt an understanding of the economy was as important for public decision-making at the start of statehood as it was after the oil in Prudhoe Bay inspired economic growth. In the history of Alaska, Rogers found a set of economic realities that described Alaska's economy. Rogers saw the modern economy as made up of four development strands, including Native Alaska, Colonial Alaska, Military Alaska, and most recently, the State of Alaska.[4] Each strand appeared at different periods of history, but each continues to play a role in the modern Alaska economy. The strand metaphor emphasizes the limited integration of the driving forces behind Alaska's economic growth.

According to Rogers, the Alaska economy is a fragile one—an export economy with few products to sell. As an export economy that

3   George Rogers, *The Future of Alaska, the Economic Consequences of Statehood* (Baltimore: The Johns Hopkins Press, 1962), 170.
4   David Kresge, Thomas Morehouse, and George Rogers, *Issues in Alaska Development* (Seattle: University of Washington Press, 1977), 13.

sells its natural resources to the rest of the world, Alaska depends on world markets and prices. Alaska has "been dependent on one or two or three economic activities or crops. When one suffers decline this can produce a general economic recession."[5] Dependence on external markets for a limited number of products creates the instability of the boom-bust cycle.

The lack of regional connection has contributed to the instability of Alaska's economy. According to Rogers, the historic Alaska economy was not integrated across industries or regions. Alaska "was not a single integrated economy but a federation of regional and local economies with strong direct Outside economic ties. Limits to integration make it less likely that decline in one part of the state would be buoyed by growth in another part, or that people and other inputs could easily move between opportunities.

Rogers said the boom-bust cycle made its Alaska debut with the decline in fur seal and sea otter production during the last part of Russia's colonial rule. Limited crops, dependence on export markets, and lack of regional integration all contributed to the instability of Alaska's economy. Rogers thought the boom-bust cycle is here to stay.[6]

Rogers also recognized that government has been an important force in Alaska's economy throughout its history. Rules and regulations have determined both the types and amounts of economic activity that could prosper in Alaska, and government investment in transportation connections promoting aviation, roads, and railroads also added to increased regional integration. Federal government spending, beginning with the World War II military buildup, provided the basis for a more stable economy. However, government didn't eliminate the boom-bust cycle. The mid-1980s economic crash showed Rogers that the addition of federal and state governments in Alaska's economic foundation had not eliminated this economic curse of the frontier.[7]

---

5   George Rogers, "The Alaska Economy and Economic Issues: An Historical Overview," in *Alaska Public Policy Issues: Background and Perspectives*, ed. Clive Thomas (Juneau: Denali Press: 1999), 19.
6   Rogers, "The Alaska Economy and Economic Issues," 29.
7   Ibid., 27.

As an economist, George Rogers searched Alaska history for general principles that would help us understand and make predictions about the future of the economy. Terrence Cole, meanwhile, is an historian who looks at the particulars of the economy's history. He has investigated the particulars of industries, people, and communities in Alaska. These particulars help us understand the story of economic change: the economic actors and the institutions they shaped, and how these people and institutions created the economy at the time.

Terrence combines economic concepts, mostly used correctly, with Alaskan color throughout his work. Economics is evident in his explanation of branch banking, the determinants of mining costs, and the concentration in Alaska resource industries. While the economics are comforting to an economist, the real lessons come from the color and detail. The stories of the scoundrels, government dreamers, and hard-working practical men show the interplay between the frontier's eternal optimism and the challenges and constraints to economic development.

Terrence examines the causes and consequences of a number of Alaska's historic boom-bust cycles. Both the copper and salmon industries experienced booms with the outbreak of World War I, with copper as an important ore for the production of shells and other military material. Salmon was part of U.S. food exports to Europe when that continent's agriculture was shut down by war. Expansion in copper production was followed by decline when the war market for copper collapsed and prices fell. The decline was felt by the businesses and residents of the community of Cordova as well as the mine workers. The collapse in the salmon stock from wartime overfishing created a corresponding bust in coastal communities.[8]

As noted, the federal government has played a large role in the economic cycles of Alaska. Anchorage was created by the construction boom associated with the building of the Alaska Railroad. Its economy grew when thousands flocked to build the ARR, and went bust when the workers left. The construction projects resulted in two

---

8   Cole and Rasmuson, *Banking on Alaska*, 171–73.

economic disruptions—the first when construction slowed down during World War I, and the second when construction was completed in 1922.[9]

The federal government also had a role in the collapse of the gold mining industry, which provided the main support for the resident non-Native population before World War II. The first territory-wide shut-down of gold mining occurred with America's entry into World War I. Wartime inflation, the fixed gold price, and the loss of workforce to high-paying defense jobs drove gold mining and the territory into recession. Gold mining rebounded during the Great Depression, when the U.S. government increased the official price of gold by 75 percent. However, U.S. entry into World War II made it harder to get workers and supplies. In 1942, the federal government declared gold mining non-essential and ordered most gold mining in America to stop.[10] Federal government and military spending replaced mining as the primary economic force in the lives of the non-Native population.

Alaska's last great recession in the early 1980s was part of a boom-bust cycle reflecting the growth of the oil industry as the primary driver of the economy. The fiscal link between oil production and state revenues magnified the problem. Decline in the state's oil revenues created a fiscal gap, where petroleum taxes could no longer cover levels of past state spending. The resulting drop in state spending drove the economy into recession. Government was a destabilizing force.

Alaska's present season of anxiety reflects this same link between oil production and state spending. In *Blinded by Riches: The Permanent Funding Problem and the Prudhoe Bay Effect*, Cole examined the long history of resource development and public revenues that lies behind today's dilemma.[11] He shows that "In reality the 'fiscal gap' is not a

---

9   Cole and Rasmuson, *Banking on Alaska*, 130–33.

10   Terrence Cole, "The Decline of Gold Mining in Alaska," *Pacific Northwest Quarterly* 80, 2 (1989): 64–71.

11   Terrence Cole, *Blinded by Riches: The Permanent Funding Problem and the Prudhoe Bay Effect* (Anchorage: Institute of Social and Economic Research, University of Alaska, 2004).

new dilemma, but the latest manifestation of a recurring phenomenon that has plagued Alaska for at least a hundred years: the Alaska permanent funding problem.[12]

Cole identified our "permanent funding problem" as part of Alaska's fiscal history. For most of Alaska's history, natural resource revenues have been the main source of public revenues, and Alaska government expenditures have always exceeded the revenues generated in the economy. Crises have occurred whenever this permanent funding problem comes to light, as in the 1940s, when the federal military buildup expanded the population and the demand for services without a way to expand public revenues.[13] Prior to statehood, federal government subsidies masked the problem for Alaskans. More recently, the wealth of Prudhoe Bay has masked the same structural issue. However, the wealth of Prudhoe Bay has been the exception and not the rule in Alaska's resource history. As Cole states, "one Prudhoe Bay is worth more in real dollars than everything that has been dug out, cut down, caught or killed in Alaska since the beginning of time."[14]

The use of nonrecurring natural resource revenues to pay for the recurring costs of government has been called the "fiscal trap.[15] The historical perspective on the fiscal trap that Cole provides suggests that we haven't learned much from history. The fiscal trap has been a result of the combination of three things. First, the lack of diversity in the tax base exposed public revenues to the contraction of resource production.[16] This is partly a reflection of the limited number of "crops" Rogers identified, but also of a second longtime characteristic of the economic landscape. The "Kennecott syndrome" was what Secretary of the Interior Harold Ickes called the view that Alaska was a place to make money and leave—not a place to build by paying taxes.[17] Finally, the early battle over the tax system was fought between miners

---

12   Cole, *Blinded by Riches*, 5.
13   Ibid., 55.
14   Ibid., 109.
15   Ibid., 98.
16   Ibid., 29.
17   Ibid., 42.

(residents trying to export taxes) and fishing interests (nonresidents who didn't want to pay).[18] The fishing industry's large corporations had outsized political power to fight taxation. In 1949, a more broad-based tax system was introduced, including an income tax. Alaska's fiscal trap has meant that the instability of resource production is passed through to the local economy through the public sector.

JACK LONDON AND FRONTIER GROWTH

In the boom-bust story, the frontier economy is fragile. This model fits neatly into the widely used economic base models of regional growth, as in the economic base model the determinant of growth is the external demand for the region's natural resources.[19] The level of activity in the support sector is directly related to the size of this export sector. The shops, services, and trades that support the population and industry drawn to the frontier simply react to and follow resource production. The support sector of the region's economy just reacts, and firms in this sector are passive actors in this tale.

In his 1900 essay, "The Economics of the Klondike," Jack London took on the idea of the fragile frontier.[20] The essay was intended to refute critics who had described the movement of thousands to the Klondike gold fields as "a poor business decision" and "an example of human folly." London acknowledged that the value of the gold removed was less than the costs of seeking and producing the gold in the Klondike. However, he stated, the individual loss for the stampeders had "been of inestimable benefit to the Yukon country, to those who will remain in it and to those yet to come.[21] London argued that, while gold mining might have been responsible for the arrival of the supporting industries, these industries weren't passive, but played

---

18   Ibid., 31.
19   A. Krikelas, "Review of Economic Base Literature," *Federal Reserve Bank of Atlanta Economic Review* July/August (1992): 13–31.
20   Jack London, "The Economics of the Klondike," *The American Monthly Review of Reviews* 21, no. 1 (1900): 70–74.
21   London, "The Economics of the Klondike," 72.

an active role in creating the future for the frontier economy. London's argument had three parts.

First, the economic environment was changed by what went before. For example,

> The Klondike rush placed hundreds of steamers on the Yukon, opened navigation of its upper reaches and lakes, put tramways around the unnavigable Box Canyon and White Horse rapids, and built a railroad from the salt water at Skagway across the White Pass to the head of steamboat traffic on Lake Bennett.[22]

Second, as a result of these changes in the economic environment, cost conditions in the region would also change.

> Conditions will become normal and the Klondike just enter upon its true development. With necessaries and luxuries of life cheap and plentiful, with the importation of machinery which will cheapen many enterprises and render many others possible... when a sack of flour may be bought for a dollar instead of fifty, and other things in proportion, it is apparent how great a fall the scale of pay can sustain.[23]

Finally, profitable activities in the region would expand as a result of the reduction in costs:

> Living expenses being normal, a moderate wage will be possible. Nor will laborers fail to hasten there from the congested labor markets of the older countries. This is turn, will permit the employment on a large scale of much of the world's restless capital now and seeking investment.[24]

The result: the region would be a transformed as a region for economic growth.

---

22 Ibid., 73.
23 Ibid.
24 Ibid.

> The new Klondike, the Klondike of the future, will present remarkable contrasts with the Klondike of the past. Natural obstacles will be cleared away or surmounted, primitive methods abandoned, and hardship of toil and travel reduced to the smallest minimum. Exploration and transportation will be systematized... The frontiersman will yield to the laborer, the prospector to the mining engineer, the dog-driver to the engine driver, the trader and speculator to the steady going modern man of business.[25]

The real benefits of the Klondike gold rush couldn't be counted simply as the gold removed from the field. The real benefits came in the changes brought to the country that opened the region to future economic growth. Frontier natural resource booms would build something to be left behind after a bust. The boom associated with the Klondike gold rush changed the economy of the North by attracting firms that supported the miners. When the boom died, some of these firms (though certainly not all) stayed and supported new resource development throughout the country. These firms played an active role lowering costs and expanding opportunities on the frontier.

TESTING THE JACK LONDON HYPOTHESIS

"The Economics of the Klondike" provides a hypothesis about the role of the supporting industries in frontier economic growth. The Jack London hypothesis could also be stated as: *Resource development changes the support sector in ways that last beyond a particular resource boom, and that encourage future economic activity*. Although he might not have called it testing, Terrence and I have both tested this hypothesis. I used the World War I economic bust as a natural experiment for testing this hypothesis, and found that the pattern of change in the support sector after the economic collapse was consistent with London's notion that something built during a boom remains after.[26] In *Banking on Alaska*, Cole showed how banking—and in particular

---

25   Ibid., 74.
26   Lee Huskey, "Alaska's Economy: The First World War, Frontier Fragility, and Jack London," *The Northern Review* 44 (2017): 327–46.

the Bank of Alaska—grew, matured, and survived beyond an individual resource boom. The bank's survival is a test of the hypothesis, and its activities illustrate how this part of the support sector encouraged future growth.

America's entry into World War I resulted in an immediate decline in gold mining and eventual busts in the copper and fishery industries. The Jack London hypothesis would predict that supporting industries did not experience the same degree of economic decline as these root natural resource industries. If supporting industries mirror the decline in the natural resource industries, there would be no support of the Jack London hypothesis. The U.S. Census in 1910 and 1920 and the Polk Business Directories for 1915–1916 and 1923–1924 provide data about the Alaska support sector. While not perfect, each data set describes the Alaska economy before and after the World War I economic crash.

Comparing employment by major occupational group in 1910 and 1920, the U.S. Census indeed offers support for the Jack London hypothesis. While employment in all major occupational sectors declined over this period, employment in the natural resource industries fell by a larger rate than in the supporting industries. The natural resource industries in question included fisheries, farming, forestry, mining, and manufacturing. Between 1910 and 1920, this sector shrank by more than 40 percent. Transportation employment fell by over 30 percent. Employment in most categories of support sector occupations (Trade, Professional Service, Clerical Service, and Public Service) declined by *less than 10 percent*. Domestic Service was the only occupational category that decreased significantly, declining by almost 25 percent. Overall, the share of total employment represented by the supporting industries grew from 37 percent to 44 percent between 1910 and 1920.[27] These census data suggest the economic environment in Alaska was fundamentally changed by the early-twentieth-century economic boom, and that this change survived the economic bust of World War I.

---

27   Huskey, "Alaska's Economy," figure 1, 336.

The Polk Directories provide a more detailed description of the support sector than the census. They provide a count of the number of firms in each of 112 business categories. The Jack London hypothesis is further tested by comparing the change in the number of firms in each business category with the change over this same period in the resource sector activity and the overall economy. The change in the real value of mineral production between 1913 and 1923 was used as a proxy for change in the resource sector. Over this period, the real value of mineral production declined by about 40 percent. An estimate of the change in the non-Native population between 1915 and 1924 was used as a proxy for the change in the overall economy. The estimated decline in Alaska's non-Native population was 11 percent.[28]

A relative increase in the number of firms in a business category would also be consistent with the hypothesis.[29] More than two-thirds of the support industry business categories (seventy-five categories) expanded relative to the change in mineral production. Of these, fifty-five business types, almost half of the total, declined less than the 11 percent decline of Alaska's non-Native population, and increased in per-capita terms. These fifty-five business types accounted for almost two-thirds of the 1,788 support sector businesses in the 1924–1925 directory. A significant share of the support sector did not mirror the decline found in measures of the total economy and the minerals industry after World War I. This pattern was consistent with the Jack London hypothesis.[30]

Banking on Alaska also provides an industry-level "test" of Jack London's idea. Unlike mining and fishing—industries with external markets—banking in Alaska depended on the growth of a local market; banks evolved along with the market. Alaska's first banks were merchant banks located in coastal outfitting centers and gold banks in mining camps. Trading companies offered banking services to their customers. By making small loans to prospectors who were also

---

28   Huskey, "Alaska's Economy," 337–38.
29   As with the census data, a relative increase in the number of firms means either the number of firms actually increased or the number of firms declined at a lower rate than the overall economy or the staple sector.
30   Huskey, "Alaska's Economy," 339–41.

their customers, traders could expand their mercantile business. Mining camps' banks made their profits by assaying and purchasing gold dust from miners, replacing gold dust with currency and coins as the medium of exchange in the camps. Merchants and gold banks lowered the cost of trading and increased access to capital for prospectors.[31]

According to Cole, the Alaska banking industry faced five problems prior to 1913. First, banks were located in small, isolated communities. Both towns and banks could be short-term ventures. Gold camps and outfitting centers provided thin markets for bank services that lasted only as long as the gold.[32] Second, Alaska banks had limited access to capital. Since there was little capital in the market, frontier banks were undercapitalized.[33] Third, the limited communications and transportation in Alaska made it difficult to move funds between communities. Bills of exchange were of limited use when there was no way to know if the issuing bank remained in existence.[34] The fourth problem was that merchant banks could limit competition with other merchants through their lending activities.[35]

The final problem of the Alaska banking industry was the lack of government supervision. Anyone could start a bank. The 1911 failure of the Washington-Alaska Bank convinced Fairbanks business leaders that a stable banking system was needed for the economy to grow.[36] The Territorial Banking Act of 1913 brought Alaska banks under government regulation, establishing the Territorial Banking Board to define what a bank could and could not do and providing rules and conditions for establishing a bank.[37]

The Bank of Alaska was one of the first banks incorporated under the new act. Andrew Stevenson began the bank in 1916 in Skagway,

---

31 Cole and Rasmuson, *Banking on Alaska*, 3–12.
32 Ibid., 9.
33 Ibid., 19.
34 Ibid., 5.
35 Ibid., 47–49.
36 Ibid., 22–23.
37 Ibid., 42.

which was the entry point to the Yukon and interior gold fields.[38]
The bank addressed many of the problems of Alaska banking.
Commercial banks made their profits by encouraging growth of the
economy through investment. The Bank of Alaska was a commercial bank not tied to any particular merchant, so it reduced the competitive advantage of merchants with banks.[39] With major New York
stockholders, the Bank of Alaska increased Alaska's access to outside
capital. And finally, the Bank of Alaska pursued a strategy of branch
banking. Branch banking meant that the economic fortunes of a
bank would be diversified across a number of communities, mini-
mizing the risk of bank closure when a community suffered economic hardship.[40]

In *Banking on Alaska*, we see that building the supporting sector
in an economy is not simply "build it and they will come." The Bank
of Alaska faced and overcame many challenges. There were govern-
mental roadblocks, competitive encounters, and economic challenges. The branch banking system was opposed by both the
Territory's Governor and the head of the Territorial Banking Board.[41]
The Bank of Alaska faced competition when it established branches
from an established bank in Cordova and new banks in Anchorage.
Most significantly, the bank survived the numerous economic downturns that affected different industries and regions throughout the
state.[42] In Anchorage, the population decline during World War I
and after the railroad was completed caused financial trauma, as
people withdrew as depositors as they left the territory and loans
collapsed along with the local economy. The frontier optimism and
the need to make loans to generate income resulted in some self-
induced problems. Bad loans in the fish and lumber industries
drained the bank's capital. In these situations, the ability to raise
capital from outside investors proved important for keeping the
bank open. The story of the Bank of Alaska provides some insight

---

38   Ibid., 31.
39   Ibid., 48.
40   Ibid., 33.
41   Ibid., 41–42.
42   Ibid., 86, 89, 125, 131.

into the possible struggles of other businesses building Alaska's support sector.

Banks play a significant role in economic development in three particular ways. They mobilize a region's capital and provide easier access to imported capital. They reduce the costs of doing business by arranging financial transfers between producers and consumers even in different parts of a country. And banks act as boosters for the local economy and economize on entrepreneurship by providing information about business opportunities.

The Bank of Alaska contributed to the growth of the Alaska economy in each of these ways. First, bank loans to the mines, mills, and canneries throughout the territory provided more capital for their expansion. Second, the bank also reduced business costs by eliminating the exchange fees on checks written on the Bank of Alaska when cashed in Seattle.[43] This reduced the cost of purchasing supplies. Third, it played an important part in the growth of Alaska's airline industry by encouraging and investing in the airlines. The growth of Alaska's aviation industry connected communities and contributed to reducing the cost of rural economic activities.[44] As the market grew, the Bank of Alaska changed its approach and adopted more conservative loan guidelines. These conservative guidelines helped the Bank weather the real estate downturn of the 1980s.[45]

Economic booms and busts have been present throughout Alaska's history as a resource frontier. This section has presented some evidence that Jack London may have been right about the ways these cycles affected the economy. Economic expansions seem to have left something of value behind after their various declines. The Bank of Alaska weathered a number of downturns and grew and supported the growth of the Alaska economy. The supporting sector of Alaska's early-twentieth-century economy was changed during the boom years, and the economy's collapse was less dramatic than the collapse of the resource industries after the start of World War I.

---

43 Ibid., 55.
44 Ibid., 253–56.
45 Ibid., 262.

CONCLUSIONS

Booms and busts are part of Alaska's economic history. Rogers and Cole have demonstrated the reasons for these economic cycles by examining the particulars of history and drawing general principles from Alaska's experience. Even the growing importance of government to the economy after World War II and the discovery of the massive natural wealth of the Prudhoe Bay oil fields could not stabilize the economy. This history is responsible for Alaska's current economic anxiety. Jack London, however, offers some hope for the Alaska economy. The boom-bust story of the frontier assumes the economy is fragile. Jack London hypothesized that the frontier economies might be less fragile than usually assumed. He suggested that resource economic booms would build something that is left behind after the decline in natural resource production. Businesses in the supporting industries attracted to a region by a resource boom would stay behind. These left-behind businesses would create opportunities for future economic growth. This chapter offers some support for this view of economic history. The Jack London hypothesis emphasizes the build, and presents a more optimistic story of the economy after the resource boom.

BIBLIOGRAPHY

Cole, Terrence. "The Decline of Gold Mining in Alaska." *Pacific Northwest Quarterly* 80,2 (1989): 64–71.

———. *Blinded by Riches: The Permanent Funding Problem and the Prudhoe Bay Effect.* Anchorage: Institute of Social and Economic Research, University of Alaska, 2004.

Cole, Terrence, and E. Rasmuson. *Banking on Alaska: A History of NBA* (Vol. 1). Anchorage: Rasmuson Foundation, 2000.

Huskey, Lee. "Alaska's Economy: The First World War, Frontier Fragility, and Jack London." *The Northern Review* 44 (2017): 327–46.

Huskey, Lee, and T. Cole. "Searching for Bonanza: Economics and Alaska History." Presented at the Western Regional Science Annual Meetings (Hawaii), 1997.

Kresge, David, Thomas Morehouse, and George Rogers. *Issues in Alaska Development.* Seattle: University of Washington Press, 1977.

Krikelas, A. "Review of Economic Base Literature." *Federal Reserve Bank of Atlanta Economic Review* July/August (1992): 13–31.

London, Jack. "The Economics of the Klondike." *The American Monthly Review of Reviews* 21, no. (1900): 70–74.

Rogers, George. *The Future of Alaska, the Economic Consequences of Statehood,* Baltimore: The Johns Hopkins Press, 1962.

———. "The Alaska Economy and Economic Issues: An Historical Overview." In *Alaska Public Policy Issues: Background and Perspectives,* ed. Clive Thomas. Juneau: Denali Press, 1999.

A Note About David Eric Jessup

David Eric Jessup is an instructor of Swedish in the Department of Scandinavian Studies at Gustavus Adolphus College in St. Peter, Minnesota, and an instructor in the Department of History at St. Olaf College in Northfield, Minnesota. In 2001, he completed an MA in Northern Studies at the University of Alaska Fairbanks, where Terrence Cole served as the chairman of his thesis committee. The article appearing here is based on material in his thesis, "James Church McCook and American Consular Diplomacy in the Klondike, 1898–1901." Following in Dr. Cole's footsteps, David entered the PhD program in history at the University of Washington. His first published article, "The Rise and Fall of Katalla: The 'Coming Metropolis of Alaska,'" began as a paper assignment in one of Dr. Cole's classes. It won the Alaska History award in 2005.

BETWEEN TWO EMPIRES

Canada and the Alaska Boundary Dispute

David Eric Jessup

The Alaska boundary dispute was a disagreement over the location of the border defining the shape of the Alaska panhandle, and superficially, this dispute was between Great Britain and the United States. In reality, it was a dispute between Canada and the United States, but Canadians had little say in the matter. At the turn of the twentieth century, Canadian sovereignty remained somewhat ill-defined. The Dominion of Canada, created by the British North America Act on July 1, 1867, existed as a distinct confederation within the British Empire. Although autonomous in the conduct of its domestic affairs, the government in Ottawa did not play an international role; Canadian foreign policy was the responsibility of London. With the emergence of the U.S. as a world power in the 1890s, and as the relationship between the United States and Great Britain grew in importance, Canada was left in the awkward position of sharing a continent with one power and being utterly beholden to the other. The Alaska boundary dispute, precipitated by the Klondike gold rush, seemed to underscore Canadian weakness.

However, the United States had become so entangled in so many engagements around the world that American interest in Canada was necessarily limited, and venerable American ideas about swallowing Canada whole were fading away. With its neighbor distracted, Canada escaped the Alaska boundary dispute relatively unscathed, though

MERELY A SUGGESTION

U. S.—There Little Girl, Don't Cry, Why Bother About Any Boundary Lines at All.

Two days before the Alaska Boundary Tribunal officially announced its decision, the front page of the *Minneapolis Journal* featured a cartoon mocking Canadian anger over the boundary dispute while "suggesting" that Canada should belong to the United States, an idea long popular among powerful American politicians. *Minneapolis Journal, October 19, 1903.*

the dispute demonstrated the limits of its influence, caught as it was between an old British Empire and a new American one.

To the United States, the Klondike gold rush was an insignificant diplomatic event, despite the fact that it saw over 30,000 people, mostly Americans, pour into the Canadian Yukon in a single year. Had it occurred a decade earlier, the gold rush would have excited

JOHN BULL: "Yes, 'e's makin' a lot of noise, Sam, but 'e'll get over it."—From the *North American* (Philadelphia).

Canadians' feelings that Canada had been betrayed by Great Britain in the Alaska boundary dispute is understandable in light of U.S. cartoons like this one, in which Uncle Sam and John Bull determine the location of the Alaska boundary without consulting Canada, depicted as a crying child. *American Monthly Review of Reviews (New York), Vol. 28, No. 6,* December 1903.

more interest at the State Department, but in the late 1890s American statesmen were engaged in diplomatic maneuvering in Venezuela, Hawaii, Cuba, the Philippines, Samoa, China, South Africa, and Central America. President William McKinley's December 1898 annual message to Congress, which ran to forty-six pages when printed, made no mention of the gold rush at all.[1] The view from Canada was understandably quite different, and Ottawa made a swift and concerted effort to assert Canadian sovereignty in the Klondike. Between 1896 and 1898, the Canadian government increased the North West Mounted Police force in the Yukon from twenty to nearly two hundred, and sent an additional two hundred soldiers on top of that to supplement the police in the fall of 1898. That military detachment, the Yukon Field Force, represented one quarter of the Canadian militia.[2] These

---

1   U.S. Congress. House. Papers Relating to the Foreign Relations of the United States, with the Annual Message of the President Transmitted to Congress December 5, 1898. 55th Cong., 3d sess. 1901. H. Doc. 1, xlix–xcv.

2   David R. Morrison, *The Politics of the Yukon Territory, 1898–1909* (Toronto:

moves reflected the traditional uneasiness with which the Dominion viewed the United States.

Canadian unease was understandable. American annexation of Canada had long been a topic of serious consideration on both sides of the border. William H. Seward, the Secretary of State under Presidents Abraham Lincoln and Andrew Johnson, is described by historian Richard H. Miller as having "coalesced the fragmented approaches of his predecessors into an expansionist master plan."[3] Seward negotiated the purchase of Alaska from Russia as a step in the direction of even greater North American expansion. The Senate ratified the treaty of sale on April 9, 1867, ten days after Queen Victoria had given her royal sanction to the British North America Act. In the debate over the appropriation of the $7.2 million the United States had agreed to pay for Alaska, California Representative William Higby revealed the ultimate aim of many expansionist proponents of the purchase in his speech on the floor of the House:

> Alaska will soon have a hardy, active people; trade and commerce will grow up to great importance. Its growth and thrift on the north, the same as that on the south in Washington and Idaho Territories, will make British Columbia sicken and die as a British province and cause it to spring into newness of life as a territory of the United States.[4]

Over time, the discourse surrounding annexation shifted in focus from the notion of a military or political takeover of Canada to the idea of a voluntary merger or commercial union. Still, the American attitude toward Canada was ambiguous. Alice Felt Tyler, biographer of

---

University of Toronto Press, 1968); William R. Morrison, *Showing the Flag: The Mounted Police and Canadian Sovereignty in the North, 1894–1925* (Vancouver: University of British Columbia Press, 1985), 30–31.

3   Richard H. Miller, ed. *American Imperialism in 1898: The Quest for National Fulfillment* (New York: John Wiley and Sons, 1970), 5.

4   William Higby, *Speech of Hon. William Higby, of California, Delivered in the House of Representatives the 21st Day of March, 1868, on the Treaty Between the United States and the Russian Government on the Transfer of Alaska* (Washington, D.C.: Turner, Printer), 8.

Benjamin Harrison's Secretary of State, James G. Blaine, described Blaine's attitude regarding Canada as "a queer combination of a rather suspicious dislike and a conviction that Canada must sometime in the probably far distant future become a part of the United States."[5] As late as 1891, Blaine wrote to the president, "The fact is we do not want any intercourse with Canada, except through the medium of a tariff, and she will find that she has a hard row to hoe and will ultimately, I believe, seek admission to the Union."[6] That same year, former Oxford history professor Goldwin Smith published his book *Canada and the Canadian Question*, in which he argued that his adopted Canada was an artificial creation that naturally should belong to the United States. Prime Minister John A. Macdonald and his Conservative Party won Canada's 1891 election after turning annexation fears into a political issue.[7] Meanwhile in the U.S., the Continental Union League, calling for the integration of the two countries, could boast a membership that included Andrew Carnegie, Theodore Roosevelt, and John Hay.[8] More significant perhaps was a line in the 1896 Republican Party platform on which William McKinley campaigned: "We hopefully look forward to the eventual withdrawal of the European powers from this hemisphere, to the ultimate union of all the English-speaking parts of the continent by the free consent of its inhabitants."[9] By the late 1890s, however, as U.S. expansionism approached its zenith, a number of factors actually turned American imperialist attention away from Canada.

The Great Rapprochement between the United States and Great Britain of the late 1890s saw the traditional feelings, born in the Revolution, of hostility and suspicion between Americans and Britons

---

5   Alice Felt Tyler, *The Foreign Policy of James G. Blaine* (Minneapolis: University of Minnesota Press, 1927. Reprint, Hamden, CT: Archon Books, 1965), 351.

6   James G. Blaine to Benjamin Harrison, September 23, 1891, in Albert T. Volwiler, ed., The *Correspondence Between Benjamin Harrison and James G. Blaine 1882–1893, Memoirs of the American Philosophical Society* (Philadelphia: American Philosophical Society, 1940), 194.

7   J. L. Granatstein and Norman Hillmer, *For Better or for Worse: Canada and the United States to the 1990s* (Toronto: Copp Clark Pitman, 1991), 25–27.

8   David Healy, *US Expansionism: The Imperialist Urge in the 1890s* (Madison: University of Wisconsin Press, 1970), 49–50; Granatstein and Hillmer, 20–22.

9   Paolo E. Coletta, ed. *Threshhold to American Internationalism: Essays on the Foreign Policies of William McKinley* (New York: Exposition Press, 1970), 22.

transformed into a common understanding that lasted through both world wars. Oddly enough, the new relationship took hold after the United States made an aggressive move aimed directly at thwarting British interests in South America. The unsettled location of the border between British Guyana and Venezuela, and Great Britain's refusal to submit the question to arbitration, led the Venezuelan government to angrily suspend diplomatic relations with London in 1887. President Grover Cleveland authorized Secretary of State Richard Olney to send an ultimatum on the Venezuelan boundary question to British Prime Minister Lord Salisbury on July 20, 1895.[10] In the 10,000-word note, which Cleveland called a "twenty inch gun," Olney invoked the Monroe Doctrine, arguing that British interference in the New World amounted to aggression toward the United States, and that the only proof of British goodwill in the present situation was to submit the boundary question to arbitration. Lord Salisbury's November reply, which made it clear Britain would not arbitrate the matter, prompted Cleveland to make an impassioned message to Congress on December 17, 1895, in which he not only suggested the possibility of war but called for a commission of Americans to determine the location of the boundary.[11]

Events far from Venezuela softened British resistance to U.S. demands. On January 3, 1896, after the Jameson Raid had failed to spark an uprising of British subjects against the Republic of South Africa, Kaiser Wilhelm II sent a congratulatory telegram to Boer President Paul Kruger. News of the telegram caused concern in London over German intentions and a reason to improve relations with the United States.[12] In February 1897, the British agreed to submit the matter of the Venezuela boundary to a board of arbitration, which determined the final boundary line on October 3, 1899. Although the boundary itself was never of major significance to Britain, its arbitration concession, according to historian David Healy, "cleared the air and calmed old suspicions." More importantly, it prompted British

---

10   Healy, 23–30; Thomas A. Bailey, *A Diplomatic History of the American People* (New York: F. S. Crofts and Co., 1940), 477–93.

11   Bailey, 485–86.

12   R. G. Neale, *Great Britain and United States Expansion: 1898–1900* (East Lansing: Michigan State University Press, 1966), xiv–xviii; Bailey, 488–89.

recognition of "Americans into the ranks of the civilizing powers."[13] Thereafter, events around the world drove Britain toward the realization that a strong American ally was ever more important. In September 1898, French and British forces met at Fashoda in present-day South Sudan. An Anglo-French convention in 1899 ended the African dispute diplomatically, though the French also had designs on China, where British economic interests were enormous. Moreover, by the middle of 1898, the Germans had seized the port of Kiaochow (Jiaozhou), and the Russians had taken both Port Arthur (Lushun) and Talienwan (Dalian).[14]

That same year, the United States entered the scene in Asia as a result of a war ostensibly fought to aid Cubans resisting oppressive Spanish rule. On April 11, 1898, President McKinley asked Congress for a declaration of war against Spain, "in the name of humanity, in the name of civilization, in behalf of endangered American interests which give us the right and the duty to speak and to act."[15] Hostilities in the four-month-long Spanish-American War ended on August 12, 1898. On February 6, 1899, the Senate ratified the Treaty of Paris, which ceded to the United States the former Spanish colonies of Guam, the Philippines, and Puerto Rico, while Cuba became an independent American protectorate. The U.S. had become an imperial power in what historian Samuel Flagg Bemis characterized as the "great aberration of 1898."[16] At the outset of the war, the U.S. Asiatic squadron under Admiral George Dewey had steamed from Hong Kong to the Philippines and devastated the Spanish fleet in Manila Bay before American soldiers had even set foot in Cuba. After the battle, Dewey waited for the arrival of American troops to capture Manila. A variety of European ships sent to look after local business

---

13 Healy, 29–30.

14 Julius W. Pratt, *Expansionists of 1898: The Acquisition of Hawaii and the Spanish Islands* (Baltimore: Johns Hopkins Press, 1936. Reprint, Gloucester: Peter Smith, 1959), 260–61; Neale, xiv–xvi.

15 U.S. Congress. House. Papers Relating to the Foreign Relations of the United States, with the Annual Message of the President Transmitted to Congress December 5, 1898. 55th Cong., 3d sess. 1901. H. Doc. 1, 760.

16 Samuel F. Bemis, "The Great Aberration of 1898," in Theodore P. Greene, ed., *American Imperialism in 1898* (Boston: D. C. Heath and Co., 1955), 84–92.

interests soon joined his squadron, including five German battle-ships, which, despite their neutral purpose, comprised a force stron-ger than the American fleet preparing to take the city.[17] Two British warships, however, were also in the bay, and rumors began on both sides of the Atlantic that the British had protected the American fleet from German aggression.[18]

Public and congressional debates over the cession of the Philippine Islands were fierce, but President William McKinley, with thin Senate approval, chose to annex the entire archipelago. The decision gave rise to the Filipino Insurrection, a costly quagmire for the U.S. military, which eventually resorted to suppression techniques not unlike those once employed by the Spanish in Cuba. The need to supply and fortify the new American foothold in the Philippines created the perfect excuse for the annexation of Hawaii, which was finalized by a joint resolution of Congress on July 7, 1898. Nine years earlier, the United States had agreed to a tripartite protectorate over the autonomous South Pacific islands of Samoa, in cooperation with Germany and Great Britain.[19] But when the Samoan king died in August 1898, and a civil war erupted on the islands, the protecting powers reassessed their interests. Late in 1899, Germany and the United States split Samoa between them, while Britain accepted compensation elsewhere.[20] The German pres-ence in Samoa was indicative of far greater imperialist aspirations, and British concerns over German intentions, particularly in Asia, were mounting. This worked to the benefit of the United States. Perceiving the U.S. as a counter-balance to its European neighbors, Britain shielded the United States from widespread criticism before and during the Spanish-American War. In April 1898, six European envoys had met in Washington to recommend that their governments send a common message to American diplomats in opposition to intervention in Cuba,

---

17 Bailey, 514–15.
18 Charles S. Campbell, Jr., "Anglo-American Relations, 1897–1901," in Paolo E. Coletta, ed., *Threshhold to American Internationalism: Essays on the Foreign Policies of William McKinley* (New York: Exposition Press, 1970), 226; Bailey, 214.
19 Pratt, 200; Bailey, 466.
20 Campbell, 234.

but London barred its ambassador from supporting the measure.[21] At the war's end, Britain encouraged American annexation of Hawaii and the Philippines, preferring a larger U.S. role in the Pacific to land-grabbing by its European rivals.

Though the American economic stake in China was considerably smaller than that of Great Britain, Washington and London now shared a determination to protect their respective Asian interests. On September 6, 1899, and March 20, 1900, Secretary of State John Hay sent his famous Open Door Notes to the capitals of Europe, affirming American commitment to the British assertion that open access to Chinese markets should be maintained by all Western powers. Shortly after the issuance of the second Open Door Note, the United States contributed 2,500 troops to the international expeditionary force of 20,000 that marched on Beijing on August 14, 1900, to rescue besieged Westerners held in the wake of the Boxer Rebellion.[22]

Meanwhile, the Second Boer War erupted in South Africa in October 1899. Just as Britain had lent tacit approval to the United States in the Spanish-American War, the U.S. now showed its sympathy with the British cause by declaring neutrality. Before the war, in a letter to Henry White, the First Secretary of the American Embassy in London, Secretary of State John Hay acknowledged that "all the Irish, and many Germans" believed that Washington should support the Boers, but wrote, "I hope, if it comes to blows, that England will make quick work of Uncle Paul [Kruger]. Sooner or later, her influence must be dominant there, and the sooner, the better."[23] In June 1900, after the Boers had proven themselves extremely difficult to defeat, Hay expressed his exasperation: "We do occasionally kill a Filipino, but what man has ever seen a dead Boer?"[24] In just three years, the United States had gone from clamoring to defend Venezuelan sovereignty in the face

---

21   Campbell, 225.
22   Bailey, 526–30.
23   John Hay to Henry White, September 24, 1889, in William Roscoe Thayer, *The Life and Letters of John Hay* (Boston: Houghton Mifflin Co., 1915. Reprint, Kraus Reprint Co., 1969), 221.
24   John Hay to Henry Adams, June 15, 1900, in Thayer, 232.

of perceived imperialist bullying to defending the interests of a fellow colonizing power.

Great Britain and the United States had developed a mutual need for each other. This being the case, there were still several unresolved issues between London and Washington, including the poorly defined boundary between Southeast Alaska and British Columbia. In the aftermath of the Venezuela boundary dispute, the British ambassador to Washington, Sir Julian Pauncefote, and U.S. Secretary of State Richard Olney signed a general arbitration treaty on January 11, 1897. The agreement would have paved the way for the negotiation of all outstanding Anglo-American disputes. President McKinley, who assumed office before the Senate vote on ratification, strongly supported the treaty, but the Senate rejected it. Many senators were unwilling to yield American foreign policy decisions to an arbitration board, while others did not share in the suddenly friendly disposition toward the British. Regarding the 1900 Republican Party convention, Hay wrote: "We had great trouble to prevent the Convention from declaring in favor of the Boers, and of the annexation of Canada."[25]

Four decades before the United States purchased Alaska, the Anglo-Russian Convention of 1825 established the boundaries between Russian America and the British possessions in the Northwest. The northern portion of the border followed a straight line down the 141st meridian, but the boundary of southeastern Alaska followed a much more complicated path. In the words of the treaty (translated from the original French):

> The line of demarcation between the possessions of the High Contracting Parties...Commencing from the southernmost point of the island called Prince of Wales Island...shall ascend to the North, along the channel called Portland Channel, as far as the . . . 56th degree of north latitude; from this last-mentioned point the line of demarcation shall follow the summit of the mountains situated parallel to the coast as far as the...141st degree of west longitude.

---

25   John Hay to John W. Foster, June 23, 1900, in Tyler Dennett, *John Hay: From Poetry to Politics* (Port Washington, NY: Kennikat Press, 1963), 333.

... That whenever the summit of the mountains which extend in a direction parallel to the coast ... shall prove to be at a distance of more than 10 marine leagues from the ocean, the limit between the British possessions and the line of coast which is to belong to Russia ... shall be formed by a line parallel to the windings of the coast, and which shall never exceed the distance of 10 marine leagues therefrom.[26]

The 1867 purchase treaty recognized the boundary established by the 1825 convention between Russia and Great Britain. But the exact location of the line was indefinite. There was little geographic information available about the territory in question, and it was not clear what were the "mountains situated parallel to the coast." At the time of the purchase, however, neither the Americans nor the British considered the matter pressing.

Five years later, news of the Cassiar gold strike in British Columbia drew the attention of President Ulysses S. Grant to the imprecise boundary. In 1872, he called for the appointment of a joint commission to settle the issue, but Congress was unwilling to act.[27] Twenty more years passed before Secretary of State Blaine negotiated an 1892 treaty that provided for eleven teams, four American and seven Canadian, to undertake a border survey. In December 1895, the surveyors presented a joint topographic report and maps to be used as the basis for a boundary settlement, but their work went largely ignored.[28] Then, in July 1897, when word of the gold discovery in the Klondike reached Seattle, thousands of Americans began charging northward.

The quickest route to the gold fields took miners through the archipelago of Southeast Alaska and up Lynn Canal. Two American towns, Skagway and Dyea, sprung up at the end of the deep inlet where

---

26   "Convention Between Great Britain and Russia, signed at St. Petersburg, February 28/10, 1825," in John A. Munro, ed., *The Alaska Boundary Dispute* (Toronto: Copp Clark Publishing Co., 1970), 9.

27   Norman Penlington, *The Alaska Boundary Dispute: A Critical Reappraisal* (Toronto: McGraw-Hill Ryerson Ltd., 1972), 20–21.

28   Lewis Green, *The Boundary Hunters: Surveying the 141st Meridian and the Alaska Panhandle* (Vancouver: University of British Columbia Press, 1982), 54–63.

miners disembarked to begin their journey overland to the Yukon River tributaries in Canada. In February 1898, months after the founding of the two towns, Canadian Interior Minister Clifford Sifton and Prime Minister Sir Wilfrid Laurier made statements before the Canadian Parliament calling the head of Lynn Canal "disputed territory."[29] This was cause for the United States to take new interest in the matter.

In May 1898, representatives of Great Britain and Canada, meeting with American officials in Washington, established a Joint High Commission for the resolution of the boundary question.[30] Canada began the negotiations by making the sweeping claim that, according to the terms of the 1825 treaty, the heads of all the inlets in Southeast Alaska were actually in Canada. The U.S. commissioners observed that Canada had never asserted sovereignty over the inlets before the Klondike gold rush, but they were nonetheless initially willing to offer Canada partial control of the port of Pyramid Harbor at the head of the Chilkat Trail. However, news of the proposed arrangement was leaked, and strong opposition from the western states prompted the American commissioners to withdraw the Pyramid Harbor offer. The commission adjourned having settled nothing in February 1899.

It was not until October of that year that Secretary of State John Hay and Reginald Tower, the British chargé d'affaires in Washington, agreed to a *modus vivendi* creating a provisional boundary across the Chilkoot Pass, the White Pass, and the Chilkat Pass, the three main routes into the interior from Lynn Canal. The agreement included the understanding "that the citizens or subjects of either power, found by this agreement within the temporary jurisdiction of the other, shall suffer no diminution of the rights and privileges which they now enjoy."[31] The boundary dispute undoubtedly contributed to nationalist posturing in the Yukon, but throughout the gold rush,

---

29 Penlington, 37.

30 John Herd Thompson and Stephen J. Randall, *Canada and the United States: Ambivalent Allies* (Athens: University of Georgia Press, 1994), 67.

31 U.S. Congress. House. Papers Relating to the Foreign Relations of the United States, with the Annual Message of the President Transmitted to Congress December 5, 1899. 56th Cong., 1st sess., 1901. H. Doc. 1, 330.

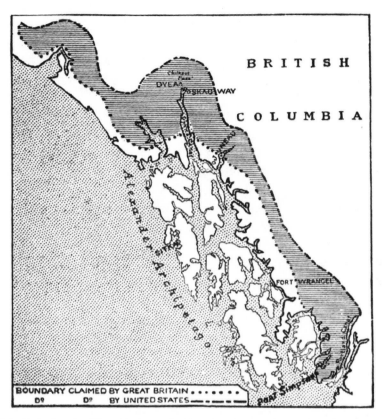

If the Alaska Boundary Tribunal had recognized Canada's claims, the heads of Lynn Canal and Glacier Bay, as well as other Southeast Alaska inlets, would have been located in Canada, giving Canada greater access to the Pacific. *American Monthly Review of Reviews (New York), Vol. 28, No. 5, November 1903.*

American and Canadian authorities respected the provisional arrangements.

At the same time, foreign policy makers in the United States were focused on various plans for the construction of an isthmian canal across Central America. In 1850, Great Britain and the United States had signed the Clayton-Bulwer Treaty, which stipulated that canal construction across the isthmus was to be a joint Anglo-American effort. But the U.S., emboldened by the war with Spain, now looked to building and controlling a canal unilaterally. Early in 1899, British ambassador Sir Julian Pauncefote and John Hay had drawn up a draft treaty that would have allowed the U.S. to do just that, but British Prime Minister Lord Salisbury would not consent to the accord without first consulting Canada in regard to the Alaska boundary. Ottawa urged London to make no changes to the original canal treaty until the U.S. agreed to submit the disputed Alaska boundary to arbitration.[32] The U.S. Senate, meanwhile, passed a bill sponsored by Senator John Morgan of Alabama that called for the construction of a canal through Nicaragua, and President McKinley appointed a commission to study various canal routes. On May 2, 1900, the House of Representatives overwhelmingly passed a canal bill put forward by Congressman William Hepburn of Iowa.[33] Both the Morgan and Hepburn bills were in flagrant violation of the Clayton-Bulwer Treaty.

As American intentions became clearer, the British found themselves ever more deeply embroiled in the Boer War, and increasingly determined to maintain positive relations with the United States. Although Canada was faithfully sending troops to aid the Empire in South Africa, Britain felt less and less compelled to hold up the renegotiation of the 1850 treaty in order to secure American consent to arbitration on the boundary issue. In January 1900, London appealed to Ottawa to acquiesce on the subject of the treaty, and the Canadian government, in no position to refuse, agreed not to object. The first Hay-Pauncefote Treaty of February 5, 1900, would have abrogated the Clayton-Bulwer Treaty, and allowed for U.S. construction and ownership of an isthmian canal. The Senate, however, rejected the treaty because of its ban on fortification of the waterway, and the House subsequently passed the Hepburn bill. On even this point the British proved willing to concede, and on November 18, 1901, the second Hay-Pauncefote Treaty paved the way for an American-built, -owned, and -fortified isthmian canal.[34] All the while, Canadian demands for arbitration of the Alaska boundary dispute went unheeded.

---

32 Campbell, 232.
33 Campbell, 239–42.
34 Bailey, 533–35.

The American refusal to arbitrate the Alaska boundary issue is ironic in light of the U.S. demands leveled at Britain in 1895 over the Venezuelan boundary, but the United States now found itself in a favorable bargaining position. U.S. aversion to arbitration stemmed, at least in part, from a previous Alaska diplomatic dispute that took place just before the improvement in Anglo-American relations. In 1881, the U.S. Treasury Department had declared what was essentially a *mare clausum* in the Bering Sea, in reaction to foreign competition for the valuable northern fur seals that spent the summer months on breeding grounds on Alaska's Pribilof Islands. Pelagic sealing, the practice of killing seals from boats on the open ocean during the animals' 2,000-mile annual migration from California, severely threatened the survival of the seal population. It had also begun to cut into the profits of the Alaska Commercial Company, to which the U.S. government had granted exclusive Pribilof sealing rights in 1870. Over twenty years, the federal government had earned over $6 million from the rent and taxes remitted by Alaska Commercial, which approached the original purchase price of Alaska. In 1886, when the Revenue Marine Service, the forerunner of the U.S. Coast Guard, began seizing pelagic sealing vessels in the Bering Sea, the Governor General of Canada protested on the grounds that such action violated the principle of Freedom of the Seas.[35]

The United States and Great Britain submitted their dispute in the Bering Sea to an international arbitration tribunal comprised of two Americans, two Britons, and one member each from France, Italy, and the Kingdom of Sweden and Norway. The U.S. argued that the seals summered on American soil and were therefore the property of the United States, no matter where they traveled. Senator John Morgan, who served as a member of the tribunal, contended that the United States "have such rights over these fur-seals as any owner of land animals would have over domestic or domesticated animals, when found on the public highways."[36] Not surprisingly, on August

---

35   Gerald Williams, *The Bering Sea Fur Seal Dispute* (Eugene, OR: Alaska Maritime Publications, 1984), 7–15.

36   United States, *Bering Sea Tribunal of Arbitration: Opinion of Senator Morgan at the Conference in Paris* (Washington, D.C.: Government Printing Office, 1893), 71.

15, 1893, the tribunal ruled against the United States on all five points considered in the dispute. The U.S. reluctantly agreed to the terms and enacted legislation accordingly. In their ruling, the arbitrators established a series of regulations intended to protect the declining seal herds, but the decision allowed pelagic sealing on the open ocean during most of the year. In just the first season following the arbitration, record-setting harvests drove the seals to the brink of annihilation. The situation was so dire that the House of Representatives voted, in December 1894, to slaughter the entire herd so as to keep any remaining profits in the United States, but the bill was tabled when it was thought that the British might agree to amend the new restrictions.[37] Frustrated by American reluctance to pay damage claims for vessels seized on the open sea, the British refused to renegotiate. As a result, seals became scarce, the industry declined, and the United States was left with a bitter arbitration experience.

When the U.S. finally agreed to address the Alaska boundary question, it did so on its own terms, and well after the Klondike gold rush had seen its heyday. By then, President McKinley had been assassinated in September 1901 (in the seventh month of his second term in office), and Theodore Roosevelt had ascended to the presidency. In recognition of American neutrality in the Boer War, Britain agreed to a U.S. adjudication plan. A convention established the Alaskan Boundary Tribunal on January 24, 1903. There were to be no third-party participants this time, and both sides would have equal representation. "The tribunal," the agreement read, "shall consist of six impartial jurists of repute."[38] Canadian officials were under the impression that these jurists were to come from the bench, or from some other "impartial" setting. Great Britain appointed two Canadians, the Lieutenant-Governor of Quebec, Sir Louis Jetté, and Allen Aylesworth, a prominent Ontario attorney, to the tribunal. The Lord Chief Justice of England, Lord Alverstone, joined them. Taking no chances, President Theodore Roosevelt appointed Secretary

---

37 Williams, 50–51.
38 Canada. Parliament. Sessional Papers, 1903, No. 149, "Correspondence and Papers Relating to the Alaska Boundary Question," 3.

THE NEWS REACHES BOGOTA.—From the *Herald* (New York).

Britain agreed to allow the United States to build, own, and unilaterally fortify, what would become the Panama Canal in 1901, despite Ottawa's attempts to secure a guarantee from London that the Alaska boundary would be arbitrated first. However, U.S. involvement in Central America, depicted here by a giant Teddy Roosevelt digging the canal himself, represented one of several new foreign policy fronts diverting American attention away from the old idea of annexing Canada. *American Monthly Review of Reviews (New York), Vol. 28, No. 6, December 1903.*

of War Elihu Root, Senator Henry Cabot Lodge of Massachusetts, and Senator George Turner of Washington.[39] All three had previously voiced their opinions on the proper location of the boundary. In a letter to the Colonial Office in London, Lord Minto, the Governor General of Canada, expressed his concerns over the American appointments: "The appointment to the tribunal by the United States government of gentlemen who are not judges, and whose views leave no room for expectation of a judicial consideration of the question, changes the whole situation."[40] Indeed, Roosevelt had

---

39   U.S. Congress. Senate. Alaskan Boundary Tribunal: Proceedings of the Alaskan Boundary Tribunal, Vol. 1. 58th Cong., 2d sess. 1904. S. Doc. 162, 15.

40   Lord Minto to Colonial Office, March 6, 1903, in Canada. Parliament.

made careful political choices, having no intention of conceding any U.S. territory to Great Britain.

On October 21, 1903, the tribunal issued its decision, and the U.S. was largely vindicated. Former Secretary of State John W. Foster, the attorney presenting the American case, described the verdict as "a substantial acceptance of the most material claim of this country, and the result has been so regarded on both sides."[41] Canadians certainly viewed it as a diplomatic defeat. Lord Alverstone had voted with the three Americans in a 4–2 decision. In his published opinion, he wrote, "After most careful examination, I have been unable to find any passage which supports the view that Great Britain was directly or indirectly putting forward a claim to the shores or ports at the head of the inlets."[42] The two Canadian representatives refused to sign the award, and published a statement declaring that the majority had "ignored the just rights of Canada."[43] Alverstone was accused of sacrificing Canadian interests for the sake of Anglo-American relations. As W. L. Morton described it, "The Alaska boundary award was a humiliating experience for Canada. Canadians felt they had been treated with contempt by the Americans and let down by the British."[44] The public reaction among Canadians was strong. The author of an anonymously published 1904 booklet, *Canada's Alaskan Dismemberment*, alleged that the U.S. position on the boundary was "part of a policy of aggression upon the Territorial rights of the Dominion of Canada . . . that might be immediately relieved by secession from the Empire, and alliance with the States."[45]

Sessional Papers, 1904, No. 46a, "Correspondence Respecting the Alaska Boundary, together with the Award of the Alaska Boundary Tribunal," 62.

41   John W. Foster, "The Alaskan Boundary Tribunal: A Lecture Delivered in His Course in American Diplomacy in Columbian University, Washington, D.C., December 8, 1903," *Columbian University Bulletin* 2, no. 3 (December 1903), 9.

42   U.S. Congress. Senate. Alaskan Boundary Tribunal: Proceedings of the Alaskan Boundary Tribunal, Vol. 1. 58th Cong., 2d sess. 1904. S. Doc. 162, 40.

43   "Statement by the Canadian Commissioners," *London Times*, October 21, 1903, in Munro, ed., 62.

44   W. L. Morton, *The Canadian Identity* (Toronto: University of Toronto Press, 1961), 67–69 in Munro, ed., 164.

45   *Canada's Alaskan Dismemberment: An Analytical Examination of the Fallacies Underlying the Tribunal Award* (Niagara-on-the-Lake, ON: Charles Thonger, Printer, 1904), 1.

Historian Norman Penlington came to the straightforward conclusion that the "United States had the better case, the superior diplomatic skill, and the greater power to ensure victory."[46] The Boer War
had weakened Britain's diplomatic influence, and Canada had limited
control of its own foreign policy. There was also an undercurrent of
American conceit throughout the affair, evident in both President
Roosevelt's appointments to the tribunal and even more so in a letter
he wrote to Supreme Court Justice Oliver Wendell Holmes on July 25,
1903, before the tribunal had convened:

> I wish to make one last effort to bring about an agreement through
> the commission . . . But if there is a disagreement I wish it distinctly
> understood, not only that there will be no arbitration of the matter,
> but that in my message to Congress I shall take a position which
> will prevent any arbitration hereafter; a position, I am inclined to
> believe, which will render it necessary for Congress to give me the
> authority to run the line as we claim it, by our own people, without
> any further regard to the attitude of England and Canada.[47]

Such rhetoric may not have helped the cause of Anglo-American
relations, but the stronger the United States grew, the tighter its bonds
to Britain became. Over the next decade, meanwhile, Ottawa grew in
confidence, and began to take a greater role in the conduct of its foreign relations, establishing the Department of External Affairs in
1909. "All governments have found it necessary to have a department
whose only business shall be to deal with relations with foreign countries," Prime Minister Laurier told the House of Commons, "and in
our judgment Canada has a reached a period in her history when we
should follow the example of other countries."[48] On Dominion Day
that year, the crew of the Canadian vessel *Arctic* disembarked from

---

46 Penlington, 116.
47 Theodore Roosevelt to Oliver Wendell Holmes, July 25, 1903, in Elting E.
Morrison, ed., *The Letters of Theodore Roosevelt*, Vol. 3 (Cambridge, MA: Harvard
University Press, 1954), 529–31 in Munro, ed., 57.
48 Canada. Parliament. House of Commons. Debates, 11th Parl., 1st sess.,
March 4, 1909.

Melville Island in the Northwest Territories and installed a plaque on Parry's Rock "to commemorate the taking possession for the Dominion of Canada of the whole Arctic Archipelago, lying to the north of America from long. 60° w. to 141° w. up to latitude 90° n."[49] By this measure, Canada now extended all the way to the North Pole. Its land claims in the Alaska boundary dispute were modest in comparison.

BIBLIOGRAPHY

Bailey, Thomas A. *A Diplomatic History of the American People*. New York: F. S. Crofts and Co., 1940.

Bemis, Samuel F. "The Great Aberration of 1898," in Theodore P. Greene, ed., *American Imperialism in 1898*. Boston: D. C. Heath and Co., 1955.

Campbell, Charles S., Jr. "Anglo-American Relations, 1897–1901," in Paolo E. Coletta, ed. *Threshold to American Internationalism: Essays on the Foreign Policies of William McKinley*. New York: Exposition Press, 1970.

Canada. Parliament. Sessional Papers, 1903, No. 149, "Correspondence and Papers Relating to the Alaska Boundary Question," 3.

Canada. Parliament. Sessional Papers, 1904, No. 46a, "Correspondence Respecting the Alaska Boundary, together with the Award of the Alaska Boundary Tribunal," 62.

Canada. Parliament. House of Commons. *Debates*, 11th Parl., 1st sess., March 4, 1909.

Canada's Alaskan Dismemberment: An Analytical Examination of the Fallacies Underlying the Tribunal Award (Niagara-on-the-Lake, ON: Charles Thonger, Printer, 1904), 1.

Coletta, Paolo E., ed. *Threshold to American Internationalism: Essays on the Foreign Policies of William McKinley*. New York: Exposition Press, 1970.

Dennett, Tyler. *John Hay: From Poetry to Politics*. Port Washington, NY: Kennikat Press, 1963.

Foster, John W. "The Alaskan Boundary Tribunal: A Lecture Delivered in His Course in American Diplomacy in Columbian University,

---

49 David Eric Jessup, "J. E. Bernier and the Assertion of Canadian Sovereignty in the Arctic," *American Review of Canadian Studies* 38, no. 4 (Winter 2008), 409–27; 417.

Washington, D.C., December 8, 1903." *Columbian University Bulletin*, 2, no. 3 (December 1903), 9.

Granatsein, J. L., and N. Hillmer. *For Better or for Worse: Canada and the United States to the 1990s*. Toronto: Copp Clark Pitman, 1991.

Green, Lewis. *The Boundary Hunters: Surveying the 141st Meridian and the Alaska Panhandle*. Vancouver: University of British Columbia Press, 1982.

Healy, David. *US Expansionism: The Imperialist Urge in the 1890s*. Madison: University of Wisconsin Press, 1970.

Higby, William. *Speech of Hon. William Higby, of California, Delivered in the House of Representatives the 21st Day of March, 1868, on the Treaty Between the United States and the Russian Government on the Transfer of Alaska*. Washington, D.C.: Turner, Printer, 1868.

Jessup, David Eric. "J. E. Bernier and the Assertion of Canadian Sovereignty in the Arctic," *American Review of Canadian Studies* 38, no 4 (Winter 2008), 409–27.

Morrison, David R. *The Politics of the Yukon Territory, 1898–1909*. Toronto: University of Toronto Press, 1968.

Morrison, William R. *Showing the Flag: The Mounted Police and Canadian Sovereignty in the North, 1894–1925* Vancouver: University of British Columbia Press, 1985.

Miller, Richard H., ed. *American Imperialism in 1898: The Quest for National Fulfillment*. New York: John Wiley and Sons, 1970.

Munro, John A., ed. *The Alaska Boundary Dispute*. Toronto: Copp Clark Publishing Co., 1970.

Neael, R. G. *Great Britain and United States Expansion: 1898–1900*. East Lansing: Michigan State University Press, 1966.

Penlington, Norman. *The Alaska Boundary Dispute: A Critical Reappraisal*. Toronto: McGraw-Hill Ryerson Ltd., 1972.

Pratt, Julius W. *Expansionists of 1898: The Acquisition of Hawaii and the Spanish Islands*. Baltimore: Johns Hopkins Press, 1936. Reprint, Gloucester: Peter Smith, 1959.

Thayer, William R. *The Life and Letters of John Hay*. Boston: Houghton Mifflin Co., 1915. Reprint, Kraus Reprint Co., 1969.

Thompson, John H., and Randall, S. J. *Canada and the United States: Ambivalent Allies*. Athens: University of Georgia Press, 1994.

Tyler, Alice F. *The Foreign Policy of James G. Blaine*. Minneapolis: University of Minnesota Press, 1927. Reprint, Hamden, CT: Archon Books, 1965.

United States. *Bering Sea Tribunal of Arbitration: Opinion of Senator Morgan at the Conference in Paris* (Washington, D.C.: Government Printing Office, 1893), 71.

U.S. Congress. Senate. *Alaskan Boundary Tribunal: Proceedings of the Alaskan Boundary Tribunal*, Vol. 1. 58th Cong., 2d sess. 1904. S. Doc. 162, 15.

U.S. Congress. House. *Papers Relating to the Foreign Relations of the United States, with the Annual Message of the President Transmitted to Congress December 5, 1898*. 55th Cong., 3d sess. 1901. H. Doc. 1, 760.

U.S. Congress. House. *Papers Relating to the Foreign Relations of the United States, with the Annual Message of the President Transmitted to Congress December 5, 1899*. 56th Cong., 1st sess., 1901. H. Doc. 1, 330.

U.S. Congress. Senate. *Alaskan Boundary Tribunal: Proceedings of the Alaskan Boundary Tribunal*, Vol. 1. 58th Cong., 2d sess. 1904. S. Doc. 162, 40.

U.S. Congress. House. *Papers Relating to the Foreign Relations of the United States, with the Annual Message of the President Transmitted to Congress December 5, 1898*. 55th Cong., 3d sess. 1901. H. Doc. 1, xlix–wxcv.

Volwiler, Albert T., ed. *The Correspondence Between Benjamin Harrison and James G. Blaine 1882–1893*, Memoirs of the American Philosophical Society. Philadelphia: American Philosophical Society, 1940.

Williams, Gerald. *The Bering Sea Fur Seal Dispute*. Eugene, OR: Alaska Maritime Publications, 1984.

A Note from Dan O'Neill

Terrence and I became pals thirty-odd years ago at the University of Alaska, where he was teaching history and I was doing research at the oral history office. He kindly read my first book manuscript— several times—and from that I absorbed many of his standards, making them my methodological mantras thereafter. We argued and discussed any and all historical and contemporary affairs, often as a rapid-fire, cross-talking, verbal brawl, one Irishman at another. He oozed passion, burned an inexhaustible energy, understood like few others how to reach a wide audience, and was a kick in the butt to be around. When I took him on his first dip-net fishing trip to Chitina, he packed a briefcase, hauling it down the cliffs to grade papers during lulls.

THE HUNTER & THE COPPER-EYED BUG FROM MARS

Food Moralists, Meet Alaska

Dan O'Neill

When I began to reread Michael Pollan's generally excellent *The Omnivore's Dilemma*, I saw from my earlier margin notes that I had not begun to quibble with the writer's ideas until well into . . . the first page. Actually, the table of contents. Chapter eight is titled "All Flesh Is Grass," and alongside is my penciled reaction, a compound word for grass in a postdigestion state.

Pollan deploys the grass adage frequently, citing the Old Testament as its source. But, doubting Thomas that I am, I looked it up. The reference is from 1 Peter 1:24, but I see that Pollan has left out a word—a tiny but significant one. The actual quote is "All flesh is *as* grass," and the full quotation gives the sense of it: "For all flesh is as grass, and all the glory of man as the flower of grass. The grass withereth, and the flower thereof falleth away, but the word of the Lord endures forever."

So it turns out St. Peter was not metaphorically illustrating whence all meat derives, as the author implies; rather, Peter was comparing humanity to grass and man's achievements to its flower, in order to signify the temporality of both.

I won't continue in a Talmudic vein, but I will add one small historical detail: St. Peter was a fisherman. It's a safe bet he knew that fish did not sit atop a food chain anchored in pastureland. I'd also note, on behalf of my fellow Northerners, that the meat we traditionally eat—the animals of the tundra and boreal forest (moose, caribou,

bears, muskoxen, beaver, ducks, geese); sea mammals (whales, wal-
rus, seals, belugas); sea birds and their eggs (cormorants, gulls, murres,
puffins); animals of the coastal rainforest (deer and bears); mountain
animals (goats and sheep); fish (salmon, halibut, cod, flounder, gray-
ling, whitefish, pike); and assorted ocean creatures (crabs, shrimp,
clams, mussels, sea urchins)—these have been food staples of Northern
peoples for thousands of years, and that not one of them is dependent
on grass. Dry grasslands have not been common in northern North
America since the Pleistocene.

Pollan is not exceptional in discounting the North in his treatise
on eating. America is not a northward-looking nation.[1] But for that
very reason, it seems instructive to consider whether Pollan's ideas,
and those of other foodists, hold up very well when applied to northern situations around the globe. Because many of the moral, philosophical discussions swirling around food (viz., vegetarianism,
veganism, the ethics of hunting) always seem to arise from a southern,
urbanist worldview. Not so well accounted for are the rural and indigenous folks who populate most communities in Alaska and the rest
of the Circumpolar North, and the dignity and rectitude of their
foodways.

The Omnivore's Dilemma is sorted into three parts. The first follows
industrially grown corn through feedlots and slaughterhouses, ending with a meal at McDonald's. The second section focuses on grasslands and first tracks industrial organic food production, then Joel
Salatin's small-scale organic farm, and culminates in home-cooked
meals associated with each source. In the final section, Pollan joins
hunting and foraging adepts to assemble a "personally hunted, gathered, and grown meal."

---

1   Alaska's tourist office is frequently asked whether visas are required of
visitors from the lower states and what currency is used up here. During the
Chernobyl accident, National Public Radio reported that radioactive fallout
would first enter U.S. airspace when it crossed into Washington State from the
northwest; and Alaskans realize that internet merchants do not mean it when
they say, "Free shipping in the continental US." (Though we wonder, if not North
America, which continent do they think we're on?)

For the most part, these forays take Pollan into pastoral landscapes, but not beyond. Salatin's farm, for example, is roughly ten minutes' drive from a town of 25,000, an hour from a town of 50,000, and three hours from a metropolitan area of six million. Even Pollan's hunting trip takes place within California's Bay Area, not far from his Berkeley home. Unobserved here are the foodways and cultural norms of those rural folk who are less involved with fenced pastures than with obtaining food directly from nature in a backcountry or wild setting. Bayou Cajuns, for one example, typically make use of boats and camps, gathering wild catfish, shrimp, turtles, frogs, crawfish, and alligators. In Alaska, even into the twenty-first century, some groups of rural people derive as much as 80 percent of their diet, and all of their protein requirements, from hunting and fishing.[2] Pollan occasionally gives a nod to deeply rural cultures, albeit dismissively, while slipping into an urban chauvinism: "So though a hunter-gatherer food chain still exists here and there to one degree or another, it seems to me its chief value for us at this point is not so much economic or practical but didactic." It's clear enough who Pollan's "us" excludes: the people for whom hunting and fishing *are* economic and practical (not to mention healthy, culturally important, and educative in such realms as natural history, ecology, and assorted outdoor competencies).

Pollan goes on, beguiled by a "hunting as play" conceit that he appears to have picked up from the Spanish philosopher and hunting enthusiast José Ortega y Gassett.[3] In his 1972 *Meditations on Hunting*, Ortega sees hunting as mainly a leisure activity of the aristocracy, listing it alongside horse racing, exercise competitions, and parties that feature dancing.[4] He speaks of "the almost universally privileged nature of the sport of hunting," and styles hunting forays as "vacations from the human condition."[5] Yet, except for "poachers," Ortega

---

2   Ken Meter and Megan Phillips Goldenberg, *Building Food Security in Alaska*, Alaska Department of Health and Social Services, 2014, p. 9.

3   In his bibliography, Pollan notes re. Ortega's *Meditations on Hunting*, "My own meditations owe a large debt to Ortega's."

4   José Ortega y Gassett, *Meditations on Hunting*, New York: Charles Scribner's Sons, 1972, p. 33.

5   Ibid., p. 125.

completely overlooks people whose hunting and fishing pursuits are better understood *as* economic activity, rather than vacations from it. "If one were to present the sportsman with the death of the animal as a gift, he would refuse it," says Ortega. "What he is after is having to win it, to conquer the surly brute through his own effort and skill." Ortega's sportsman would be a perfect stranger in rural Alaska, where the people, including hunters, would be only too happy to receive such a gift. What matters to them *is* the meat, not some virility-bolstering conquest.

Pollan is not unconscious of the hunting ethos of rural folk, declaring at the outset that hunting a meal would "perforce teach me things about the ecology and ethics of eating that I could not get in a super-market or fast-food chain or even on a farm." Yet it seems that as quickly as this penetrative light is switched on, it is again switched off. Hunting, he insists, should be seen as an adolescent amusement, at best. "For most of us today hunting and gathering and growing our own food is by and large a form of play." Again: "Like other important forms of play, it promises to teach us something about who we are beneath the crust of our civilized, practical, grown-up lives." And again: "Irony—the outside perspective—easily withers everything about hunting, shrinks it to the proportions of boy's play or atavism." I wonder if Pollan would push his "boy's play" narrative quite so insistently if he were speaking to a distinctly rural audience—say, an audience of Iñupiat Alaska Natives in a whaling village along the Chukchi Sea coast. Because I believe it would quickly sink in for him that for the Iñupiat, hunting and fishing hold a seriousness quite beyond the native New Yorker's compass. The incongruity here is profound, the gulf between his world and theirs immense.

Pollan's discussion of hunting is both my favorite and least favorite section of the book. He opens it with these lines: "Walking with a loaded rifle in an unfamiliar forest bristling with the signs of your prey is thrilling. It embarrasses me to write that, but it is true." I thought he might go on to explain his confliction a bit, but he does not. He must assume we share his chastity in the matter of guns and so understand his predicament, which I guess amounts to this: Just *carrying* a rifle is bad enough, but a *loaded* rifle? And to feel a *thrill* on top of that?! That's the ethical lapse that prompts his little confession. Of course, if Pollan got out amongst country people more, he'd know that what would embarrass *them* would be to go off hunting with an *un*loaded rifle.

The reader understands what's going on here: the moral inoculation that Pollan feels he needs before joining the boys with guns heading into the woods. And we are given to understand that his is no loutish *Field and Stream* sensibility, and this is no unmindful conversion: "I never could stomach the straight-faced reveling in primitivism, the barely concealed bloodlust, the whole macho conceit...." And when he catches himself warming to the subject a bit and mentioning some archetypical patterns that hunting brings into view, another confession gets him out ahead of the anticipated criticism: "Wait a minute. Did I just write that last paragraph? Without irony? That's embarrassing. I'm actually writing about the hunter's 'instinct,' suggesting that the hunt represents some sort of primordial union between two kinds of animals, one of which is *me*? . . . I recognize this kind of prose: hunter porn."

Right. Well, let's review. Pollan finds the hunt thrilling—but wait, that's embarrassing. He's moved by its connections to ancestral ways, but embarrassed anew for having noticed them. He confesses to slipping into "the hunter's ecstatic purple," but then accepts as inevitable an "overheated prose ignorant of irony." Back forth, back forth. I think country people would recognize *this* kind of prose too: New Yorker neurosis porn. Maybe not quite as axel-wrapped as Woody Allen or as fast-talking and jittery as Larry David, but when Michael Pollan exhibitionalistically prepares his mind to go hunting, he is every bit as comically angst-ridden and autocolonoscopic.[6]

---

6   What to make of Pollan's repeated reference to irony? He seems to say he's naked without it, a gunslinger without his gun. But I wonder if this irony, "the outside perspective" that "easily withers everything about hunting," is more urban trope than clear thinking. Where it begins to sound snooty and superior—a putdown of country people and their ways—I can hear Thoreau chiming in: "We cannot but pity the boy who has never fired a gun; he is no more humane, while his education has been sadly neglected."

As a teenager, Pollan lived on the eleventh floor of a doorman-attended Upper East Side apartment building in New York City. There, at one point, he kept a piglet. When summer came, the pig joined the family on Martha's Vineyard, a one-way trip for the rapidly growing and increasingly rowdy sow. Seeking new pig quarters, Pollan imprudently introduced her to the pen of a massive and bad-tempered sow, and that was that.[7] Regarded as more pet than pork, she was buried rather than barbecued. Against this backdrop, it is creditable that, years later, the journalist Pollan succeeded in convincing the urbanized Pollan that he needed to experience a hunt. And, after a great deal of intentional and duly noted handwringing, he becomes more or less ethically settled about hunting feral pigs, and heads into the wilds (or at least onto a sprawling estate in Sonoma County).

I won't go into detail about Pollan's hunt, which would be painful to retell,[8] except to note that even in the context of this boutique expedition (breakfast at home, drive to where you start hunting, hunt by walking on gravel roads, a gourmet picnic with wine, napkins, and silverware, home by dark for a shower, dinner, and to sleep in your own bed), it's still disappointing to see that Pollan never becomes more than a visitor, a reporter, and uncomfortable and ill-fitted to the landscapes and the animals and the rhythms he moves among. You might say this hunt amounts to his be-wilderness experience, for he is bewildered in both the contemporary figurative sense and in the older, literal one: "lost in a pathless place."

■ ■ ■

Notwithstanding, Pollan makes a significant contribution to our understanding of hunting, and he does so before he ever picks up a

---

7   Interestingly, the death and burial occurred on James Taylor's property, the killer being the singer's sow, Mona, about whom Taylor recorded the eponymous song, wherein she is described as "too damned old to eat" and "pushing up a pine tree in my field."

8   Nightmarish, really, to a hunter: a high-powered rifle discharges accidentally; other erratic bullets are sent flying; a wounded animal hobbles off into the brush, unretrieved (*Omnivore*, p. 352).

gun. He is a far better stalker and marksman when the quarry is an elusive moral conundrum.[9] In a solid chapter called "The Ethics of Eating Animals," Pollan very effectively engages Peter Singer, point by metaphysical point. Peter Albert David Singer is the Ira W. DeCamp Professor of Bioethics at Princeton University and the author of the canonical *Animal Liberation*. Singer offers a rigid vegetarian world-view grounded in resisting "speciesism," such as "the slaughter of wild animals by hunters."[10] But Pollan sniffs out biases, noting that such ideas could not possibly arise from other than a very urbanist mindset (a point, I'm arguing, that Pollan himself sometimes misses). He quotes Singer: "In our normal life, there is no serious clash of interests between human and nonhuman animals."[11] Pollan counters, saying that "no farmer—indeed, no gardener" would recognize Singer's "normal life." Farms displace wild animals, says Pollan, and even gardeners compete with the birds and mice and voles and hares who would claim the whole harvest if they could. Well done, but my own rebuttal would have also invoked Alaska Natives, or any rural residents of entire circumpolar nations. A thought experiment: Imagine that Peter Singer boards a jet airplane in New Jersey and flies 2,400 miles to Seattle, and then another 1,500 miles to Anchorage. Then he boards a turbo-prop for a 550-mile leg to Kotzebue. Then crams himself into a little twin-engine bush plane for the final 180-mile hop to Point Hope, Alaska, a coastal community of Iñupiat (pop. 702). Tikiġaq, as the local people call it, is situated 125 miles north of the Arctic Circle on a low spit of land jutting into the Chukchi Sea (*Tikiġaq* is the Iñupiaq word for index finger). For most of the year, the spit is snowy and windswept, standing barely above the almost indistinguishable snowy and windswept frozen sea. The Tikiġaġmuit have occupied this place, not for hundreds of

---

9   Interestingly, citing Plato and Thomas Aquinas, Ortega notes "the extraordinary fact that, with maximum frequency, when a philosopher wanted to name the attitude in which he operated when musing, he compared himself with the hunter" (*Meditations*, p. 151).

10   Peter Singer, *Animal Liberation*, Harper Collins, New York, 2002 ed., p. 230.

11   Michael Pollan, *The Omnivore's Dilemma*, The Penguin Press, New York, 2006, p. 326.

years, but for thousands. Some scholars believe it is the oldest continuously occupied site of human habitation in North America. It has endured as a village largely because of its proximity to the sea lanes of migrating bowhead whales. For millennia, the people have subsisted on bowhead whales, seals, and beluga from the sea, as well as the caribou that drift through the adjacent hills. A good-sized *aġvik* (bowhead whale) can provide a village with several tons of food. And the total whale harvest across the North Slope of Alaska, when shared, might end up supplementing the diet of ten thousand people. At the same time, approximately the only edible vegetative matter that grows during the brief Arctic summer and that can be frozen for use over the long winter are wild berries.

In our experiment, Mr. Singer's mission is to sell the people on the economic, nutritional, and ethical benefits of a diet restricted to vegetables. Speaking in the community hall, Singer presents tofu as the people's protein solution. Questions you might hear from any of Alaska's bush people are called out from the floor:

Man: "Did you say *bean curd*? What is a *bean curd*?"

Man #2: "Where would you place the bullet to get a lung shot?"

Woman: "Is the hide good for anything?"

Maybe Mr. Singer could bring it off. Maybe vegetarianism would take hold among the Iñupiat. But not soon, I think. A little story to illustrate the meat/vegetable divide in Alaska villages: Some years ago I spent a week at a remote Iñupiat village, staying at the home of a man named Francis. One day I started to cook a stew using some moose meat I'd brought from home. There were no veggies in the refrigerator, so I gave Francis a few bucks to pick some up at the village store. I was browning the meat when the phone rang.

Francis, calling from the store: "What do you call those things that come in sticks like carrots, but they're green?"

Me: "Um, celery?"

Francis: "I guess so. Are they any good in stew?"

To get a further sense of how celery can be a UFO (unidentified flown-in object), consider that while there is usually a small grocery store in Native villages, the quality of fresh vegetables is usually as low as the prices are high. There are perhaps five kinds of vegetables in such a store at any one time—things like potatoes, carrots, celery, cabbage, and lettuce. No item is reliably stocked. The vegetables are flown to the village in small commuter planes after, in most cases, having already flown in a jet from California or Mexico—if not Guatemala or Chile, the last being roughly half the planet away, at one end of a carbon-y contrail 8,500 miles long. These carrots and celery are usually "bendy," as the people say, but nevertheless cost eight dollars a bunch. A head of lettuce may be brown and slimy and yet cost more than ten dollars. The price of carrots nears five dollars per pound. And so on, *ad carnivorism*. In short, the air importation of perishable fresh vegetables from lands thousands of miles distant is a costly and energy-*in*efficient way to deliver food that is nutritionally depleted and culinarily dreary.[12]

Peter Singer and other vegetarians might suggest gardens, which are possible in these areas of northern Alaska, but only in a limited way. The summertime air temperature at Point Hope, for example, averages nine degrees above freezing. Virtually all of the ground in the Arctic and most in the Subarctic is permafrost—that is, frozen as hard as concrete, year-round, just inches below the surface. Above-ground boxes can be built of lumber, but often only at considerable expense (the nearest trees to Point Hope, which is surrounded by tundra, are 100 miles away). And the people traditionally leave the village in summer for fish camps, and so cannot tend a garden in town. Some determined folks will grow a small garden at their fish camps, perhaps a potato patch, but good soil is not common, and the work of fishing is already labor intensive and exhausting.

My sister-in-law grows two small gardens at her family's fish camp on the Yukon River, one inside a derelict flat-bottom riverboat, the other inside a little old V-hull that was mostly done-for before the kids bought it for a runabout.[13] These boats have been winched up

---

12   Of course, the meat in village stores is expensive too. An October 2017 photo of a turkey in the Alaska Commercial Co. store in Kotzebue became something of an internet meme, as the price tag read $92.25 (*Arctic Sounder*, 2/11/18).

13   This boat was so forlorn and leprotic that the kids christened it, with shaky hand-lettering on the bows, the *Cirrhosis of the River*.

onto the bank, set up on logs, and punched full of holes. For fill, the family laboriously dug bucketsful of a loamy soil from a cutbank upriver, packed the buckets down to their riverboat, motored back to their fish camp, and lugged them up the bank to spread inside the garden boats. Dozens of boat trips, hundreds of bucket-loads. Mighty labor-intensive. But like many Third World solutions, this one is also brilliantly resourceful. Apart from recycling these worn-out boats, the soil in these gardens is rockless and loose, and weeds and roots cannot encroach from the terrestrial perimeter. And most importantly, the elevated soil is considerably warmer than the cold ground. Boat gardens like these are a realistic size. As a result, they provide fresh salad fixings during the summer, but they do not yield enough to preserve for nine months of winter use.

Not to prejudice the possibility of change (greenhouses, for example, may have an increasingly valuable role in food production in the rural far North), but in general, if conventional gardening on a scale much more intensive than a boat garden made economic sense for people in northern bush Alaska, then a lot of the people there would be gardening. Meanwhile, hundreds of thousands of oil-rich and succulent salmon, each one a banquet, carry themselves from the far-off ocean, like delivery drones from Amazon.com, right up to the doorstep of the village. And a single moose can feed a family of six for a *year*.

One thing Peter Singer would surely twig onto if he spent time among the Iñupiat or Athabascans would be the way in which these peoples' identities are entwined with their food habits—the acts of obtaining it, the techniques used to process it, the customs observed in sharing and eating it. And not just the subsistence economy, but much of the wider culture—even aspects of religion—are also borne along by animals. In fact, in traditional Athabascan culture it is considered presumptuous for a hunter to even say aloud that he is "going hunting." He will say instead that he is "going for a walk." It is not a hunter's cunning or aggressiveness that is rewarded, but his humility, his quiet, his respect for the animals, his soft-spoken reverence for the business he is about. As anthropologist Richard Nelson has observed, to Athabascans it is essentially this state of grace that puts a hunter in a position for the animal to offer itself.[14] That is where luck comes from. To disrupt these people's relationship with animals is to tinker fundamentally with their culture. If food moralists would ban the people's use of animals for food, it would not differ importantly from those times when missionaries forbade the speaking of the Native languages as primitive, and their songs and dances as pagan.

And, hard as it might be for some to credit, that same deep consanguinity between animals and man also exists where white people rely on wild animals for their food. Moreover, not all of these folks are bush people living a mainly subsistence lifestyle. Some live in towns and cities along the road system, yet depend on hunting and fishing to reduce the need for high-cost, imported, and often processed food. I know I feel it deeply if the season ends and I have no moose. It is a feeling of being detached from a source of my spiritual soundness, as if I am living some other person's life, where there is no corned moose for breakfast, no roast moose sandwiches for lunch, no moose stew bubbling in the crock pot and scenting the house when I get home, no prospect of company coming over for mooseburgers or smoked moose sausages or barbecued moose ribs, no special-occasion dinners highlighted by thick-cut tenderloin steaks.

Even the United States Congress understood the special relationship between Alaska's rural people and animals. In the Alaska National Interest Lands Conservation Act of 1980, Congress recognized not just the existence but the *value* of subsistence lifestyles in Alaska. Likely the most significant land conservation act in American history, ANILCA in one stroke radically increased the number and size of the nation's national parks, national wildlife refuges, wilderness preserves, wild and scenic rivers, national conservation areas, national recreation areas, and national forests. Yet even in the context of this monumental validation of conservationism, the proponents of ANILCA understood the difference between backcountry in the lower states and wilderness in Alaska. Most especially, it understood the singular fact that there were

---

14   Richard Nelson, *The Island Within*, North Point Press, San Francisco, 1989, p. 277.

people—both Native and white—who lived in or near these wild places, and that their livelihood depended on their ability to hunt, fish, gather, and cut trees. And this way of life in Alaska, the Congress noted, "may be the last major remnant of the subsistence culture alive today in North America." Consequently, the subsistence life-style was declared a "cultural value" and its continuance (by both Natives and whites) was to be allowed in the new Alaska conserva-tion units. If environmentalists have for thirty-five years understood the validity of people killing wild animals in these parklands, then perhaps there is hope that one day food moralists will too.

■ ■ ■

Michael Pollan's *Omnivore's Dilemma* is a well-researched and topically important book. It very usefully encourages saner approaches to eat-ing and food policies. And Pollan is a graceful, intelligent, and witty writer. But occasionally his thinking seems to issue from a small kitchen, his ideas over-marinated in political correctitude. Let us turn the tables. I think what would mortify an Alaskan hunter if he found himself abroad along Pollan's rustic byways—say, hiking along the trails in the Berkeley hills—would be if he turned a corner and saw racing down upon him one of those wheeled things with an external skull bone, scary, orange, reflective, wrap-around eyes, and a thorax of shining green spandex. For the Alaska hunter, it would be like sud-denly confronting a giant bug from Mars diving silently and fast and *right at him*. He'd flinch as the thing zoomed on by. But hanging in the air along with the dust, and about to settle on the hunter, would be a residue of embarrassment that the bug-thing exuded but did not claim. I have no idea what Michael Pollan would think of such an encounter if he were the one afoot. But I get the strong feeling that to the urban ethicist, it is the mountain biker, not the hunter, who is the morally sanctioned outdoorsperson.

Which suggests one more thought experiment. Imagine a crisp fall day in 1851, with sixty-six-year-old John James Audubon, thirty-four-year-old Henry David Thoreau, and thirteen-year-old John Muir venturing along a trail in a New England forest. The three rustics chat about the value of wilderness and the perils of creeping materialism. Shortly, they encounter a woodsman with a shotgun over his shoulder and a brace of grouse at his belt. Imagine their conversation. Cordial, I think, with the local man advising about the trail ahead and what birds or game or waterfalls might be seen up ahead. After a bit, they bid each other good day and continue on. A little while later, alerted by a sudden sound, the three wise men are startled spitless as a rocketing copper-eyed bug from Mars bears right down on them. Can you visualize their reaction? I can: Poof! Poof! Poof! Three puffs of dust and the bottoms of three sets of moccasins. The iconic defenders of wilderness—the patron saints of the Audubon Society and the Sierra Club—have dived terrified into the brambles. It's true, isn't it? Wouldn't the three woods-wise philosophers likely have seen in the hunter what Aldo Leopold saw in him: "a distinctly American tradition of self-reliance, hardihood, woodcraft, and marksmanship"?[15] But what on earth would they have made of the whizzing thing in neon green and eyes of mirrored copper?

One of the many things Pollan gets right in *The Omnivore's Dilemma* is his selection of a guide to take him pig hunting in the Bay Area, an Italian immigrant named Angelo Garro. Garro embodies that mingling of soul and stomach that marks people who produce their own food. Pollan refers to Angelo as "my Virgil," which irritates me only every time he does it. The possessive pronoun clunks all the way down the spiral staircase of my cochlea, and the needle of my snoot-meter swings into the "Condescension" range, both with regard to Angelo and with regard to Angelo's métier. Recall that in the *Divine Comedy*, Dante conscripts the Roman poet Virgil to guide him through *hell*, and safely past dangerous beasts:

> Behold the beast, for which I have turned back;
> Do thou protect me from her, famous Sage,
> For she doth make my veins and pulses tremble.[16]

---

15   Aldo Leopold, "Wildlife in American Culture," in *A Sand County Almanac*, Ballantine Books, New York, 1990, p. 213.
16   Dante Alighieri, *Inferno*, Canto I.

When he meets Angelo, Pollan is trying out vegetarianism as part of his book's conceit and soon is well stocked with the piety of the celibate. A vegetarian, but not a vegan, he explains, since "eggs and milk can be coaxed from animals without hurting or killing them—or so at least I thought." He will be willing to eat "animals without faces," he says, because faces are indicators of the capacity to suffer. Et cetera. Mercifully, Angelo does not partake of this delicate theology. He seems the perfect person to guide our author into the dark underworld of hunting because for Angelo, hunting's *raison d'être* has everything to do with sharing with others the good food he has obtained and processed himself. He hunts ducks and wild pigs. He makes prosciutto, salami, and paté. He forages for mushrooms, fennel, and rapini. He makes wine and cures olives. And Angelo's talk, free of campy irony, flows like a tonic:

> For me it is all about the eating. Not the sport. I am not what you call a trophy hunter. I take what I need, enough to make a nice dinner for me and my friends, maybe some salami, a prosciutto, but then: That's it, I go home.

And:

> I have the passion of cooking, pickling, curing salamis, sausage, making wine in the fall. This is my life. I do this with my friends. It is to my heart.

■ ■ ■

In a section called "Vegan Utopia," Pollan sorts out the ethical considerations that undergird veganism and various notions about animal rights, and tries to square all that with biological reality. "If our goal is to kill as few animals as possible," he writes, "people should probably try to eat the largest possible animal that can live on the least cultivated land: grass-finished steaks for everyone." Aside from the quip, there's some sense here. And by this standard, Alaskans may be in the vanguard of animal rights metaphysics (who'd have thought?). But we do eat some mighty large animals, like whale and moose (even their names signify colossality), and they all flourish on the least cultivated land.

There is also the matter of what is being called "food security." A recent study has shown that a staggering 95 percent of the $2 billion of food Alaskans buy is imported. Even when Alaskans buy seafood caught in Alaska, it has often been shipped a thousand miles to Seattle for processing, then a thousand miles back to sell. More and more, Alaska salmon is frozen and exported to China, where it is thawed, processed, refrozen, packaged, and shipped back to be sold in the USA, a round-trip of more than 8,000 miles. All these supply chains are extremely long and potentially vulnerable, coming by ship, airplane, and truck from the Lower 48, Mexico, South America, Asia, and Europe. Against $2 billion in food imports, Alaska home-grown farm products accounted for a mere $59 million in sales in 2012. By far, the most important source of local food in Alaska—worth $500 million in replacement cost—is wild food gathered by people for their own use.[17] Four percent of that comes from wild plants, the other 96 percent from animals. And none of those animals were ever caged or fenced; none were injected with anything; the food is not industrially processed; the supply lines are short; the associated costs are minimal. Lay it out, and the ethical equation pretty well solves itself.

Within our fervent national colloquy on food—veganism, vegetarianism, speciesism, locavorism, carbon footprint—Alaska's food story has gone unnoticed. That's too bad, because not every logic that answers for life in the lower states can withstand a reality check as fierce as Alaska's. You might say that Alaska is the place to bring your proposition if you want to give it a *reductio ad absurdum* test. Reckoning with Alaskans' food realities requires of food moralists a new understanding of the hunter's relationship with nature and with food. In fact, it requires the *old* understanding. Because too often food evangelists dismiss as alien that which is traditional, economical, healthy, and wise.

---

17   Meter and Phillips, p. 35–37.

BIBLIOGRAPHY

Dante Alighieri. *Dante's Inferno*. Translated by Mark Musa. Bloomington: Indiana University Press, 1971.

Leopold, Aldo. "Wildlife in American Culture," in *A Sand County Almanac*, Ballantine Books, New York, 1990, p. 213.

Meter, Ken, and Goldenberg, M. P. *Building Food Security in Alaska*, Alaska Department of Health and Social Services, 2014.

Nelson, Richard. *The Island Within*, North Point Press, San Francisco, 1989.

Ortega Y Gasset, José. *Meditations on Hunting*. New York: Scribner, 1972.

Pollan, Michael. *The Omnivore's Dilemma*, The Penguin Press, New York, 2006.

Singer, Peter. *Animal Liberation*, Harper Collins, New York, 2002 ed.

A Note from Leighton M. Quarles

I had no idea when I started my MA in Northern Studies at UAF in 2008 that the intense, hilarious professor in the T-shirt and sport coat would become a close family friend. To say he has changed my life would be trite. Of course he has. Terrence is the most selfless person that I've ever met; he's always on the lookout and goes out of his way to provide opportunities for others. He gave me my start in public history, and also tirelessly encouraged my wife in her library career. Terrence has a way of making you feel like you can accomplish anything if you would just pay attention and get after it, and you know he'll be there to help you along the way. His calling cards are his sense of humor and unflagging curiosity (he's just about the most irrepressible person I've ever met), but I will remember most his generosity and the way that he lifts up others. When my wife was pregnant, we decided right away that if it were a boy we would give him the middle name Terrence because we wanted our child to have the wonderful qualities that Terrence embodies to us. We had a girl, so that went out the window. But to honor my friend I will do my best to lift up others, help them see in themselves what they can't, and support them and cheer them to success any way I can, as Terrence did for me. Even if he still hasn't forgiven me for calling Pierre Berton's classic *The Klondike Fever* a literary trainwreck.

SITE SUMMIT

Preserving a Cold War Legacy Property

Leighton M. Quarles

The following presents the historic preservation of an Alaskan Cold War military property, Nike Site Summit. This chapter presents historical context for the Nike missile, a brief operational history, a discussion of Cold War historic preservation more broadly—and finally, a comparison of Site Summit's historic preservation with that of another Nike site no longer in military hands. This research followed two tracks: the contextual track traces the history of the weapons system the site was built to house, its purpose, its operational cycle, and, to an extent, the broader Cold War context that elucidates both why a Nike missile site would be built and why it should be preserved. The second track recounts the preservation process, the players involved, and the reasons invoked to preserve the facilities. The project invites a much more comprehensive examination of military historic preservation in Alaska, a state so impacted by the military-industrial complex that geographer Laurel J. Hummel described it as a "militarized landscape."[1] And what better proof of that assertion than the examination of a missile site extensively incorporated into the municipality of Anchorage's cultural life?

For a conflict that never entered a phase of active aggression, the Cold War left an enormous physical record across North America.

---

1   Hummel, Laurel J. "The U.S. Military as Geographical Agent: The Case of Cold War Alaska." *Geographical Review* 95, no. 1 (January 2005), 47–72, 47.

This extensive military-built environment has prompted many studies while posing developers both obstacles and opportunities. Fort Douglas, Utah, provides an excellent example: the University of Utah took over and preserved an entire military installation, adaptively reusing it in partnership with the federal government, the preservation community, and the Church of Jesus Christ of Latter Day Saints. The Presidio in San Francisco represents a larger example. The architect, planner, or developer ought to be aware of military properties in general, and Cold War sites in particular, due to their proliferation across the country, their potential historical significance, and the possibilities for adaptive reuse, which range from simple preservation and interpretation to wilder schemes, including the reuse of ICBM silos for private homes. Moreover, as this narrative will demonstrate, anyone interested in making use of a property like Site Summit should recognize the labyrinthine and lengthy process involved in preserving, modifying, or even demolishing any historic property on military land.

HISTORICAL CONTEXT

An examination of the historic preservation of a Nike missile site requires consideration of the historical context. Nike sites are merely a tiny component of a vast physical record that the gargantuan spending contest and game of brinksmanship known as the Cold War left behind. The United States lavished billions of dollars not only on offensive weapons systems and overseas adventures in containment, but also on elaborate defensive networks. The Nike surface-to-air missile sprang from and soon fell victim to a need to keep up with continuous air power innovations. Conceived as a "last line of defense" designed to protect ground sites from nuclear attack by Soviet bombers—an especially tangible threat between the late 1940s and the early 1960s, when the Soviets developed intercontinental ballistic missiles and rendered the program obsolete—Nike, developed on contract to the U.S. Army by Western Electric and Douglas Aircraft, reflected the technological peak of the bomber-interception mission foremost in defense planners' minds during the 1950s.

The first Nike system entered service in 1954, spurred by the Berlin Crisis, the Korean War, and the 1949 revelation that the Soviets indeed possessed nuclear weapons. Named Nike Ajax, the missile replaced all conventional anti-aircraft artillery by 1958.[2] Supersonic and with a ceiling of sixty thousand feet, Nike rendered anti-aircraft guns of any type obsolete.[3] The Nike Ajax never arrived in Alaska, but its successor served there from 1959 into the 1970s.

Even as sites around the United States received the Ajax, the next-generation Nike appeared and soon replaced it. The new nuclear-capable Nike Hercules could engage a 1,500-knot maneuvering aircraft, at ranges up to eighty-five nautical miles and altitudes exceeding eighty thousand feet. Moreover, it could be pressed into service as a short-range surface-to-surface missile and could be made semi-mobile.[4] By the mid-1960s, Nike Hercules had replaced its smaller, conventional predecessor and was already on its way to phase-out in favor of even newer missiles. In Alaska, Nike Hercules remained operational until 1979.

NIKE EMPLACEMENT IN ALASKA

The first Alaska Nike facility, Site Bay outside Anchorage, opened in March 1959. By May, sites Point and Summit, also at Anchorage, and sites Jig, Peter, Tare, and Mike near Fairbanks, were operational. The last, Site Love at Fairbanks, came online in 1960. These eight sites with nine batteries (analogous to companies) served as the Alaskan Command's entire air defense artillery complement. The Army, rather than the Air Force, oversaw Nike and other "point-defense" weapons,

---

2   Unless otherwise noted, the following extensive detail is found in Denfeld, D. Colt. *Nike Missile Defenses in Alaska: 1958–1979. U.S. Army Corps of Engineers Alaska District*, January 1988. The prolific Dr. Denfeld's name appears, it seems, on half the cultural resources documents produced in Alaska between the 1970s and 1990s. Denfeld, D. Colt. *Nike Missile Defenses in Alaska: 1958–1970*. Anchorage: US Army Corps of Engineers, 1988, 2.

3   Alaskan Air Command History, 1 January–30 June 1958. Elmendorf AFB, Alaska, 16.

4   Alaska Command History, 1 January–30 June 1958, Elmendorf AFB, Alaska, 16.

A Nike Hercules missile test fires at Site Summit. *US Army photo.*

and its Air Defense Group directed two missile battalions, stationed at Fort Wainwright and Fort Richardson. Fort Wainwright supplied logistical support for the 2nd Missile Battalion, 562nd Artillery. Fort Richardson supported the 4th (redesignated the 1st in 1972) Missile Battalion, 43rd Artillery.[5]

Site Summit and Site Peter in Fairbanks were the only two Nike Hercules batteries in the United States to conduct live-fire exercises, and launched missiles at both computer-generated points and tiny drones. The year 1964 saw the last Site Summit live fire.[6] Historian William J. Seidler summarizes the significance of the Nike package overall:

> Nike Hercules sites were critical elements in the overall U.S. air defense network. They provided a demanding American public a technologically advanced defense against Soviet bombers striking the American heartland [...]

---

5   Denfeld, *Alaskan Air Command History*, 1 July–31 December 1956, 10.
6   Denfeld, 2.

Nike combined Cold War cutting edge technologies of computer-
ization, rocketry, and nuclear warheads into a lethal weapon
system.[7]

Technology during the Cold War advanced so rapidly that the Nike
system, designed to intercept bombers and emplaced in an age of
ICBMs, was obsolete by the time it was fully deployed.[8] And thanks
to the 1972 Salt II agreement with the Soviet Union, the new Patriot
anti-ballistic missile platforms achieved only limited placement. The
Army shuttered the final Nike batteries in Alaska in May 1979, some
of the last decommissioned in the United States.[9]

THE NIKE LEGACY

Although Nike Hercules operations ended in Alaska in 1979, the program's legacy remains in the form of physical properties. Alaska sites
came to various ends. Many were looted, and most were later demolished or repurposed by military and civilian agencies. Sites Peter and
Mike, on military land near Fairbanks, have vanished. The Army Corps
of Engineers and the Fairbanks North Star Borough retain the first
and second launch buildings at the former Site Tare near Fairbanks,
along with a warhead storage igloo. The Battery Control facilities at
Site Bay served from 1983 to 1986 as a minimum-security prison for
the Alaska Department of Corrections. By 2008, Site Bay had joined
hundreds of other disused and partially demolished relics of Alaska's
Cold War built environment. Only its abandoned, crumbling rein-
forced concrete components remained.[10] Lastly, Site Point became

---

7   Seidler, William J. *The Coldest Front: Cold War Military Properties in Alaska.*
Draft. Anchorage: Alaska Department of History and Archeology, 1996, 28.

8   Hollinger, Kristy. *Nike Hercules Operations in Alaska: 1959–1979.*
Conservation Branch, Directorate of Public Works, U.S. Army Garrison Alaska,
July 2004, 61.

9   Alaska Office of History and Archaeology, Department of Natural
Resources. Site Summit Nike Hercules Missile Installation. Anchorage, Alaska,
June 1996, 15.

10   Site Bay, Alaska. Charlie Battery of the Last Operational U.S. Nike-
Hercules Missile Battalion. http://nikealaska.org/bay/sitebay.html.

Anchorage's Kincaid Park, with some of its buildings remaining intact.[11] Due to its status as the only remaining complete Nike facility, Site Summit, 12.5 miles from Anchorage, joined the National Register of Historic Places (NRHP) in 1996.[12]

NIKE SITE FACILITIES

The two Nike Hercules sites in Alaska left a significant imprint on the landscape, comprising as many as thirty buildings spread over the two adjoined sites. Patterns varied according to terrain, but typically extended over two separate areas: the launch area and the battery control area. The launch area included two structures to house and launch missiles; a building for operations and launch control; missile maintenance and motor repair shops; a warhead magazine; a fuse and detonator magazine; and dog kennels. An alarmed double fence and constant dog patrols protected active sites. The battery control area contained the operations building, which housed missile tracking and target tracking radars; barracks; and a High Power Acquisition Radar (HIPAR) building, with its accompanying radar and repair shop. The system required a specific line of sight, dictating that the battery control area be at a higher elevation than the launch control area. Alaska military facilities differ from those in the Lower 48 in that they are designed to operate in much harsher conditions. Nike batteries were no exception, particularly at Site Summit, which featured distinctive clamshell covers for radar, heated concrete launch aprons, and utilidors to permit easy access to and maintenance of utilities and communications equipment. Owing to permafrost conditions, launchers were built aboveground.[13] These Nike sites were no small operations. As many as 125 personnel operated a Nike site at any given time. The

---

11   Hollinger, 63–64.
12   Site Summit Retention Plan, Fort Richardson, Alaska. Anchorage, Alaska: CH2M Hill, August 2010.
13   Denfeld, 11.

Site Summit's Integrated Fire Control/Battery Fire Control Area. Note extensive terrain leveling. *US Air Force Photo.*

batteries were on alert twenty-four hours a day, with shifts of over fifty people onsite.[14]

Site Summit on Joint Base Elmendorf Richardson, adjacent to Anchorage, is the archetypal Alaska Nike site. Situated on the southwest flank of Mount Gordon Lyon at between 3,100 and 3,900 feet elevation, it overlooks the city and the military installation. A 1.5-mile gravel road connects an Upper Site and a Lower Site. Patti-McDonald Company, M-B Contracting Company, and Connelly Construction Company built Site Summit over two summers, beginning in May 1957 and culminating in September 1958. Contractors blew sixty feet off a mountain peak to make room for the Integrated

---

14   Hollinger, 39. Kristy Hollinger's 2004 historic context for the U.S. Army Garrison, Alaska, goes far beyond mere building and manpower documentation or even Cold War big-picture themes and captures the rich social history of Alaskan Nike battery life.

Fire Control Area/Battery Control Area, and placed the Missile Launch and Storage Area on a leveled ridge nearby. This significant terrain alteration left Site Summit a prominent, visible feature of the Anchorage skyline.

Site Summit is distinctive for another reason, one that continues today. Since 1960, the Army Garrison, Alaska (USAGAK), has displayed an illuminated five-pointed star on the mountainside just below the lower site. Demonstrating the military establishment's connection with the community, the Army lights the star in a ceremony coincident to the Anchorage Christmas tree lighting festivities, and keeps it lit until the conclusion of the Iditarod Trail Sled Dog Race in March.[15] The star itself has not been considered for inclusion on the National Register, perhaps because most of the preservation process for Site Summit occurred before the fifty-year eligibility marker.[16] However, it remains as proof of the Nike facility's link with the community and helps explain locals' attachment to what is otherwise one of a great many Cold War relics in Alaska.

PRESERVING COLD WAR MILITARY PROPERTIES

Alaska has a significant number of Cold War properties throughout the state, many of which, regardless of their historical significance, have been demolished or are returning quietly and messily to nature. Site Summit's selection and inclusion on the NRHP makes more sense when viewed in the context of the broader national push to save Cold War artifacts, and the priorities assigned thereto. After its closure in 1979, Site Summit languished until the mid-1990s. The Army used it for occasional training operations, and despite its

---

15 "Star at Arctic Valley Sheds Light on Anchorage's Holiday Season." *Alaska Dispatch*, 30 November 2013. https://www.alaskadispatch.com/article/20131130/star-arctic-valley-sheds-light-anchorages-holiday-season.

16 The "fifty year rule," established in the Historic Sites Act of 1935, has a long list of exceptions. Presidential and nuclear sites are automatically eligible for inclusion on the National Register regardless of age. For a thoughtful discussion see John H. Sprinkle, Jr., "Of Exceptional Importance: The Origins of the 'Fifty Year Rule' in Historic Preservation," *The Public Historian* 29, no. 2 (Spring 2007), 81–103.

location on what was then Fort Richardson, the site was extensively vandalized. Severe weather, always a potentiality in Alaska, further degraded the property. Site Summit's trajectory changed, however, with the end of the Cold War. Well shy of the standard fifty-year minimum cutoff for listing on the NRHP, the registry identified Site Summit in 1996 as "an outstanding example of a Cold War era Nike Hercules missile site."[17]

Its timeline played a significant role in the site's nomination. No sooner had the Cold War ended than Congress instructed the Department of Defense to "inventory, protect, and conserve" the enormous physical and cultural resources left behind.[18] To that end, the Legacy Resource Management Program was written into the 1991 DoD Appropriations Act. DoD promptly established the Cold War Task Area, which consulted scholars and other knowledgeable people, made site visits all over the country, and determined what to preserve and how to preserve it. These activities consumed much of the early 1990s and significantly expanded the NRHP. In Alaska, the Legacy Resource Management Program worked with the Alaska Department of History and Archaeology to produce an initial statewide survey, *The Coldest Front: Cold War Military Properties in Alaska*. Site Summit escaped the fifty-year cutoff for a specific reason: while only 3 percent of properties in the NRHP were listed before the fifty-year mark, a disproportional number were related to missiles and nuclear facilities.[19] Indeed, Site Summit relates to both—having been designed to protect American cities from nuclear bombs, and using nuclear-capable surface-to-air missiles, Nike sites were clearly eligible. Moreover, in relation to Cold War resources, the fifty-year marker may have impeded preservation of the nation's heritage. As the authors of a definitive DoD report on the Legacy Project argue, "Even though the Cold War ended only recently, it was unquestionably of exceptional importance in our Nation's history. Experience

---

17   Friends of Nike Site Summit, www.nikesitesummit.net.

18   *Coming in from the Cold: Military Heritage in the Cold War.* Report on the Department of Defense Legacy Cold War Project. Washington, DC: Department of Defense, 1996, 35.

19   *Coming In,* 15.

shows that waiting 50 years before engaging in historic preservation activities would result in the loss of many historic resources."[20] One need look no further than the other Nike sites in Alaska to find confirmation. Nearly all other Nike sites have been demolished or are deteriorating. A notable exception is Anchorage's Kincaid Park.

SITE POINT/KINCAID PARK: AN EXAMPLE OF ADAPTIVE REUSE

The former Site Point in Anchorage, deactivated in 1979, is the best-preserved Alaska Nike site other than Summit. It was released to the Municipality of Anchorage in 1980 under the Federal Land Surplus Act, and over the 1980s was incorporated into a large outdoor recreation area, known as Kincaid Park.[21] The Integrated Fire Control area has been demolished, but most of the launch area buildings remain intact. Four launch structures, the warhead storage igloo, two ammunition storage bunkers, and a launch control building are all in good shape. The municipality has taken no steps to disguise the park's origins. Indeed, Kincaid Park's landscape designers have consciously replicated the original functional design of Site Point's facilities in the angular shape of other park buildings. The bunkers once used to house ordnance and military equipment now house skis and recreation equipment, and are used for events from weddings to fashion shows.[22] In her 2004 historic context for the U.S. Army Garrison, Alaska, historian Kristy Hollinger asserted that Kincaid Park's Nike site, due to the condition of its buildings and its accessible location, showed "excellent potential for historic interpretation."[23] Such work lies in the future.

---

20 *Coming In*, 52.
21 "Kincaid Park." Parks Department, Municipality of Anchorage. http://www.muni.org/Departments/parks/Pages/Kincaid%20Park%201.pdf.
22 Dunham, Mike. "Soul of Kincaid Park: Landscape Architecture Transforms Old Missile Sites into Beloved Public Park." *Anchorage Daily News*, 1 April 2007. http://www.adn.com/2007/04/01/151102/soul-of-kincaid-park.html.
23 Hollinger, 64.

PRESERVATION OF OTHER NIKE SITES

Due to Nike sites' closure in the 1970s and their locations in and around cities, which hastened selloff and demolition, the Legacy program came too late for most. As early as 1991, the Army Corps of Engineers, New England Division, had already formulated a programmatic agreement to survey Nike sites in the Northeast before they disappeared.[24] Similar Historic American Building Survey/Historic American Engineering Record surveys were being conducted throughout the country by the mid-1990s. In Alaska, the Corps of Engineers began a long-term documentation project for all Cold War sites, including Nike facilities.

In 1998, only two years after Site Summit was listed and the glacial process of actually preserving it commenced, Nike Site SF-88 in San Francisco was preserved and interpreted, the first and currently only Nike site to achieve that distinction.[25] And yet, construction-wise, SF-88 is far less remarkable than Site Summit, due to the engineering innovations prompted by its Arctic conditions.

THE PRESERVATION PROCESS FOR SITE SUMMIT

Listing Site Summit on the NRHP in 1996 did not guarantee its survival. Over the following thirteen years, plans were developed to retain and revamp the facility. Certain fundamental concerns delayed the process and made the retention of Site Summit more difficult than originally anticipated. Its location presented serious challenges. Site Summit lies on currently used military land, and its access road crosses a live fire range. Moreover, the events of September 11, 2001, heightened concerns about base security, and the Army rejected free civilian access to its property. For the same reason, the Army declined to allow a civilian agency to operate the site alone. Funding posed a major obstacle to preserving and managing Site Summit.

---

24 *Coming In*, 44.
25 Martini, John A., and Stephen A. Haller. *What We Have We Shall Defend: An Interim History and Preservation Plan for Nike Site SF-88L, Fort Barry, California.* National Park Service Golden Gate National Recreation Area, San Francisco, California, 1998, vi.

The Army and the Alaska State Historic Preservation Officer produced a number of documents and weighed various options, but real progress in preserving Site Summit came with the Army's 2008 *Final Finding of No Significant Impact and Environmental Assessment, Management of Nike Site Summit*. Seeking to implement a management strategy that met training needs, prevented vandalism, protected health, and complied with Section 106 of the National Historic Preservation Act, the Army proposed four options, ranging from no action to full demolition.[26] While their preferred course of action was "selective retention," which involved demolishing twelve buildings, the *Final Finding* demonstrated the military's interest in preserving the bulk of Site Summit.[27] In early 2007 the Army met with federal, state, and tribal governments, informed them of an agency scoping meeting, and solicited comments. Shortly thereafter, they published notices in Alaska newspapers with the same goal.

PUBLIC PARTICIPATION

Public participation in the scoping process demonstrated the community's interest in the Site Summit retention project and helped secure its success. Eighty-seven comments were received during the scoping period, mostly from the general public and Nike veterans. Public comment focused on preserving Site Summit for two reasons: first, "to keep Site Summit's rich heritage and unique role

---

26 Section 106 of the National Historic Preservation Act of 1966 lies behind most Army—indeed, most federal agencies'—interest in documenting historic sites. The Act "requires Federal agencies to take into account the effects of their undertakings on historic properties, and afford the Advisory Council on Historic Preservation a reasonable opportunity to comment." Its intended effect is to prevent careless destruction of property and foster consultation between the agency considering a change to its property, the State Historic Preservation Officer, the Advisory Council on Historic Preservation, and the public. Advisory Council on Historic Preservation, Section 106 Regulations Summary. http://www.achp.gov/106summary.html; King, Thomas F. *Cultural Resource Laws and Practice*. Lanham, MD: AltaMira Press, 2013, 105–7.

27 *Final Finding of No Significant Impact and Environmental Assessment, Management of Nike Site Summit*. Fort Richardson: Department of the Army, United States Army Garrison, Alaska, 2008, 2.

in the Cold War"; and second, to educate and entertain the Anchorage public and tourists. Moreover, individual commenters addressed preservation to remedy what was increasingly seen as a "visual eyesore" and expressed hope that the site would become a state or national park.[28] Government agencies, including the National Park Service (NPS), Alaska Office of History and Archaeology, Bureau of Land Management, and Municipality of Anchorage expressed support, and the municipality offered its assistance in creating preservation, interpretation, and recreational resources for the area. The comment process, and especially remarks from NPS and Alaska's State Historic Preservation Officer (SHPO), spurred the Army to begin Section 106 consultation.[29] Two key outcomes resulted from the Army's *Final Finding*: first, the scoping process made the issue of whether to save Site Summit a public one, and second, the Army document spurred the Army to ask NPS to review its findings.

The National Park Service, after thorough surveys of all the twenty-seven buildings at Site Summit, determined that nine of the twelve proposed for demolition could be stabilized. They reluctantly concluded that the other three buildings' loss could be mitigated through interpretation. Interestingly, the entire exchange with NPS occurred under Section 213 of the NHPA, though on an "informal" footing. Section 213 is reserved for problematic or controversial situations, and allows the Advisory Council on Historic Preservation (ACHP) to request the Secretary of the Interior's input. The copious NPS documentation bears no mention of any controversy. Indeed, it hardly seems to fit Section 213 at all. Far from indicating a problem, using Section 213 seems to have been a clever bureaucratic method of coordinating multiagency support and, by ensuring the NPS and ACHP would work together, preventing needless complexity. It also demonstrates a pleasing level of cooperation between the Army, the NPS, and the ACHP.[30] Indeed, the NPS report and subsequent negotiations

---

28 *Final Finding*, 1-9.

29 *Final Finding*, 1-10–1-11.

30 The agreement's authors are coy about Section 213, and spend over a page explaining its fortuitous if mysterious use. Using Section 213 evidently permitted the NPS to work more closely with the ACHP in its role as special advisor to

between the Army and other interested parties ensured the Site Summit retention plan's success.

Site Summit's future was assured when, in 2009, the Army entered into a Programmatic Agreement (PA) to save the facility. DoD frequently uses Programmatic Agreements to meet NHPA compliance requirements. These agreements are multilateral, and involve a government agency, the State Historic Preservation Officer, and the AC.[31] The PA engaged the NPS, the SHPO, the Alaska Association for Historic Preservation, the ACHP, the National Trust, numerous other organizations including the Native Village of Eklutna, and, significantly, a civilian volunteer organization, the Friends of Nike Site Summit (FONSS), affiliated with the SHPO, NPS, and the Alaska Veterans Museum.[32] FONSS agreed to "stabilize and restore" five buildings themselves. In 2010, the Department of Defense created Joint Base Elmendorf Richardson from Elmendorf Air Force Base and Fort Richardson.[33] The Air Force, as base operator, assumed the Army's responsibility for the project. Restoration work began in 2010, with JBER providing security and working to restore the rest of the buildings.[34] In fall 2012, the first public tour took place.[35]

---

the Site Summit restoration process. "Evaluation of the Impact of the US Army's Proposed Management Strategy on Nike Site Summit Historic District and Recommendations for the Avoidance, Minimization, and Mitigation of Adverse Effects." Anchorage: National Park Service, Alaska District, 2008, 1–3.

31 *Coming In*, 16.

32 AK-MOA-270, Programmatic Agreement Among the United States Department of the Army, The Alaska Historic Preservation Officer, and the Advisory Council on Historic Preservation Regarding Management of Nike Site Summit Historic District at Fort Richardson, Alaska, 2009.

33 JBER is the product of 2005's Base Realignment and Closure Commission recommendation and joins a number of other joint bases. Newcomers. Joint Base Elmendorf Richardson. http://www.jber.jb.mil/Info/Newcomers/.

34 "Nike Site Summit: A Piece of History Worth Preserving." Joint Base Elmendorf Richardson. http://www.jber.jb.mil/Services-Resources/Environmental/Nike/Restoration.aspx.

35 Friends of Nike Site Summit. http://www.nikesitesummit.net/.

CONCLUSION

This history of the establishment and preservation of Site Summit proves instructive in several ways. For developers and military personnel, the history illustrates the sheer complexity and tediousness of the historic preservation process. "There is no doubt," the NPS report of 2008 asserts, "about the significance of Nike Site Summit." And yet thirteen years passed before the preservation program came to fruition. Moreover, the final programmatic agreement between the Army and various parties relied heavily on the restoration efforts of a volunteer group. Not only is the process slow, but funding may not support the full implementation of the Legacy project or other national heritage–oriented preservation projects. Municipal or local governments might find the example of Kincaid Park, an undertaking completed without the burden of multiple levels of consultation, more appealing.

For community interest groups, however, Site Summit presents a heartening example of cooperation between the military, the National Park Service, state and city governments, and civilians. A notable absence of acrimony on all sides marked the Site Summit retention process. Even the Army officials, who might be forgiven for simply wanting to demolish the entire site to protect post boundaries and facilitate training programs, wanted to keep at least some of Site Summit open. Likewise, the local NPS branch went out of their way to conduct an unofficial Section 213 consult with the Army, rather than simply referring the matter to Washington, D.C.

This project is hardly complete. Future research could provide a better-rounded comparison between community reuse projects and military or joint preservation efforts under the umbrella of the NHPA. Meanwhile, the city of Anchorage enjoys a well preserved "militarized landscape" that offers multiple lessons for the student of historic preservation.

BIBLIOGRAPHY (PARTIAL)

AK-MOA-270, Programmatic Agreement Among the United States Department of the Army, the Alaska Historic Preservation Officer, and the Advisory Council on Historic Preservation Regarding Management of Nike Site Summit Historic District at Fort Richardson, Alaska, 2009. http://www.nikesitesummit.org/Received%20Documents/Programmit %20Agreement.pdf.

Alaska Office of History and Archaeology, Department of Natural Resources. *Site Summit Nike Hercules Missile Installation.* Anchorage, June 1996.

Coming in from the Cold: Military Heritage in the Cold War. Report on the Department of Defense Legacy Cold War Project. Washington, D.C: Department of Defense, 1996.

Dunham, Mike. "Soul of Kincaid Park: Landscape Architecture Transforms Old Missile Sites into Beloved Public Park." *Anchorage Daily News*, 1 April 2007. http://www.adn.com/2007/04/01/151102/soul-of-kincaid-park.html.

Final Finding of No Significant Impact and Environmental Assessment, Management of Nike Site Summit.

Forthollinger, Kristy. *Nike Hercules Operations in Alaska: 1959–1979.* Conservation Branch, Directorate of Public Works, U.S. Army Garrison Alaska, July 2004.

Hummel, Laurel J. "The U.S. Military as Geographical Agent: The Case of Cold War Alaska." *Geographical Review* 95, no. 1 (January 2005), 47–72.

King, Thomas F. *Cultural Resource Laws and Practice.* Lanham, MD: AltaMira Press, 2013.

Martini, John A., and Haller, S. A. *What We Have We Shall Defend: An Interim History and Preservation Plan for Nike Site SF-88L, Fort Barry, California.* National Park Service Golden Gate National Recreation Area, San Francisco, California, 1998.

Richardson, AK: Department of the Army, United States Army Garrison, Alaska, 2008.

Seidler, William J. *The Coldest Front: Cold War Military Properties in Alaska.* Draft. Anchorage: Alaska Department of History and Archaeology, 1996.

Site Summit Retention Plan, Fort Richardson, Alaska. Anchorage: CH2M Hill, August 2010.

A Note from Katherine Ringsmuth

I entered the Northern Studies master's program in 1998. That year I took my first Alaska history course with Terrence, who'd always been popular with graduate students. To convince him to be my advisor, I theatrically donned fish slimer bibs, rain boots, hairnet, and cannery cap to present my class research paper, aptly titled "Red Gold: Fish and Fishing on the Naknek River." Terrence found my presentation hysterical and spirited (if a little gutsy). He agreed to take me on as his student, which led to even more crazy stories and memories. Twenty years later, the subject of that paper has become the focus of my academic pursuits, culminating with the <NN> Cannery History Project, launched in 2015. Through it all, Terrence has been there to help me keep my sense of humor, support my unorthodox approaches, and has ceaselessly served as my mentor and friend.

THE \<NN\> CANNERY HISTORY PROJECT

Documenting Cannery Work, People, and Place

Katherine Ringsmuth

Open the page and let the stories crawl in by themselves.
> —John Steinbeck, *Cannery Row*

The \<NN\> Cannery History Project is a three-tiered collaboration between the Alaska Association for Historic Preservation (AAHP), Tundra Vision: Public History Consultants, University of Alaska Fairbanks (UAF), National Park Service (NPS), the Office of History and Archaeology (OHA), the Alaska State Museum (ASM), Trident Seafoods, and local Bristol Bay groups to collect, share, and preserve the stories of the diverse, and often invisible, cannery workers whose activities are reflected by and embedded in the industrial landscape contained within the historic \<NN\> Cannery at South Naknek, Alaska. Whether they came from China, the Philippines, or simply upriver, cannery people found dignity through their laborious interactions and forged a deep connection to the surrounding environment. Their diverse traditions left a mark on Alaska history and culture. Their work mattered.

The \<NN\> Cannery History Project is a public history endeavor that infuses education, preservation, and interpretation with community engagement, and it does what the National Historic Preservation Act aspires to do: inspire, benefit, and remember the voices of the people.

<NN> Cannery at South Naknek, Alaska, ca. 1980. *Courtesy of Gary Johnson.*

The <NN> Cannery History Project aims to meet three objectives by 2021:

- List the <NN> Cannery complex at South Naknek in the National Register of Historic Places;
- Develop a digital storytelling pilot program that teaches local students to craft films based on cannery work and culture, in order to stimulate community participation and project longevity; and
- Curate and design a traveling exhibition with the Alaska State Museum (ASM) called *Mug-Up* to ensure that the lives of cannery people will be better understood and valued by the general public.

The relationship between cannery and community cannot be overstated. The <NN> Cannery supported thousands of residents, transient workers, and fishermen, and gave each a unique identity and lifeway. The cannery connects Bristol Bay to an extensive community web, and its closure in 2016 marked the end of an era. Collectively, the project's three objectives will create from the cannery's slow erosion a "humanities" community and present to the public an introspective, unique, and colorful depiction of cannery peoples' lifeways and history—to do as Steinbeck once wrote: "To open the page and let the stories crawl in by themselves."

PROJECT BACKGROUND

The <NN> Cannery is situated on the south side of the Naknek River, one of the five major waterways that constitute the Bristol Bay salmon fishery—Alaska's largest and most sustainable commercial fishery. Tides fronting the cannery ebb and flow twenty-two feet twice a day, pushing by waves of salmon, destined for natural streams radiating from the Naknek Lake system located approximately twenty miles upriver. Just as the strong runs of salmon supported canneries, the salmon provided a stable resource for Native communities. Packers Creek, which runs beneath the cannery and intersects the historic property, stands out for its archaeological potential to shed light on the region's Indigenous past, due to its proximity to the coast, confluence with the Naknek River, and source of reliable freshwater.

For over a century, the San Francisco–based Alaska Packers Association's (APA) <NN> Cannery served as the centerpiece of the Bristol Bay salmon fishery. Because the facility endured neither fire nor reconstruction, and functioned almost continuously between 1895 and 2015, it has maintained architectural integrity and remains one of the most historically significant remnants of the industry on the West Coast. APA dominated Alaska's salmon market, accounting for 70 percent of the total salmon pack.[1] As one expert put it, "Canneries

---

1 Steven Haycox, *Alaska, an American Colony* (Seattle: University of Washington Press, 2002), 241.

transformed this entire area and represent the Industrial Revolution of the North."[2] APA assigned for the cannery the initials NN, possibly for NakNek, and drew a diamond (an accounting symbol called a chevron signifying "at") around the cannery abbreviations—hence, APA's well-known trademark: the diamond canneries.

For over 120 seasons, the <NN> Cannery brought together a mix of people: Chinese, Japanese, Filipinos, Croatians, Italians, Scandinavians, Unungan, Alutiiq, and Dena'ina, men as well as women, the young and the seasoned. APA employed mostly immigrants from Europe to gillnet salmon in double-ender sailboats in the early days. These men were from fishing nations like Italy, Croatia, Greece, Norway, and Sweden. Others came from Germany, Russia, Algeria—even as far away as Australia.[3] Besides fishing, skilled immigrants built both the cannery and the salmon boats. To process the salmon, the cannery hired Asian crews—first from China, then Japan, and later the Philippines. Indigenous Alaskans also worked at the cannery, becoming major contributors to and caretakers of the operation. APA's <NN> Cannery in South Naknek is historically significant because the structures, objects, and the industrial landscape collectively tell the story of these varied yet forgotten people.

In 2015, a contingent of Alaska historians, curators, filmmakers, and culture bearers, led by the public history consultant company Tundra Vision, came together with the goal of preserving the history of the 128-year-old <NN> Cannery in South Naknek, Alaska, which had been slated for closure and ultimately abandonment by the facility's current owners, Trident Seafoods. In November 2016, Trident authorized the launch of the <NN> Cannery History Project. In January 2017, the Alaska Association of Historic Preservation (AAHP) 501(c)(3) agreed to add the <NN> Cannery History Project to its programs, fulfilling the project's administrative and fiduciary duties.

---

2   Alan Boraas, "Turning Point: Photo Exhibition." *Peninsula Clarion*, November 21, 1996.

3   Bob King, "Iron Men of Bristol Bay," Alaska Historical Society Blog, posted December 7, 1015.

Thanks to the technical assistance provided by NPS, initial field-work begun in summer 2016 resulted in the completion of a Building Inventory and Assessment of the site's fifty-plus buildings. In 2017, fieldwork assignments consisted of collecting Alaska Historic Resource Survey data, conducting an archeological resource survey, interviewing former cannery workers, and consulting local residents about the project during a "Mug-Up Community Conversation" session at the South Naknek Library. To date, the <NN> Cannery History Project has produced a seven-minute interpretive video, been reported on by print and radio media, participated in numerous public engagement events, and developed an interactive project website.

In summer 2018, our team will return to the site with museum curators to collect both artifacts and recently discovered APA records (which will be accessioned into the Alaska State Archives), while a National Park Service's historic architect will scan the "White House," one of the cannery's most historically significant buildings. High-definition laser scanning is a fairly new technology used to help cultural resource practitioners accurately document large sites and structures that would otherwise be too expensive or time-consuming using traditional methods. The scanner can capture small-scale architectural features and details while simultaneously scanning large objects and site context within a 360-degree radius. These capabilities, paired with the fact that it can be operated by one person, make it a cost-effective and powerful tool for easily capturing large datasets in a short period of time. The resulting data from a single scan position is a three-dimensional representation (or "point cloud") of the surrounding area, and can be used for interpretive purposes, developing architectural and engineering drawings, facility maintenance, and heritage documentation projects.

Besides the technical assistance supplied by NPS, financial support for the <NN> Cannery History Project has come from multiple sources. Between August 2017 and December 2017, the National Endowment for the Humanities awarded the project a $60,000 Creating Humanities Community Grant for exhibit development; the Alaska Association for Historic Preservation awarded $2,600 for research/travel; and the National Park Service awarded a $48,668 Underrepresented

Communities Grant for the National Register nomination and digital storytelling workshop. So far the <NN> Cannery History Project has also raised $10,000 in individual donations. A $50,000 NPS Maritime Heritage Grant proposal has been submitted in collaboration with the University of Alaska Fairbanks, for conducting interviews with ten former cannery workers. If funded, these interviews will supply firsthand accounts for the nomination and exhibit, as well as form the basis for a "Histories of Fisheries and Canneries in Alaska" Project Jukebox, the university's oral history digital archive.

OBJECTIVE 1—FROM LOCAL TO GLOBAL: DOCUMENTING UNDERREPRESENTED CANNERY COMMUNITIES

The <NN> Cannery's design and function serve as an excellent representation of a typical salmon cannery, and reflect a broad range of historic contexts: corporate, technological, economic, social, cultural, and environmental. The work and ancillary activities that took place within the cannery's fifty-plus structures—several of which are recognized to be historically significant in their own right—affected local, state, national, and even global activities and people. The <NN> Cannery employed hundreds of residents and thousands of transient workers, who together produced more canned salmon than any cannery in Alaska. Over time, these cannery people developed unique identities and stories, which today remain little known or understood. Although hundreds of canneries were built in Alaska, few left standing possess the integrity of location, design, setting, materials, workmanship, feeling, and association of the <NN> cannery, which meets all the criteria for historic evaluation.

Currently, only two Alaska canneries are listed in the National Register of Historic Places (NRHP), and neither represent Bristol Bay, the largest red salmon fishery in the world. Considering the historical importance of the canned-salmon industry to Alaska, listing the <NN> Cannery would fill a gap in the state's historic preservation program and set the standard for future cannery documentation projects. Moreover, the cannery's termination by Trident Seafoods magnifies threats, such as adverse weather, looting and vandalism, shrubbery

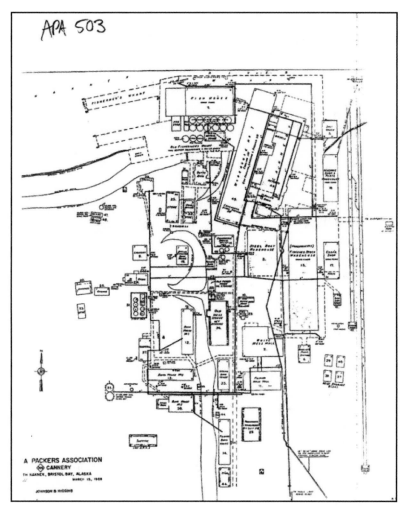

<NN> Cannery Plat, 1968. *APA Collection, Alaska State Archives, Library, and Museum, Juneau, Alaska.*

overgrowth, and fire. Thus, property documentation will capture the stories of cannery workers before the buildings that reflect their intersected activities disappear forever.

In July 2016, I collaborated with historian Bob King and NPS historic architect John Wachtel to conduct an historic and architectural survey of the cannery buildings at South Naknek. Using a 1968 cannery plat and building inventory, our survey aimed to determine:

- The general condition of the buildings;
- The buildings' historical/cultural/social associations;
- The buildings' historic and current function;
- If a building had moved or was modified from its historic use;
- The meaning or reasons behind change; and
- How the interconnected parts worked to create a unified system.

In December 2017, the <NN> Cannery History Project received funding from the National Park Service to research, document, and nominate the salmon cannery as a historic district to the National Register of Historic Places, and to uncover the stories of the cannery's underrepresented communities.

This matters because a vast majority of historical narratives interpret, explain, and personify Alaska's salmon industry through the activities of fishermen—the so-called "Iron Men of Bristol Bay"—rather than the processors, often minorities, whose collective knowledge of the mechanical operation, physical labor, and salmon themselves formed the cannery's industrial backbone. Several of the <NN> Cannery's individual structures convey the collective and personal experiences of cannery workers—a community of people practically invisible to the historic record. Although numerous groups of people labored at the <NN>, the national register will highlight two distinct yet interrelated stories: the Alaska Native laborers, whose homeland the cannery occupied, and the Asian cannery workers, whose customs and traditions shaped the cannery's workscape and directly linked the Alaska cannery to the broader Pacific world.

The Local Story: Cannery Caretakers

The Indigenous Alaskans who worked at the cannery were descendants of Katmai people and are culturally connected to the Brooks River Area's Archeological District and National Historic Landmark at Katmai National Park and Preserve. Villagers migrated downriver and established South Naknek after Novarupta volcano destroyed Savonoski village and created the Valley of 10,000 Smokes in 1912. The red salmon crash of 1919 drove Native residents to seek cannery work, and despite a cultural lifeway lost to cannery life, Native people became integral contributors to and caretakers of the operation. Historically, they supplied salmon to the cannery, constituted the "spring/fall" crew that readied and winterized the operation, and served as winter watchmen, protecting the collective structures and storing boats throughout the off-season. The cannery's operational longevity is a testament to local vigilance. Cannery buildings that convey the Native experience and influence on cannery work include the Laundry, where Native women not only found jobs but controlled the work space and activities therein. Equally significant are the Native Bunkhouse and the "white" Mess Hall, both of which reveal the ethnic and racial segregation policies that were prevalent in all Alaska salmon canneries.

The most significant <NN> Cannery building representing the Alaska Native experience, however, is the Old Hospital. The <NN> Hospital served as the only site for health care prior to statehood and supplied health services to all residents, regardless of employee status. Its historical significance derives from association with the Spanish influenza pandemic, which killed more Alaskans per capita than anywhere in the world, including the two hundred people who died on the Naknek River alone.[4] When the epidemic hit Bristol Bay in spring of 1919, cannery doctors treated Native residents ravaged by the disease. Ancillary to the hospital was the Radio Shack, which

---

4   Alfred W. Crosby, *America's Forgotten Pandemic: The Influenza of 1918* (Cambridge University Press, 2003), 241–57; Alaska Packers Association, "Report on 1919 Influenza Epidemic, Naknek Station, Bristol Bay Alaska," APA Collection, Alaska State Library, Archives and Museum, Juneau, Alaska.

was the largest and most efficient wireless apparatus in Bristol Bay.[5] The building handled all communications between the cannery and the outside world, and was critical during the outbreak. A cannery doctor and a nurse attended to people inflicted with the flu, most of whom died, leaving behind an orphaned generation. These health-care providers saved many Native children, but they would grow up disconnected from their earlier culture.

Documenting the Old Hospital, and shedding light on the historic events that occurred there, will help uncover the industry's under-lying value to local residents, as well as its costs. Historic designation will not only add to the National Register the first Alaska property associated with the Spanish influenza pandemic—one of the most historically significant events of the twentieth century—but by bring-ing this story to the forefront, we will articulate the complexities between residents and the cannery and help to heal a community still suffering from the residual impacts of cultural loss.

The Global Story: Pacific Connections

The second underrepresented cannery group is the Asian crew, hired first from China, then Japan, and later the Philippines via labor con-tractors located in the West Coast hubs of San Francisco and Seattle. These workers were hired to process salmon and, in the early years, soldered by hand the tin cans on the long voyage northward. The industry's most telling—and unapologetic—depiction of the Asian cannery worker is a machine called the "Iron Ch**k," which was invented to replace the task of butchering salmon by human hand—a critical task assigned to the Chinese workers. Machines, however, did not supplant Asian processors, as indicated by numerous cannery buildings built in later years to accommodate Asian workers.

The four small Chinese bunkhouses are some of the cannery's old-est structures. The fact that they were built to house the earliest can-nery processors indicate that Asian workers were vital to the operation

---

5   APA, "Report on 1919 Influenza Epidemic, Naknek Station, Bristol Bay Alaska."

A wooden barrel filled with bolts, likely transported from San Francisco to Bristol Bay aboard an APA star ship, is stamped "APA 1899 <NN>." Near the top of the barrel is a Chinese character. The marking illustrates the Asian influence on the cannery work experience and directly represents the Chinese laborers at the <NN> Cannery at South Naknek. *Courtesy of Katherine Ringsmuth.*

from the beginning. Although Asian cannery workers were necessary, they were nevertheless isolated from the rest of the cannery complex, suggesting policies of segregation and pacification. The plain design of these four structures represents the "no-frills" architecture that served a purely functional purpose. Moving Asian workers from the four bunkhouses to a larger, two-story building in later years suggests the Asian workforce was actually surging as cannery lines mechanized. But the change in the building's name from "China House" to "Filipino Bunkhouse" denotes the impact of national laws such as the 1882 Chinese Exclusion Act and the 1902 Geary Act that made permanent the exclusion of Chinese immigrants, which together sparked a generational transition that eventually replaced Chinese and Japanese laborers with Filipino and Native labor.

Likewise, the construction of the <NN> Cannery's Filipino Mess Hall suggests that crew size was relatively large and necessary to the canning operation. But like the Native cannery workers, the Filipino Mess Hall reveals a darker story of racial segregation. The presence of a separate "white" Mess Hall from the Filipino Mess Hall underscores this discrimination, while the eventual closing of the Filipino Mess Hall (converted to a provisions warehouse and fishermen's laundry) and the construction of a single Mess Hall for all cannery workers, signifies a shift in an industry-wide policy that eventually integrated the workforce.

Despite Asian cannery workers' contributions to the industry, historians know very little about them. We know that the Superintendent's House included a "servant qtrs" room attached to the kitchen, used by a Chinese worker, but beyond that we know little else about this individual. The Chinese graveyard near the original bunkhouses may yield new information about these workers—specifically, who they were and from where they originated. The ground around the bunkhouses also has the potential to yield important archeological evidence, furthering our understanding of the Asian cannery experience under National Register Criterion D (Information Potential). Of all the buildings associated with underrepresented communities, the Chinese bunkhouses and graveyard are most at risk from threats such as vegetation overgrowth, erosion, and natural deterioration. And despite being used as storage for decades, the bunkhouses, with their precariously leaning walls etched with graffiti, still maintain structural integrity; together the four structures and graveyard are physical reminders that reflect the contributions made by the contracted China crew, and ultimately all the Asian cannery workers who gave their lives to the industry.

Over the decades, Asian workers experienced upward mobility within the cannery order.[6] Prior to the Great Depression, Filipino

---

6   Chris Friday, *Organizing Asian American Labor: The Pacific Coast Canned-Salmon Industry, 1870–1942* (Philadelphia: Temple University Press, 1994).

schoolboys—the *Alaskeros*—made their way to Alaska canneries to seek work before college, and transformed the labor system through the power of the union by the 1930s. The postwar years saw Filipino workers transition into skilled positions such as machinists and carpenters. Japan's rise as a major player in Alaska's canned salmon international market also impacted labor hierarchy. The fairly recent introduction of the Egg House reflects the economic importance of packed salmon roe, a specialty food prepared for Asian palates. Salmon roe, or fish eggs, was packed by Japanese technicians, sold by Japanese brokers, and considered far more valuable than the canned fish product. Bilingual Japanese personnel were hired to supervise both the Fish House and Egg House. Understanding the ability for these groups to adapt to their circumstances, and even move beyond them, broadens our interpretation of both the Native and the Asian experiences in Alaska canneries.

Perceiving Alaska's "Invisible" People

The <NN> Cannery is eligible for listing in the National Register under the program's Criterion A (properties "associated events that have made a significant contribution to the broad patterns of our history") and possibly D (yielding "information important in prehistory or history"), and is significant for its association with over a century of laborers, people who were vital to the cannery's longtime success. Despite their skill and labor, cannery workers existed in the shadows, only to be marginalized, exoticized, or ignored by popular writers, academics, curators, and even park rangers in the narratives of Alaska's most important salmon fishery. Collectively, these workers constitute Alaska's "invisible cannery people," a population that is multiethnic and multicultural but poorly understood. The <NN> Cannery History Project aspires to explain how cannery workers were discriminated against, segregated, and oppressed, while simultaneously looking at how these workers and their ability to can salmon moved beyond constraints and shaped our nation's history. Through the interpretation of the cannery's built history, the nomination will move these processors from the margins into a more central position in Alaska history.

OBJECTIVE 2—FROM FISH CANNERY TO A HUMANITIES COMMUNITY

The <NN> Cannery's closure in 2015 severely impacted Bristol Bay residents. Contained in the local community are memories of the "exotic" workers with whom Native people bartered for foodstuffs, shared a graveyard, and, in some cases, exchanged DNA. Indeed, the Cannery is a place that holds extraordinary community value and history, and therefore public participation in the project's documentation process will hopefully have the *intended* consequence of creating a humanities community that will infuse the project with authentic voices, protect resources, and underpin future educational endeavors to recruit, train, and instill the value of history in the next generation. History activities ignited by the project will revive and raise awareness for a multicultural working community that has existed in canneries throughout the Pacific slope for over a century. Thus, ancillary to the National Register nomination is the development of a digital storytelling workshop designed for village youth.

The group targeted to participate in the workshop includes the children and grandchildren of former cannery workers—the "spring/fall" crew, the winter watchmen, the laundry ladies. A digital storytelling workshop derived from research uncovered during the National Register process will connect the present generation with a past once lost to them; this program will help explain devastating episodes such as the flu pandemic, and perhaps even soothe old wounds; and hopefully the program will boost self-esteem by giving dignity and validity to the work of their elders.

Inspiration for a storytelling workshop comes from a defunct local history program, *Uutuqtwa: An Historical Magazine of the Bristol Bay Area*, which was produced by Bristol Bay high school students in the 1970s and 1980s. *Uutuqtwa* shows Bristol Bay's penchant for local history, and the likelihood of parents passing down the value of "doing history" to their own children and grandchildren. The two-week digital storytelling workshop will serve as a pilot program, which if successful will leverage long-term funding for future courses, ideally granting program facilitation to the Bristol Bay School District. The aim, then, is to continue the local traditional identity of the "caretaker."

Japanese technicians enjoy a cup of coffee on the cannery dock at Mug Up, circa 1988. *Courtesy of Katherine Ringsmuth.*

Instead of cannery caretakers, the storytelling program will provide local youth with the skills, responsibility, and confidence to become caretakers of cannery history and curators of cannery people's stories.

Naknek resident Sharon Thompson of Steelbird Productions will lead the digital storytelling workshop. Thompson has created commercials, documentaries, crowdfunding videos, and advocacy pieces and worked with national broadcasters, as well as filmed many oral histories—most recently with regional Native elders on a project for the Bristol Bay Historical Society. With a bachelor of arts degree in English and theater and a certificate in feature film writing, Thompson strives for meaningful storytelling. Where oftentimes educators lack the experience and/or skills in filmmaking, Thompson is an expert. Steelbird Productions has boots on the ground in Bristol Bay, always camera-ready, resourceful, and willing to collaborate.

To provide Thompson with a roadmap needed to facilitate the digital storytelling workshop, the <NN> Cannery History Project will collaborate with an Anchorage-based educational consulting firm, See Stories, which specializes in digital storytelling for youth. See Stories will organize the workshop structure, provide a curriculum design, and lead four two-hour training sessions with Thompson. See Stories is nationally recognized for its work, from Barrow to Uganda. In 2016, See Stories received the National Youth Arts and Humanities Program Award from former First Lady Michelle Obama on behalf of the President's Committee on the Arts and Humanities for its five-year humanities youth film workshop program with a local museum in Kodiak, Alaska.

Another significant aim for the digital storytelling workshop is to support local institutions so that collected material can be permanently cared for by an enthused and skilled community. The <NN> Cannery History Project's collaborative approach may also be an effective model for creating options for other private owners and local stakeholders across Alaska. A vocal and engaged cannery community can inform private owners that properties oftentimes maintain historic, as well as economic, value and perhaps in the future may persuade owners to consider history and culture when managing their property. Participatory history turns potential looters or vandals into stewards—vigilant protectors of the past. The <NN> Cannery is a place that holds extraordinary community values and history, and therefore the public's involvement in our research and exhibit development—indeed, the creation of an active "humanities" community around the end of era—will infuse the project with authentic voices, protect resources, and underpin future humanities community endeavors.

OBJECTIVE 3—*MUG-UP* EXHIBITION: A COSMOPOLITAN WORKING EXPERIENCE

A history exhibition can serve as an educational and empathetic device that conveys to the public the importance of the seafood industry in Alaska. Exhibitions are uniquely suited to give voice to the countless underrepresented people who contributed to the industry. Objects, artifacts, and digital "interactives" can communicate stories such as commercialization and the art of marketing, cultural representation in technology, migrations and diversity in the far North, and canned salmon's wartime roles. Importantly, exhibitions can also create an experience, interpreting to the visitor cannery life from the vantage point of the people who worked there. The display of cannery items, combined with creative interactives and firsthand narratives, can develop new interpretive programming, bolster cultural institutions, and potentially boost the local economy.

The Alaska State Museum has agreed to partner with the <NN> Cannery History Project to build and install a traveling exhibition that will inform visitors from near and far of the cannery workscape. The Museum will serve as a repository for material gathered during the course of the project, and will make it available for future research. The Museum has the expert staff and professional connections for developing an exhibit and, in doing so, will foster relationships with fishermen and cannery folk, and add signature acquisitions to their collection of seafood history objects.

The planned exhibition is titled *Mug-Up*, the cannery community's colloquial word for coffee break. Mug-Up fueled cannery workers with caffeine and pastries, provided a respite from the monotony of the slime line or patching table, and momentarily brought people together from around the world. In addition to the lap of tides, the squawk of seagulls, and the rumbling of fishing boats, scores of languages might be heard on the dock at Mug-Up. Simply put, Mug-Up celebrates the diversity reflected on the cannery floor.

The *Mug-Up* exhibition, then, will aspire to explain to the broader public why the task of canning salmon shaped history. It will pull in processors from the margins of history by highlighting how Filipino crews endured cannery life in charismatic ways, how women workers related to the environment, and how Mug-Up served as a hub of global and cultural exchange. Contrary to the belief that early cannery life was gloomy and inhospitable, aspects of cannery culture depict a multiethnic, multigenerational community that played games, made music, and took comfort in the bonds of friendship. As one cannery worker described it, "we were intimate strangers." Nevertheless, the exhibit will also address difficult, even heartbreaking, stories, as it is only through reminders of the past that we truly understand the industry's value and its costs.

Bringing a Cannery into a Museum

One of the challenges for the exhibit will be to condense a massive industrial campus into a 30,000-square-foot museum space. Framing the exhibit narrative will be the <NN> Cannery's ten most significant features, which will serve as interpretive stations for visitors to learn more about the individual cannery spaces and the people who worked within them. The ten stations include:

1. Fish House/Egg House Complex
2. Cannery Complex
3. Carpenter Shop Complex
4. Mess Hall Complex
5. Chinese Bunkhouses & Graveyard
6. Fishermen & Filipino Bunkhouses
7. Laundry
8. Hospital & Old Radio Shack
9. Store/Rec Hall
10. Management Complex (Office and Superintendent's Residence)

In addition to objects, artifacts, and other visuals that will be displayed within each station, recorded interviews with cannery people will speak to the work activities taking place within the structures. Interviewees may include superintendents, company personnel, carpenters, machinists, beach gang, quality control, cooks, laundry workers, villagers, egg-house technicians, fishermen, slimers, pilots, local residents, and industry experts. To explain how the ten stations are connected, our plan is to build a scale model of the <NN> Cannery from ca. 1979. To show change over time, NPS will also help create a digital site evolution, depicting development from 1890 to the present. Encompassing the exhibit will be panels providing the broader history of the canned-salmon industry in Alaska. Students enrolled in the digital storytelling workshop will supply the soundscape for the exhibit.

The midnight sun bathes a Filipino cannery worker after a sixteen-hour work day, which was typical during the season peak, circa 1988. *Courtesy of Katherine Ringsmuth.*

CONCLUSION—THE WHOLE IS GREATER THAN THE SUM OF ITS PARTS

Today, most buildings at the<NN> Cannery still convey their original function and purpose, and all provide insight into the working lives of cannery people. Few written accounts of these cannery workers exist today, as most had no time to write down their story. They did not keep journals, and few wrote letters. Even company records used position titles, rather than personal names, to identify workers. The cannery's structures, artifacts, and surrounding industrial landscape contain these stories. Discarded machine parts, broken boardwalks, skeletal remains of bunkhouses, and graffiti etchings are the enduring reminders of the past that gives voice to the cannery people. Williwaw winds, alders, or fire will inevitably reclaim the <NN>

Cannery, but as one cannery worker put it, "Until the last chunk of cannery machinery sinks into the earth, it still means something to someone." Together, the three <NN> Cannery History Project deliverables—a National Register nomination, digital storytelling workshop, and museum exhibition—will assign value to the so-called industrial "junk" and will fortify cannery communities across the Pacific. They will convey the message that beyond putting fish into a tin can for over a century, the <NN> Cannery was a cultural crossroads with far-reaching historical dimensions, and that this cannery's work, people, and place perfectly epitomize how *the whole is greater than the sum of its parts.*

The purpose, then, for the <NN> Cannery History Project is to put history and culture on par with economics, biology, and politics when depicting Alaska's seafood industry. It provides cannery communities a platform to share their stories, thus bringing historical meaning to their work. Dialogues framed by history and culture will help to reconcile the confused identities canneries left in their wake. By exploring these topics through the exhibit, we hope to obtain empathy, mutual understanding, and respect. From the Scandinavian carpenter, to the Chinese butcher, to the Native Laundry lady, to the Filipino cook, to the superintendent—these forgotten voices will remind the public that no one group or individual associated with the <NN> Cannery experienced life there in the same way. And that is an important lesson in itself—not only for how we explain the past but for how we relate to and perceive each other today.

BIBLIOGRAPHY

Alaska Packers Association. "Report on 1919 Influenza Epidemic, Naknek Station, Bristol Bay Alaska." APA Collection, Alaska State Library, Archives and Museum. Juneau, Alaska.

Boraas, Alan. "Turning Point: Photo Exhibition." *Peninsula Clarion*, November 21, 1996.

Crosby, Alfred W. *America's Forgotten Pandemic: The Influenza of 1918*. Cambridge University Press, 2003.

Friday, Chris. *Organizing Asian American Labor: The Pacific Coast Canned-Salmon Industry, 1870–1942.* Philadelphia: Temple University Press, 1994.

Haycox, Steven. *Alaska, an American Colony.* Seattle: University of Washington Press, 2002.

King, Bob. "Iron Men of Bristol Bay." Alaska Historical Society Blog, posted December 7, 2015.

A Note from Dirk Tordoff

Recipe for a great one-of-a-kind human being:

Take equal parts:
Victor Borge, Benjamin Franklin, Tommy
Smothers, Winston Churchill, Carol Burnett,
Mark Twain, Studs Terkel;

Combine with
Essence of Absent-Minded Professor; and
Bake in a pinball machine, until it tilts.
And *voilà* . . .

There are plenty of great people in the world, but extraordinary ones are few and far between. If you meet one, and providence grants, that person will become a true friend.

Luck has been mine. I've had the good fortune to call Terrence a friend in the twentieth and twenty-first centuries. He inspires, entertains, continues to amaze, and most of all encourages me to achieve. That association makes my life, and subsequently that of my family, better. In the words of Buzz Lightyear, "To infinity . . . and beyond."

ROADS VERSUS RUNWAYS

Transportation Development in Territorial Alaska

Dirk Tordoff

Travel by aircraft is a luxury in much of the world, but an absolute necessity in Alaska. Throughout the United States small towns are linked by road systems, but rural Alaskans, depending on the season, use off-road vehicles, snowmobiles, and motorboats for local travel and moving between villages. Limited surface transportation options in these regions make airplanes the critical link to the rest of the world. Residents of such rural hubs as Utqiagvik, Kotzebue, Nome, Bethel, and Dillingham have no road connections to the major highway system in the state. In the event of medical emergencies, more than 64,000 other Alaskans in 201 towns and villages with year-round populations of twenty or more people have no road access to reach in-patient hospitals.[1]

Throughout the state, commercial air services operate small air taxis, regularly delivering passengers, mail, medicine, supplies, and other necessities of life to small communities. Their single- and twin-engine planes typically carry between three and twenty passengers.[2] From high school basketball teams flying to regional

---

1   Aviation Access to Remote Locations in Alaska, Recommendations to Increase Aviation Access to Medical Facilities, Federal Aviation Administration Study for the House and Senate Appropriations Committees, May 2001, House Report 106-940 accompanying H. R. 4475, FY 2001 (DOT Appropriations), 1–8.

2   Air Taxis, BusinessDictionary.com. Web Finance, Inc., accessed March 18, 2018 [http://www.businessdictionary.com/definition/air-taxi].

tournaments to a final flight home for the recently deceased, Alaska air taxis are the only reliable year-round transportation in most of the state.[3] The largest of the more than twenty air services operating in the state, Ravn Alaska, serves more than a hundred rural communities.[4]

Why are so many places isolated from the road system, and how did Alaska's airplane-dependent transportation system evolve? In many ways, airplanes aren't merely the solution to limited road access but were a major contributing factor to how it came about. Comparing transportation development in the continental states with that in Alaska shows that the mold that isolated Territorial communities from surface transportation was cast by World War II.

Alaska has four essential modes of public transportation allowing people to travel within the state and connect to the rest of the world. The highway system provides access to a relatively narrow portion of Alaska and connects to the ALCAN (Alaska-Canada) Highway, Canada, and the contiguous forty-eight United States. The Alaska Marine Highway System serves isolated coastal communities with connections to seaports in Canada and Washington State. The Alaska Railroad (ARR) originates at tidewater in Seward and provides passengers and cargo a single line through several highway-connected communities up to Fairbanks.[5] Compared to these other three systems, Alaska air taxis link far more, and nearly all, Alaska villages and towns to the highway systems, urban areas, and air routes out of the state.

Until the early 1900s, Alaska's road system development mirrored what had occurred in the continental United States. Westward expansion beyond the Mississippi River during the early 1800s was almost exclusively overland. Settlers seeking land and opportunity traveled on foot or relied on some combination of horse, mule, oxen, or other livestock to move their belongings to new homes in the west. Routes

---

3   Larger multi-engine aircraft deliver passengers, freight, and fuel to villages with adequate runways.

4   "Flying with Ravn," Ravn Alaska, accessed March 18, 2018 [https://www.flyravn.com/flying-with-ravn/route/map/].

5   White Pass and Yukon Railroad (WP&YRR) also starts in Alaska but ends in Canada.

were based on previously established Native American or wildlife trails or blazed through wilderness by trappers and explorers. As time progressed, much of the trail system was improved for wagon travel and, after automobiles were introduced, to modern roads and highways.[6]

Steam power became a driving force in world transportation by the mid-1800s, and in the continental U.S., steam-powered ocean, river, and lake steamers soon connected ports and cities to others around the world. With completion of the Transcontinental Railroad in 1869, steam-powered locomotives sped U.S. travelers coast to coast. Distances that had taken months of arduous travel were accomplished in mere days.

Early explorers, fishermen, whalers, gold seekers, fur traders, and adventurers heading to Alaska, meanwhile, had been limited to sailing ships. But by the 1870s, ocean steamships outperformed sailing ships, and steam-powered paddle-wheel riverboats were operating on the Yukon River.[7] When rivers flowed ice-free, riverboats carried freight and passengers throughout the Yukon River system.[8]

Word of gold discoveries in the Klondike and Alaska reached the world in 1897, and thousands of fortune seekers stampeded north. A traveler with a forty-dollar ticket could board the train in Boston on Monday and arrive in Seattle or San Francisco four days later. For another ten-dollar ticket they were bound for Skagway or Dyea, Alaska.[9] Once in Alaska, however, the majority of newcomers were limited to travel modes proven by indigenous Alaska Natives: foot, small boats, and dog teams. Prospectors faced a slow and exhausting journey on foot up the Chilkoot or White Pass, then had to build a raft

---

6   Sara E. Quay, *Westward Expansion* (Westport, CT: Greenwood Press, 2002), 212.

7   Barry C. Anderson, *Lifeline to the Yukon: A History of Yukon River Navigation* (Seattle: Superior Publishing Co., 1983), 37.

8   Riverboats eventually operated on the Kuskokwim River and other river systems in the territory.

9   Kathryn Taylor Morse, *The Nature of Gold: An Environmental History of the Klondike Gold Rush* (Seattle: University of Washington Press, 2003), 47.

or boat to cross Lake Bennett, then float down the Yukon River to arrive at gold camps.[10]

Meanwhile, those with the financial means had the option of traveling in relative luxury. Steamships from the West Coast of the U.S. carried them to St. Michael at the mouth of the Yukon River, where they transferred to commercial riverboats for travel up the river system to gold camps, hoping to strike it rich.

Fueled by gold fever, Alaska's immigrant population of fewer than five hundred people in 1880 grew to more than thirty thousand people by 1900. During that boom, growing demands for mining equipment and other freight for the lucrative goldfields prompted entrepreneur-funded railroad construction. The first railroad, the White Pass & Yukon Rail (WP&YRR), was completed in 1900 and connected coastal Skagway, Alaska, to Whitehorse, Yukon Territory, in Canada and to the Yukon River.[11]

Within a few years, three small short-line railroads totaling less than forty miles of track were built on the Seward Peninsula. Like the WP&YRR, each was supporting gold mining in the region.[12] The next significant project, the land-locked Tanana Mines Railroad, renamed the Tanana Valley Railroad (TVRR), was completed in 1905.[13] Mining equipment shipped to the Interior on riverboats was transferred to the TVRR at the town of Chena on the Tanana River for delivery to Fairbanks and gold mining operations in the Goldstream and Chatanika Valleys.

As mining regions and towns grew in the territory, increasing pressure from miners for better trails led the federal government to establish the Board of Road Commissioners for Alaska during 1905. Eventually operating as the Alaska Road Commission (ARC), the board

---

10　These were the most popular routes, although other more difficult travel options existe,d including the Dalton Trail and Valdez Glacier routes.

11　Howard Clifford, *Rails North: The Railroads of Alaska and the Yukon* (Seattle: Superior Publishing Co., 1981).

12　Edward Sanford Harrison, *Nome and Seward Peninsula: History, Description, Biographies, and Stories* (Seattle: Metropolitan Press, 1905), 169.

13　Nicholas Deely, *Tanana Valley Railroad: The Gold Dust Line, Alaska* (Fairbanks: Denali Publishing, 1996).

was tasked with surveying, building, and maintaining what would become a far-reaching system of trails, sled roads, roads, and tramways linking villages and towns in the Interior of the territory with coastal communities based on commercial needs.[14]

Resource development, and most significantly gold mining, was the major determining force for what routes were developed. Construction priority was based on popular routes to gold mining regions; trails to nonmining regions had no standing.

The act establishing the Board of Road Commissioners was not designed to provide access for everyone in the Territory. Instead, it only allowed construction of trails and roads for development of commerce:

> The Board shall have the power, and it shall be their duty, upon their own motion or upon petition, to locate, lay out, construct, and maintain wagon roads and pack trails from any point on the navigable waters of said district to any town, mining, or industrial camp or settlement, between any such town, camps or settlements therein, if in their judgment such roads are needed and will be of permanent value for the development of the district; but no such road or trail shall be constructed to any town, camp, or settlement which is wholly transitory or of no substantial value or importance for mining, trade, agriculture, or manufacturing purposes.[15]

These goals were lofty, and funding never met what was needed to accomplish all that was demanded of the ARC.[16]

At its inception, ARC's system incorporated existing summer walking and winter dogsled trails. Many of the routes followed previously

---

14   The Board of Road Commissioners eventually operated as the ARC, and for purposes of simplification, ARC is used universally here; Annual Report of the Chief of Engineers, Extract, Board of Road Commissioners, *Construction and Maintenance of Military and Post Roads, Bridges and Trails, Alaska* (Washington, D.C., 1919), 2097.

15   Ibid., 2097.

16   Grace Edman, Alice Hudson, Sam Johnson, *Alaska Division of Highways: Fifty Years of Highways* (Nome: Alaska Department of Public Works, Division of Highways), 261.

established trails and much of the Washington-Alaska Military Cable and Telegraph System (WAMCATS) telegraph routes, which had been built between 1900 and 1904. The 1,056-mile WAMCATS system of telegraph lines stretched from Valdez to Eagle, Fairbanks, Rampart, Tanana, Fort Saint Michael, Port Safety, and Nome.[17]

To build and maintain routes, ARC workers marked trails with regularly placed tripods, bridged creeks, and, starting in 1917, built a series of shelter cabins.[18] Cabins were built from native materials where available and furnished with a woodstove and stock of dry firewood. Designed to protect travelers from inclement weather, cabins "were spaced to suit the condition of the trail, the loads that were to be hauled and were placed in sheltered areas."[19]

Far from mere paths, basic trails were cleared to a width of eight feet. Winter sled roads were twelve feet wide, and wagon roads were sixteen feet wide with fourteen-foot-wide bridges.[20] Maintaining this trail system was no small feat—it was difficult and expensive. Initially, workers were limited to hand tools and performed thousands of man-hours of strenuous labor each year. Requests to expand the system far outstripped ARC's budget being "far beyond its ability to meet with funds available. . . ."[21]

Similar to development in the contiguous states, demand grew and as budgets permitted, dog team and walking trails were improved for pack-train use, horse-drawn wagons, and winter sleighs. Eventually, a few trails became roads groomed for automobiles.

Popular, well-traveled trails and wagon roads featured commercial roadhouses, offering basic food and shelter. Roadhouses were spaced

---

17   Claus-M. Naske, *Alaska Road Commission Historical Narrative: Final Report* (Fairbanks: State of Alaska Department of Transportation & Public Facilities, 1983), 13.

18   Biennial report of the Alaska Territorial Highway Engineer and Superintendent of Public Works, 1935–1936, 29.

19   Grace Edman, Alice Hudson, Sam Johnson, *Alaska Division of Highways: Fifty Years of Highways* (Nome: Alaska Department of Public Works, Division of Highways), 7

20   Major General A. W. Greely, U.S.A., *Handbook of Alaska* (New York: Charles Scribner and Sons, 1925), 44.

21   War Department, *Report of the Board of Road Commissioners for Alaska, 1912* (Washington, D.C.: Government Printing Office, 1912), 6.

at varying distances, usually between fifteen and thirty miles, and travelers could usually walk from one to the next along the trail in a single day. Larger well-equipped roadhouses provided shelter for horses and dog teams.[22]

In 1913, on the eve of World War I, train travel throughout the United States was commonplace over an ever-expanding web of rails. Road systems grew, and although still uncommon, daring intrepid motorists could drive from the Atlantic to the Pacific.[23] A few automobiles had reached one hundred miles per hour, and Henry Ford launched his new moving assembly line, revolutionizing automobile construction.[24]

That same year, ARC reported 829 miles of wagon road and more than 2,000 miles of trails and sled roads, with 450 miles of winter-only trails.[25] Between Valdez and Fairbanks, 380 miles of trails had been improved to a primitive wagon road, allowing summer or winter horse-drawn travel.[26] In any season the trip was slow, and travelers relied heavily on the roadhouse system. One official government party inspecting ARC work progress traveled nearly two weeks along the route, leaving Valdez on September 30 and reaching Fairbanks on October 12. The team rode on horse-drawn buckboards and the mail stage, and finished the final forty miles in an automobile.[27]

The Wright Flyer lifted off at Kitty Hawk, North Carolina, in 1903 and ushered the nation into the age of airplanes. In the following decade, flying grew from a curiosity to a burgeoning industry. Major American manufacturers including Boeing, Curtiss, and Wright refined their designs and built ever-improved models of aircraft. Intrepid pilots routinely set and reset speed, altitude, and distance records.[28]

---

22 Herbert L. Heller, *Sourdough Sagas* (Sausalito: Comstock Editions Inc., 1972), 171–77.

23 Douglas Brinkley, *Wheels for the World: Henry Ford his Company and a Century of Progress* (New York: Viking Penguin 2003), 116–17.

24 Ibid., 151.

25 The route was shortened over the years to 362 miles today.

26 War Department, *Report of the Board of Road Commissioners for Alaska, 1912* (Washington, D.C.: Government Printing Office, 1912), 7.

27 Ibid., 6.

28 Martin's supply of high-octane fuel hadn't arrived, so the use of a lower grade led to the unorthodox takeoff method.

At the same time, militaries around the world, including the U.S., were actively assembling squadrons of warplanes.

Aviation had become well established and thriving in the United States, but no airplanes had yet flown in Alaska skies, and no runways had been built or even planned in the territory by the ARC.

The year 1913 marked two significant milestones in Alaska travel. The first indeed involved an airplane, and although it had no immediate effects, the event dramatically changed the territory's transportation future. The second involved an automobile, and rapidly changed travel options in Interior Alaska.

Standing in the dusty, windy prop-wash, Lily Martin released the rope and freed the frail Gage-Martin Tractor Biplane to gain speed and finally lift off from a temporary airfield at Exhibition Park in Fairbanks.[29] At that moment, just past 8 p.m. on Thursday, July 3, 1913, the seeds of aviation were planted in Alaska. It took another decade for those seeds to germinate.[30]

Pilot of the craft James V. Martin, Lily's husband, was a Harvard-educated experienced aviator who had both designed and built the biplane. The Martins had shipped the craft to Skagway on a steamship and transferred it to the WP&YRR to Whitehorse. After a riverboat trip down the Yukon and up the Tanana and Chena Rivers, it finally arrived in Fairbanks.[31]

Following 4th of July holiday flight demonstrations, the Martins had hoped to sell the airplane. Unfortunately no buyers came forward, and so the couple re-crated the craft for a lengthy riverboat trip down the Chena, Tanana, and Yukon Rivers to St. Michaels and back to the states by steamship.[32]

The second milestone that year was an automobile trip between Fairbanks and coastal Valdez completed in only three days. Tom Gibson left Fairbanks on July 29 with two passengers, made a side

29   U.S. Aviation Firsts, www.aerofiles.com/chrono.html (accessed March 12, 2018).

30   Robert W. Stevens, *Alaskan Aviation History: Volume One 1897–1928* (Des Moines: Polynas Press, 1990), 19.

31   Ibid., 17–18.

32   Ibid, 2.

trip to Chitina, and arrived in Valdez on August 2.[33] The Copper River and Northwest Railroad (CR&NW) connected Chitina to coastal Cordova, and as a result Chitina served as an important link to the ARC trail system until the late 1930s.[34] Gibson carried passengers and freight on the Fairbanks–Valdez route via automobile for more than a decade.[35]

During winter, contract mail carriers used horse-drawn sleighs or dog teams along the ARC trail system,[36] and among the locations served by weekly mail during the winter of 1919 were Valdez, Chitina, Fairbanks, Circle, Tanana, Iditarod, McGrath, Susitna, Bettles, Kaltag, and Nome. Meanwhile, Unalakleet, Kotzebue, and Noorvik received mail every two weeks. Mail delivery trips from Kotzebue to Pt. Barrow departed on the first days of December, February, and April.[37]

In the continental states, this was the era of barnstorming. Entrepreneurial pilots, often operating from farmers' fields, criss-crossed the nation selling rides and putting on aerobatic displays for an enthusiastic public. World War I had left a ready supply of surplus military aircraft and, in many cases, military-trained pilots for the Flying Circuses.

Although Alaska transportation options were expanding, they were still limited to surface travel in 1919. ARC reported the Alaska system at the time as 1,013 miles of wagon road and more than 3,000 miles of sled road and trails in a

> connected system extending from Valdez, on the coast and Chitina, on the Copper River Railroad, to Fairbanks and vicinity, with trails extending from the road system to Eagle, to the settlements above

---

33 Nancy DeWitt, *Extreme Motoring: Alaska's First Automobiles and Their Dauntless Drivers* (Fairbanks: Fountain Antique Auto Museum, 2015), 50–52.

34 Lone E. Janson, *The Copper Spike* (Anchorage: Alaska Northwest Publishing Co., 1975), 152–58.

35 Nancy DeWitt, *Extreme Motoring: Alaska's First Automobiles and Their Dauntless Drivers* (Fairbanks: Fountain Antique Auto Museum, 2015), 62.

36 William S. Schneider, *On Time Delivery: The Dog Team Mail Carriers* (Fairbanks: University of Alaska Press, 2012), 26.

37 About the Mail, *Fairbanks Daily News-Miner*, March 24, 1919.

the Arctic Circle, to the Lower Yukon, Nome, Candle and other Seward Peninsula points.

Further the system connected to trails traveling through Iditarod, Ophir, the Innoko, Turnagain Arm, and Seward.[38]

Alaska Native villages situated along routes to gold fields could also be reached, although, as mandated by Congress, not as a primary concern of the ARC.

ARC maintained additional roads and trails in coastal gold mining, logging, and fishing communities, including Juneau, Haines, Skagway, Ketchikan, Prince of Wales Island, and Petersburg.[39]

The Valdez–Fairbanks trail, now called the Richardson Road, was the territory's most developed route, with numerous roadhouses along its length. Leaving Valdez travelers passed the Granby, Worthmann's, Beaverdam, Tiekel, Tonsina, Copper Center, and Tazlina Roadhouses before reaching Gulkana, which was only about one-third of the way to Fairbanks.[40]

By 1923, now a full twenty years after Kitty Hawk, still neither airplanes nor runways existed in Alaska, nor did ARC have plans to construct any. However, the value and importance of air travel was well established in the rest of the world. Aviation promised to turn several days of overland travel into mere hours in an airplane. It was an alluring proposition, and local businessmen made plans to bring commercial air services to Fairbanks.

As had happened a decade before, two major events in Alaska transportation unfolded in a single year. The highly anticipated arrival of President Warren G. Harding to officially open the U.S. government-owned and -built Alaska Railroad was the first. Harding drove

---

38   Board of Road Commissioners in Charge, Construction and Maintenance of Military and Post Roads, Bridges, and Trails, Alaska, Annual Report of the Chief of Engineers Extract (Washington: Government Printing Office, 1919), 2098.

39   Ibid., 3873–3875.

40   Claus-M Naske, *Paving Alaska's Trails: The Work of the Alaska Road Commission* (Boston: University Press of America, 1986), 49.

a golden spike at Nenana on July 15, 1923, to commemorate the opening, linking coastal Seward to Fairbanks in Alaska's Interior.[41]

The second event marked the true beginning of commercial aviation in the Territory.[42] Schoolteacher Ben Eielson, a former U.S. Army pilot and the only trained pilot in Fairbanks, and several local businessmen had formed the Farthest-North Airplane Company. The military surplus Curtiss "Jenny" plane they had purchased traveled by steamship to Seward, and then on the Alaska Railroad to Fairbanks.[43] It arrived June 23, 1923.[44]

Ten years to the day after Martin's flights in Fairbanks, on July 3, 1923, Eielson successfully test flew the Jenny from Weeks Field, which had recently been dedicated as an airfield by the Fairbanks City Council.[45] The Farthest-North Airplane Company, with Eielson at the controls, embarked on an ambitious plan to fly miners and freight to far-flung mining camps.

In spite of difficult conditions, requiring landings on river bars and crude runways, the Farthest-North Airplane Company enjoyed success. Eielson flew as far as Tanana, 125 miles north of Fairbanks, that summer. A particularly lucrative flight earned the company $450,[46] when Ben took a gold mine executive and mining supplies 100 miles southeast of Fairbanks and landed on a Salcha River gravel bar.[47]

The following winter Eielson made the first experimental airmail flights in the territory, flying a De Havilland biplane loaned by the U.S. Postal Service to the Farthest-North Airplane Company. The plane had been shipped via steamship from Seattle to Seward, then hauled to Fairbanks on the Alaska Railroad. Eielson flew seven trips from Weeks

---

41 Attempts the previous year in Ketchikan and Anchorage had been unsuccessful.

42 Edwin M. Fitch, *The Alaska Railroad* (New York: Praeger Publishers, 1967), 62.

43 The official opening of the Alaska Railroad took place July 15, but the line had operated for several weeks prior; Robert W. Stevens, *Alaskan Aviation History: Volume One 1897–1928* (Des Moines: Polynas Press, 1990).

44 Ibid., 123.

45 Ibid.

46. $450 in 1923 is equivalent to $6500 in 2018 dollars.

47 Robert W. Stevens, *Alaskan Aviation History: Volume One 1897–1928* (Des Moines: Polynas Press, 1990), 123.

Field in Fairbanks, landing on the frozen Kuskokwim River ice in front of the village of McGrath. Returning from McGrath on the eighth trip, the airplane nosed over onto its back upon landing due to soft thawing conditions in Fairbanks. Eielson was not injured in the accident, but the remaining planned flights for that year were canceled, and the biplane was shipped back to Seattle. Eielson had proven winter flight was possible and had chopped weeks off the time dogsled mail carriers need to cover the same distances.[48]

At this time, nearly every early Alaskan flight was a first. Pilots had few options where to land, relying on frozen rivers and lakes in winter, sandbars and rough ridge tops during summer, and a few crude landing fields. Maps were incomplete, and pilots had to deduce routes and memorize crucial landmarks for reference in future flights.[49] Weather predictions were rudimentary or nonexistent. The frail wood, fabric, and wire aircraft were easily damaged, and depended on marginally reliable engines.[50] In spite of the challenges, demand for air travel grew throughout the territory, and more aviation companies were launched. One glaring impediment to that growth, meanwhile, remained the lack of suitable runways anywhere in the territory.

The first government-funded, purpose-built runway in Alaska occurred in Nome, specifically for the first Fairbanks-to-Nome flight planned for June 1925. The Territorial legislature dedicated $5,000 to the ARC for the project, with another $1,100 pledged for construction by the newly formed Fairbanks Airplane Corporation.[51] The flight nearly ended in disaster. Pilot Noel Wien was scheduled to land on a sandbar near the town of Ruby to refuel, but high water on the Yukon River covered sandbars, and so he was forced to land on a small ball field. The plane nosed over, damaging the propeller, right wing, and rudder. Wien got back into the air after repairs were made and a replacement propeller was delivered by motorboat from Fairbanks.

---

48   Ibid., 125–26. 49

49   Ibid., 153–63.

50   By 1930, air-cooled radial engines brought increased reliability to flying, replacing the older troublesome water-cooled motors.

51   Claus-M. Naske, *Paving Alaska's Trails: The Work of the Alaska Road Commission* (Boston: University Press of America, 1986), 143.

He successfully completed the first flight to the new field in Nome on June 9, 1925.[52]

As aviation became more popular, businessmen and Alaskans from all walks of life called on the Territorial legislature to fund ARC runway construction.[53]And they did—Nome was only the beginning.

Aviation in Alaska was still twenty years behind the rest of the nation, but after the Nome project, construction of runways by ARC and development of commercial aviation in the territory took off at a dizzying pace. In 1925 the Territory and the Alaska Road Commission established a standard for aviation fields at 1,400 by 600 feet. Funding was approved by the Territorial Board of Road Commissioners to begin building standardized runways "in the direction of prevailing winds in order to permit planes to take off and land against the wind."[54]

Gold mining, still a major industry in Alaska, was the determining factor where runways were built. Mining companies often provided labor along with funds to assist the ARC in construction. Transportation-hungry communities also assisted, often providing land and labor for the projects. Landing fields built in Tokotna, Flat, Wiseman, Brooks, Circle, and Ruby were completed with a combination of mining company, community, and government funding and labor.[55] By 1928, eighteen runways were finished in the territory, and several others were planned.[56]

Another challenge faced by the ARC was the uncertain longevity of boomtowns, which affected decisions of where to expend limited resources. Iditarod is a case in point. Gold was discovered in the region

---

52   Ira Harkey, *Pioneer Bush Pilot: The Noel Wien Story* (Seattle: University of Washington Press, 1974), 136–46.

53   Claus-M. Naske, *Paving Alaska's Trails: The Work of the Alaska Road Commission* (Boston: University Press of America, 1986), 145.

54   Claus-M. Naske, *Alaska Road Commission Historical Narrative: Final Report* (Fairbanks: State of Alaska Department of Transportation & Public Facilities, 1983), 291.

55   Ibid., 291–92.

56   Board of Road Commissioners for Alaska, Report Upon the Construction and Maintenance of Military and Post Roads, Bridges, and Trails, and of Other Roads, Tramways, Ferries, Bridges, Trails, and Related Works in the Territory of Alaska, Annual Report of the Chief of Engineers Fiscal Year 1927 (Juneau, 1927), 86–87.

in 1908, and Iditarod grew to a full-fledged transportation and commerce hub for the mining district. Iditarod was incorporated as a
town under Territorial law in 1911, and at one point had a telephone
company, two newspapers, four hotels, nine saloons, a fire hall, and
numerous other businesses.[57]

Iditarod was situated along the ARC trail system, leading southwest to numerous towns and villages including Bethel, Dillingham,
and Goodnews Bay, and northeast through McGrath to Nenana.[58]
However, mining declined in the area during the 1920s, and businesses closed. The post office moved to Flat in 1929, and Iditarod was
no longer listed as an incorporated town in a governor's report of
1930.[59] The ARC could no longer justify improving trails to an area
where resource development had declined so significantly.[60]

Aviation in interior and southcentral Alaska and on the Seward
Peninsula continued to enjoy rapid expansion, and as the 1931 construction season ended, the number of runways had swelled to
seventy-four. Landing strips were completed across the Interior, reaching north from Southcentral and west to Nome. None were yet located
north of the Brooks Range, on the Alaska Peninsula, on Kodiak Island,
or along the Aleutian chain, and only one was built in Southeast.[61]
Runway standards were revised—Class A airports had two
300-by-3,000-foot runways, and smaller emergency fields were constructed with single 200-by-1,500 foot runways.[62] The largest

57   Linda Kay Thompson, *Alaska's Abandoned Towns: Case Studies for
Preservation and Interpretation*, History and Archaeology Series No. 2 (Alaska
Division of Parks, 1972), 52.

58   Claus-M. Naske, *Paving Alaska's Trails: The Work of the Alaska Road
Commission* (Boston: University Press of America 1986) 136.

59   Linda Kay Thompson, *Alaska's Abandoned Towns: Case Studies for
Preservation and Interpretation*, History and Archaeology Series No. 2 (Alaska
Division of Parks, 1972), 58; Mary Balcom, *Ghost Towns of Alaska* (Chicago:
Adams Press, 1965), 16.

60   Claus-M. Naske, *Paving Alaska's Trails: The Work of the Alaska Road
Commission* (Boston: University Press of America, 1986) 136.

61   Ibid., 146.

62   Claus-M. Naske, *Alaska Road Commission Historical Narrative: Final Report*
(Fairbanks: State of Alaska Department of Transportation &Public Facilities,
1983), 292.

fixed-base operations were located in Fairbanks, Anchorage, Valdez, and Nome. A total of 6,500 passengers were carried by thirty-one airplanes in the territory during 1931.[63]

Increased airfield spending led to close scrutiny and reduction of spending on other parts of the ARC system. One significant indicator of the changing travel patterns was reduced spending on shelter cabins located throughout the trail system.

Funding for shelter cabin construction and maintenance peaked with a high of $40,000 per year in 1927, declining thereafter—by 1933, the annual allocation was just over $4,000.[64]At that time the trail system included 226 shelter cabins.[65] Pressures eventually mounted to discontinue the system entirely, and ARC's 1933–1934 report included a dire prediction for the trail system: "There is no question that airplanes have diverted much winter travel from the land and it may be that in time no dog sled traveling will be done at all . . ."[66]

Air-mail contracts significantly affected the ARC trail system. Prior to the introduction of airplanes, U.S. Mail traveled year-round by boat along the coast and during the summer on Interior river systems. Star Routes were awarded through a bidding process. During winter, mail carriers made slow progress between towns using horse-drawn sleighs or dog teams, an excruciatingly slow process that wasn't always acceptable by the post office. One report stated:

> For some time past the mail service in Alaska has not been what it should be to aid in proper development of the Territory. There have been numerous complaints, which upon investigation have been found to be justified, and active measures are being taken

---

63 Claus-M. Naske, *Paving Alaska's Trails: The Work of the Alaska Road Commission* (Boston: University Press of America, 1986), 145.

64 Biennial report of the Alaska Territorial Highway Engineer and Superintendent of Public Works, 1937–1938 (Juneau, 1939), 58.

65 Biennial Report of the Alaska Territorial Engineer and Superintendent of Public Works, 1935–1936 (Juneau, 1937), 39.

66 Grace Edman, Alice Hudson, Sam Johnson, *Alaska Division of Highways: Fifty Years of Highways* (Nome: Alaska Department of Public Works, Division of Highways), 76.

at the present time to make a general improvement in the mail service throughout the entire Territory.[67]

Timeliness in delivery was dramatically improved by using airplanes. A 1935 report to Congress outlined the challenges and solutions in detail, pointing out that carrying mail by airplane "is materially expediting the mails; it is also proving cheaper than service by dog sleds." The report highlighted the differences between the forms of transportation on the Fairbanks-to-Nome route. "Twenty-five to fifty days are required to make the trip from Fairbanks to Nome by dog team, but less than 2 days by airplane."[68] A direct flight could have been completed in one day, but two days were required because the plane made twenty-one stops to deliver and pick -up mail along the route.[69] Postal officials favored air mail as it proved faster, more efficient, and far cheaper than overland travel.

ARC's 1936 report pointed to the dramatic changes continuing in the trail and shelter cabin system. "Since the airplane is supplanting overland travel and airmail contracts are taking the place of mail transport by dogs it is now apparent that purely from a standpoint of overland travel the shelter cabin is no longer pressing need." Ironically, the report went on to say the only shelter cabin built during that period " was on the Healy aviation field, used chiefly in transporting sick or injured miners to the hospital."[70] In the preceding year, fifty-six airplanes in the territory had flown more than a million miles combined, transporting 10,194 passengers.[71] There

---

67 United States Postal Service, *Annual Report of the Postmaster General, For the Fiscal Year Ended June 30, 1921* (Washington, D.C.: Printing Office), 53.

68 U.S. Congress, Senate, Committee on Post Offices and Post Roads, To Authorize the POSTMASTER GENERAL, TO CONTRACT FOR AIR MAIL SERVICE IN ALASKA, Report No.571 (House of Representatives, 74th Congress, 1st Session, April 1, 1935), 1.

69 Pacific Alaska Airways Operational History 1932–1941, Crosson Family Collection, File 37-F (Alaska & Polar Regions Archive, University of Alaska Fairbanks), 9.

70 Biennial Report of the Alaska Territorial Engineer and Superintendent of Public Works, 1937–1938 (Juneau, 1939), 58.

71 Biennial Report of the Alaska Territorial Engineer and Superintendent of Public Works, 1935–1936 (Juneau, 1937), 56.

were now eighty-nine runways in the territory constructed and maintained by ARC.[72]

Further, the importance of aviation in the Territory was acknowledged by the ARC: "To some communities in Alaska aviation fields are more important than roads for the reason that roads would cost millions of dollars and require years to build." The need for additional landing fields was also noted: ". . . nothing is quite so important as a place to land if the necessity arises."[73]

By 1939, the status of remote trails, shelter cabins, and their users was bluntly apparent in the ARC hierarchy of need. "Shelter cabins today are occupied and used chiefly by natives, not necessarily en route from one place to another, but using these refuge cabins for bases in their trapping operations." The report included, "No request for shelter cabins has been made by this office in the budget request since it is believed that if there is a necessity for this it becomes more properly a function of the Indian Office."[74]

On the cusp of the United States entering World War II in 1941, ARC was responsible for 8,500 miles of sled roads and trails, but had conducted no maintenance on 4,296 of those miles.

Additionally, maintenance of the shelter cabins themselves was discontinued. At the same time, the number of landing fields had grown to 155 in the Territory, with an additional ten facilities for seaplanes.[75]

ARC budgets increased during the war years, but funds were directed to road projects that aided the war effort rather than to existing trails. Territorial Governor Ernest Gruening believed that highway construction should support military needs in Alaska and recommended ARC's construction budget be set aside and replaced with

---

72 Ibid., 56.

73 Biennial Report of the Alaska Territorial Engineer and Superintendent of Public Works, 1937–1938 (Juneau, 1939), 61.

74 Grace Edman, Alice Hudson, Sam Johnson, *Alaska Division of Highways: Fifty Years of Highways* (Nome: Alaska Department of Public Works, Division of Highways), 90.

75 Biennial Report of the Alaska Territorial Engineer and Superintendent of Public Works, 1937–1938 (Juneau, 1939), 65, 69.

one more in line with needs of the military. Among Gruening's recommendations for construction was "A connecting link from the Anchorage road system to the Richardson Highway . . ." This became the modern-day Glenn Highway.[76] In addition, ARC projects during the war included replacing bridges along the Richardson Highway with ones capable of carrying fifteen-ton military loads and construction of the Tanana River bridge at Delta.[77]

Great scrutiny was exercised over where ARC spent funds and the priority of who should benefit from them. The 1943–44 Territorial Highway Report left little to the imagination:

> The theory of an equal division of the road funds between the four judicial divisions is as impracticable as it is unsound. It is obvious that a division having a population of 1600 white people does not require as much road development as one that has more than more than 18,000 white people—not that the native people are not as much entitled to the use of the roads as anyone else, but simply for the reason that they do not, for the most part, live where the roads are or use them and, therefore, a comparison of the white population served as a better index to the needs.[78]

The report went on to strengthen the diminished importance of shelter cabins: "The situation today is so different than the early days when travelers used the winter trails regularly. . . . Shelter cabins in the early days afforded a worthwhile facility, but the need for them is not believed to exist today."[79]

A decade later, the 1956 ARC Annual Report made no mention of shelter cabins at all. Down from a peak of more than 8,500 miles of trails in the early 1940s, the report now listed a total of 445 miles.

---

76 Claus-M. Naske, *Paving Alaska's Trails: The Work of the Alaska Road Commission* (Boston: University Press of America, 1986), 208.

77 Ibid., 211.

78 Grace Edman, Alice Hudson, Sam Johnson, *Alaska Division of Highways: Fifty Years of Highways* (Nome: Alaska Department of Public Works, Division of Highways), 102.

79 Biennial Report of the Alaska Territorial Engineer and Superintendent of Public Works, 1937–1938 (Juneau, 1939), 29.

These preserved routes were located primarily on the Seward Peninsula, and only 49 percent were maintained year-round.[80] The era of an interconnected trail system was past, and for much of rural Alaska, airplane travel had become the norm.

The ARC had done the job of building a system of trails and roads from tidewater to support resource development in the Territory. The organization's stated mission was never to provide surface transportation to all Alaskans in all regions of the territory, and so it didn't. The arrival of commercial aviation forced the ARC to refocus their efforts to meet the demands of resource developers, which it did by building runways wherever needed. Had commercial aviation been delayed in Alaska for another decade, there is little doubt that a map of today's road system would be much different.

The limited number of roads in Alaska today evolved from early mandates and economics. No government effort was ever dedicated to improving transportation for the general public, only for commerce. Development of a transportation system began much later in Alaska than it did in the continental United States, and during that time lag, aviation became viable. When Alaska's transportation system was developing, airplanes outcompeted ground-based vehicles in both time and money. As throughout the developed world, roads are constructed where trails have become popular. When trails and wagon roads were abandoned, Alaska lost its blueprint for more modern highways.

Today, few subjects raise emotions and debate more than proposals to construct new roads through undeveloped parts of Alaska. Regardless of personal feelings, issues such as land ownership, environmental concerns, and budget restrictions will make construction of any significant new public roads in the wilds of the state unlikely.

---

80 Grace Edman, Alice Hudson, Sam Johnson, *Alaska Division of Highways: Fifty Years of Highways* (Nome: Alaska Department of Public Works, Division of Highways), 133–34.

BIBLIOGRAPHY (PARTIAL)

Anderson, Barry C. *Lifeline to the Yukon: A History of Yukon River Navigation.* Seattle: Superior Publishing Co., 1983.

Annual Report of the Chief of Engineers, Extract, Board of Road Commissioners, *Construction and Maintenance of Military and Post Roads, Bridges and Trails, Alaska.* Washington, D.C., 1919.

Aviation Access to Remote Locations in Alaska, Recommendations to Increase Aviation Access to Medical Facilities, Federal Aviation Administration Study for the House and Senate Appropriations Committees, May 2001, House Report 106-940 accompanying H.R. 4475, FY 2001, DOT Appropriations.

Balcom, Mary. *Ghost Towns of Alaska.* Chicago: Adams Press, 1965.

Biennial Report of the Alaska Territorial Engineer and Superintendent of Public Works, 1935–1936. Juneau, 1937.

Biennial Report of the Alaska Territorial Engineer and Superintendent of Public Works, 1937–1938. Juneau, 1939.

Board of Road Commissioners for Alaska. *Report Upon the Construction and Maintenance of Military and Post Roads, Bridges, and Trails, and of Other Roads, Tramways, Ferries, Bridges, Trails, and Related Works in the Territory of Alaska*, Annual Report of the Chief of Engineers Fiscal Year 1927. Juneau, 1927.

Board of Road Commissioners in Charge. *Construction and Maintenance of Military and Post Roads, Bridges, and Trails, Alaska*, Annual Report of the Chief of Engineers Extract. Washington, D.C.: Government Printing Office, 1919.

Brinkley, Douglas. *Wheels for the World: Henry Ford, His Company and a Century of Progress.* New York: Viking Penguin, 2003.

Clifford, Howard. *Rails North: The Railroads of Alaska and the Yukon.* Seattle: Superior Publishing Co., 1981.

Deely, Nicholas. *Tanana Valley Railroad: The Gold Dust Line, Alaska.* Fairbanks: Denali Publishing, 1996.

DeWitt, Nancy. *Extreme Motoring: Alaska's First Automobiles and Their Dauntless Drivers.* Fairbanks: Fountain Antique Auto Museum, 2015.

Edman, Grace, Hudson, A., and Johnson, S. *Alaska Division of Highways: Fifty Years of Highways*. Nome: Alaska Department of Public Works, Division of Highways, 1960.

Fitch, Edwin M. *The Alaska Railroad*. New York: Praeger Publishers, 1967.

Greely, Maj. Gen. A. W. *Handbook of Alaska*. New York: Charles Scribner and Sons, 1925.

Harkey, Ira. *Pioneer Bush Pilot: The Noel Wien Story*. Seattle: University of Washington Press, 1974.

Harrison, Edward S. *Nome and Seward Peninsula: History, Description, Biographies, and Stories*. Seattle: Metropolitan Press, 1905.

Heller, Herbert L. *Sourdough Sagas*. Sausalito: Comstock Editions Inc. 1972.

Janson, Lone E. *The Copper Spike*. Anchorage: Alaska Northwest Publishing Co., 1975.

Morse, Kathryn Taylor. *The Nature of Gold: An Environmental History of the Klondike Gold Rush*. Seattle: University of Washington Press, 2003.

Naske, Claus-M. *Alaska Road Commission Historical Narrative: Final Report*. Fairbanks: State of Alaska Department of Transportation & Public Facilities, 1983.

———. *Paving Alaska's Trails: The Work of the Alaska Road Commission*. Boston: University Press of America, 1986.

Pacific Alaska Airways Operational History 1932–1941. Crosson Family Collection, File 37-F. Alaska & Polar Regions Archive, University of Alaska Fairbanks.

Quay, Sara E. *Westward Expansion*. Westport, CT: Greenwood Press, 2002

Schneider, William S. *On Time Delivery: The Dog Team Mail Carriers*. Fairbanks: University of Alaska Press, 2012.

Stevens, Robert W. *Alaskan Aviation History: Volume One 1897–1928*. Des Moines: Polynas Press, 1990.

Thompson, Linda Kay. *Alaska's Abandoned Towns: Case Studies for Preservation and Interpretation*, History and Archaeology Series No. 2. Alaska Division of Parks, 1972.

U.S. Congress, Senate, Committee on Post Offices and Post Roads, *To Authorize the POSTMASTER GENERAL, TO CONTRACT FOR AIR MAIL SERVICE IN ALASKA*, Report No. 571, House of Representatives, 74th Congress, 1st Session, April 1, 1935.

United States Postal Service. *Annual Report of the Postmaster General, For the Fiscal Year Ended June 30 1921.* Washington, D.C.: Printing Office.

War Department. *Report of the Board of Road Commissioners for Alaska, 1912.* Washington, D.C.: Government Printing Office, 1912.

A Note from Russ Vandlugt

Lieutenant Colonel Russ Vanderlugt is a University of Alaska Interdisciplinary PhD student whose dissertation focuses on the Henry Allen expedition.

I have enjoyed studying under Terrence since 2007. He served as chair on my master's degree thesis committee and is currently serving as a member of my Arctic and Northern Studies interdisciplinary dissertation committee. Terrence initially connected me with Henry Allen's 1885 expedition, now the focus of my PhD research and dissertation. He's at least partially responsible for helping me gain a position teaching American history at the United States Military Academy, and has most importantly infused me with his enthusiasm for teaching and his passion for pursuing complex questions through historical research.

THE MYSTERIOUS PROCESS
OF HISTORICAL RESEARCH

A Curious Story of How Heath Twichell found Henry Allen

Russ Vanderlugt and Heath Twichell

The origins of research projects range from assignments by professors or employers, to outgrowths of previous projects, to the most whimsical ideas from researchers themselves. An individual researcher rarely can take sole credit for his or her arrival at a specific research topic. Sometimes, the subject seems to "find" the researcher through a chain of unlikely events and circumstances. Once a topic is born, the historian's toil often becomes a labor of love, as he or she refines the grains of evidence, analysis, and writing into the gristmill of history. The ways in which researchers connect with their subjects remain mysterious and fascinating, underlining the human element of research, the importance of relationships, and the circumstance and timing inherent in any research project.

The story relayed here demonstrates one such event: a young historian (Heath Twichell) serendipitously meets an unlikely and under-recognized actor in American history (Major General Henry T. Allen), eventually publishing his biography, titled *Allen: The Biography of an Army Officer, 1859–1930.*[1] Beginning in 1962, Twichell's research, dissertation, and biography of Allen brought to light significant aspects of history not previously understood. The book dedicates only a short chapter to Allen's expedition in Alaska, titled "Twenty-Five Hundred

---

1   Heath Twichell. *Allen: The Biography of an Army Officer, 1859–1930* (New Brunswick, NJ: Rutgers University Press, 1974).

Miles on an Empty Stomach," though it presents aspects of Allen's character and life experience that shed light on that expedition's success and significance relative to other expeditions of the nineteenth century. Twichell's work facilitates the interpretation of Indigenous, Russian, and American narratives in Alaska during the nineteenth century, and provides scholars with a wealth of material for further research. In the words of John Wesley Powell, "Scholarship breeds scholarship, wisdom breeds wisdom, discovery breeds discovery"[2]—Twichell's "discovery" of Allen planted the seeds of future scholarship, with fruits of further rich and unique perspectives on the history of Alaska and North America.

I entered this realm of research in 2007, as a graduate student at the University of Alaska under the tutelage of Dr. Terrence Cole. Terrence has a remarkable gift and record for connecting students with research topics, papers, and theses, and invigorating them with his contagious curiosity and passion for historical inquiry. As an Army Captain interested in Alaska history, I was touched by Terrence's enthusiasm for his students and their research. During his fall 2007 seminar in Alaska history, Terrence posted a list titled "49 Ideas for Alaskan History Papers!"[3] Henry Allen did not make the cut. Nonetheless, Terrence pulled me aside and introduced me to Allen's 1885 expedition across Alaska, about which I knew nothing. Very few historical sources mentioned Allen, though Morgan Sherwood devoted a chapter in his 1965 book, *Exploration of Alaska, 1865–1900*, to the Allen expedition.[4] In 1974, Heath Twichell published the aforementioned Henry Allen biography, but that had been nearly two generations ago.

---

2   W. B. Allison et al. in Allison Commission, "Testimony before the Joint Commission to Consider the Present Organization of Certain Bureaus in 1886," *Senate Miscellaneous Document* 82, 49th Congress: 1st session (2345), 1082.

3   Terrence Cole, email message to author, October 1, 2007.

4   Morgan B. Sherwood, *Exploration of Alaska, 1865–1900* (New Haven: Yale University Press, 1965). Morgan Sherwood's 1962 dissertation included a chapter on the Allen Expedition titled "The Remarkable Journey of Henry Allen," which was originally published in 1965 by Yale University Press. See Morgan B. Sherwood, "American Scientific Exploration of Alaska, 1865–1900" (PhD dissertation, University of California, Berkeley, 1962). A second edition, with preface by Terrence Cole, was published in 1992. See Morgan B. Sherwood, *Exploration of Alaska, 1865–1900* (Fairbanks: University of Alaska Press, 1992).

I soon learned that Allen's expedition had been compared to that of Lewis and Clark, not only by scholars such as Sherwood but by contemporary newspaper journalists and Allen's superior, General Nelson Miles. When I told Terrence of this discovery, he responded, "Russ, this is really, really interesting...the most interesting fact about Alaskan history I have learned this year, I will tell you!"[5]

Terrence had planted the seed. Of course, Henry Allen's expedition was not the same as Lewis and Clark's, but how did it compare? Discovering the rest was up to me. I dashed off a seminar paper for Terrence, though before the semester ended I deployed to Iraq.[6] This marked the beginning of my quest to relate Alaska's history to the larger narrative of North America. Before I boarded my plane, Terrence had arranged for me to meet with Mark Hamilton, president of the University of Alaska and a retired major general. While I was serving in Iraq, letters of recommendation arrived at the History and Geography Departments at United States Military Academy from President Hamilton. Little did Terrence know, the meeting with President Hamilton was a turning point in my Army career.

Five years later, I found myself teaching American history at West Point, seeking to integrate Alaska into the broad narrative of U.S. history, despite my textbooks' authors' disinclination to do so. Unsure whether Heath Twichell was still alive, I decided to try contacting him by email. To my surprise, he wrote back the same day from Newport, Rhode Island:

> Dear Russ: I'll be glad to help you in any way I can regarding your interest in General Allen. You may not be aware, but I taught Modern European History at West Point from 1964–67, back when History was part of the Department of Social Sciences. I have often thought that almost any of the chapters in my book could easily be expanded into more depth and detail and will be happy to help

---

5   Terrence Cole, email message to the author, November 9, 2007.

6   The paper, dated December 1, 2007, was titled "The Leadership of Lieutenant Allen and His 1885 Alaska Expedition" and focused primarily on Allen's leadership decisions throughout the expedition, with a brief section that compared and contrasted the expedition to that of Lewis and Clark.

you do just that with whatever subject most interests you. Certainly Allen's 1885 Alaska expedition ranks as one of the great, but lesser known stories of the exploration of the North American continent. Both Terrence Cole and Jim Kari would also make excellent mentors, should you want to do more with this topic. I know both of them and was present in Mentasta for Henry Allen Day in 1985.[7]

With these kind words, a mentorship relationship developed, expanding and connecting the circle of scholarship initiated by Terrence. During my tour teaching history at West Point, Twichell and his wife, Mary, became family friends. They took interest in my children, and we frequently visited them at their colonial farmhouse in Newport, Rhode Island, or met them at various New England beaches. Another five years passed, and my career path continued to mirror Heath's, a half century removed. In 2017, I was stationed at Ft. Leavenworth, Kansas, as part of an Army program designed to produce PhDs. Although he was well along in years, Twichell agreed to serve on my dissertation committee, alongside Terrence Cole and committee chair Mary Ehrlander. I was honored to study with this group of mentors, allowing me to stand on the shoulders of giants. Sadly, Heath was unable to fulfill this last duty. Nonetheless, like many aged and faithful historians, he had the satisfaction of knowing he passed the torch of his passion for research and writing to the next generation. Heath Twichell's own story of finding Henry Allen and publishing his biography, recounted as follows from a first-person "as told to" perspective, is based on an interview I conducted with him at West Point in 2013.[8] The conversation arose from casual meetings between the two of us, and exemplifies how a researcher selects a

---

7   Heath Twichell, email message to author, July 17, 2012. Morgan Sherwood was present, along with Heath Twichell and Jim Kari, at the "Lieutenant Allen Day" Centennial Potlatch held to honor a military officer in Mentasta, Alaska, on June 15, 1985. Heath may have mistaken Terrence for his twin brother, Dermot, who was representing and compiling a story for the *News-Miner* at "Allen Day" (since Terrence was not present at the event in 1985).

8   The interview with Heath that includes the source material for this story occurred on March 1, 2013, at the United States Military Academy at West Point, New York.

subject through a combination of mentorship, timing, and interests. It also highlights how the relationship between mentor, student, and research topic can achieve far-reaching effects. The story is told in Twichell's voice, with only light editing, to capture the essence and character of his research. I thank Mary Twichell and Ruth Crane, their daughter, for their permission to share Heath's story of discovery. I also thank Dr. Terrence Cole for his continued mentorship and inspiration, for introducing me to the subject of Henry Allen, encouraging me to pursue teaching history at West Point (which resulted in a close friendship with Heath Twichell), serving on both my master's and PhD committees, and challenging me to understand the Allen expedition in the broader context of American history.

∎ ∎ ∎

In the spring of 1962, the Army sent me [then "Captain" Heath Twichell] to American University in Washington, D.C., for two years to get a master's degree in modern European history, to prepare me to teach at West Point. I took the required number of courses and completed my graduate degree at American University in a year and half. My master's thesis was a study of how the German Army evaded disarmament restrictions in the Treaty of Versailles after World War I.[9] I did most of my research in the National Archives, utilizing captured German documents in the original German. During my research, I ran across two books about the American occupation of the Rhineland after World War I by Major General Henry T. Allen, whom I had never heard of.[10] In his two books on the period, *My Rhineland Journal* and *The Rhineland Occupation*, Henry Allen mentioned the Allied Occupation Authorities' occasional awareness that the Germans were in fact evading disarmament restrictions.

Consequently, the Allies made sporadic flying raids to German industrial centers in the Rhineland-Ruhr area, looking for evidence

---

9   Heath Twichell, "The German Army and Disarmament during the Weimar Period" (master's thesis, American University, 1964).

10   Henry T. Allen, *My Rhineland Journal* (Boston: Houghton Mifflin, 1923) and *The Rhineland Occupation* (New York: Bobbs-Merrill, 1927).

First Lieutenant Henry Allen as an instructor in the Department of Modern Languages at West Point, 1888. *Photo courtesy the Heath and Mary Twichell Private Collection.*

of research and development in prohibited weapons. It was just a passing reference in Allen's book, but he does mention it. So I first cited Allen as a source in my master's thesis.

Since I finished my master's degree six months ahead of the Army's allotted graduate school time, I called West Point and asked, "I completed my master's degree, can I come?"

West Point responded, "No. Just keep taking more courses."

I approached my advisor, Carl G. Anthon, about the situation, and he suggested, "We'll put you on a PhD track; you might just be able to do it."[11] So they did.

I remember one of the first courses I took was an open-ended seminar where you could pick your own topic. I thought to myself, "Well, why don't I find out a little more about Henry Allen. He seems like an interesting guy."

I found my way back to the Library of Congress and opened up the card catalog. I had previously searched for Allen's name in the card catalog; that's how I found his Rhineland books. But I had not paid attention to any of the articles Allen had written or other related publications. When I opened the card catalog, I noticed that all the cards were old and thumbed and so forth, but there was one brand-new card at the front of the slide drawer. It read: "Allen Papers, Manuscript Division, Library of Congress." So I thought, "Well, I'll just check it out."

I walked into the Manuscript Division and queried the archivist, "I just noticed you have Henry Allen's papers."

The archivist looked somewhat surprised and said, "We just put that card in there yesterday, and you're the first person to ask about it."

I asked, "Well, can you show me the finding aid?"

The archivist reached into a cabinet of drawers and announced matter-of-factly, "Yeah, we just finished that." I guess they had completed the finding aid before adding the card to the catalog. The archivist handed me a loose-leaf binder. It was a list of the boxes that were donated by Henry T. Allen, Jr., Henry Allen's son.[12] Allen's papers

---

11   Carl G. Anthon was born in Wismar, Germany, in 1911, and earned his BA from the University of Chicago (1938) and his PhD from Harvard (1943) in Modern European History. After several academic positions, Anthon became a European history professor at American University from 1961–1976. In addition to his academic appointments, Anthon worked for the government as Higher Education Advisor for the U.S. High Commission for Germany (1949–1952) and Executive Secretary for the U.S. Education Commission in the German Federal Republic (1958–1960). The Carl G. Anthon Papers are held at American University.

12   The papers of Major General Henry T. Allen were donated to the Library of Congress by his son, Colonel Henry T. Allen, Jr., in 1956. See Henry T. Allen Papers, Manuscript Division, Library of Congress, Washington, D.C. (http://lccn.loc.gov/mm78010504).

consisted of seventy-three boxes; each was a standard manuscript file box.[13] Scanning through the list, one of the boxes, maybe it was "Box 1," was labeled "Diaries." I thought, "Oh, that's a good place to start." So I said, "Bring me the box with the diaries."

A few minutes later, he plunked it down on my desk. I lifted the lid. Inside were fifteen or twenty books of different sizes, shapes, and conditions. I thought, "Well, I'll just...I'll just reach in at random." Without looking, I reached in. The first thing I pulled out was this *lump*. In my hand was a very badly battered diary, obviously water-damaged. I soon discovered it was Allen's journal from his 1885 Copper River expedition. The expedition diary just happened to be the first one I pulled out of the box. I carefully opened it and began to read. I found parts of the diary were easy to read and other parts were very difficult. I spent the rest of the day completely immersed in the diary, trying to decipher Allen's smeared pencil script and making notes about the diary. Based on what I saw in the diary, I figured I would write about Allen's exploration of Alaska for a paper required for my first seminar course in the American University PhD program. I packed up my briefcase and my notes. On the way out of the Manuscript Division, I thought, "You know, Allen was 'old military.' He probably lived in the Washington, D.C., area at some point during his career." I hadn't looked at the rest of the stuff in the box, but I figured Allen may have even retired somewhere in the national capital region.

A phone booth happened to be just outside the door near the balcony area of the Library of Congress. I stepped in and opened the phone directory to "Allen." Sure enough, there was a Colonel Henry T. Allen, Jr., living on Connecticut Avenue, just northwest of the White House and less than five miles away. I put a dime in the slot. A creaky old voice answered. I told him who I was and what I was doing. He said, "Come on out, sonny. I'd like to meet ya."

That evening I drove out to Connecticut Avenue on my way home to Kensington, and stopped at Colonel Allen's apartment building. He lived on the fifteenth floor of one of Washington's huge,

---

13 The Henry T. Allen Papers consist of 15,000 items, sixty-two containers plus eleven oversize boxes, totaling twenty-two linear feet.

emblematic apartment buildings. He came to the main door and welcomed me. We had a cup of coffee and a chat. He was glad to see me; delighted, in fact, because he was the one who collected and helped organize his father's papers. He saw to it that Allen's papers were donated to the Library of Congress. He informed me that he had accomplished this several years before. My appearance on the scene was the first evidence that the Library of Congress was doing something with his dad's stuff. We became good friends and went out to dinner on numerous occasions. He loaned me things that were not in the Library of Congress collection, like Dora Allen's 1887 diary from their honeymoon. That was pretty hot stuff! Over time, I got to know Colonel Allen and he gave me souvenirs from his dad: a bolo knife from the Philippines and a few other things. But that's just the beginning of the story about the Allen book.

Meanwhile, I finished my paper for that first seminar course in my PhD program. The title of the paper was the same as it later appeared in my biography on Allen in chapter form, "Fifteen Hundred Miles on an Empty Stomach." In fact, that paper was the basis of the first chapter that I wrote for my dissertation, and later my book. I received an "A−" on the paper in May of 1964.[14] The professor was a guy by the name of Arthur A. Ekirch, Jr.[15] Arthur Ekirch was an old-time American historian. As he handed me the paper, he remarked, "Great story, Heath. Interesting. Do more." So I spent most of my free time going through Allen's papers. By the time I reported to West Point in the summer of 1964, I had looked through all seventy-three boxes in the Library of Congress, but the effort was very much just "a lick and a promise" to see what was there. The next three years I taught Modern European History at West Point. But every chance I got in between teaching I spent dipping back into that pool. After completing my

---

14 Heath later gave me his original seminar paper, dated May 1964, "Fifteen Hundred Miles on an Empty Stomach," so evidence exists of his successful grade received from Arthur Ekirch.

15 For a well-written memoriam on Arthur Ekirch (1915–2000), see Lawrence S. Wittner, "In Memoriam: Arthur A. Ekirch Jr. (1915–2000)," *Perspectives on History* 38, no. 5 (May 2000), https://www.historians.org/publications-and-directories/perspectives-on-history/may-2000/in-memoriam-arthur-a-ekirch-jr.

teaching assignment at West Point, the Army eventually gave me a year gratis to write my dissertation, but not without some drama in between.

After my first tour in Vietnam, I was stationed at Ft. Leavenworth as a Major for Command and General Staff College, from 1967 to 1968. Those were good times. I became close friends with General Norman Schwarzkopf, who was my next-door neighbor. We were all senior Majors or brand-new Lieutenant Colonels. When the time came to receive our assignments, everybody was "hot to trot" to get all the big jobs in Washington, D.C., such as Deputy Chief of Staff for Operations (DCS-Ops). We filed into a large room and they handed out assignment envelopes. I opened my envelope and it said I was going to the Chief of Military History. I thought, "Oh, shoot." Well, the Chief of the Infantry Branch had actually traveled to Ft. Leavenworth from Washington, DC with the assignments officer. He had served as my brigade commander the year before in Vietnam. He wanted me to stay and extend my assignment at Ft. Leavenworth, and I didn't want to do that. So he knew who I was.

I went in to see him and said, "Sir, you're killing me. This is a heck of an assignment! I need to go to DCS-Ops. You're sending me to Army History, and they're still writing the history of the Indian Wars . . ." Which is what they were actually doing in Washington, DC when I got there.

The Chief of Infantry Branch wasn't fazed. "Well, we have a valid requirement for a Leavenworth graduate with a master's degree in history and you're the only one; I have to fill it." And that was that.

I was assigned to the Chief of Military History's office and reported to my new boss, Brigadier General Hal Pattison. He was a World War II tanker, one of Creighton Abrams's protégés. How he ended up in Military History, I'm not quite sure.[16] I popped him a salute and said, "I'm glad to be here, sir."

---

16   Brigadier General Hal Pattison retired from the Army in 1962, but was recalled to active duty to serve as the Chief of Military History. In this capacity, he supervised the completion of the official history of the Army in World War Two and established a network of historical teams to gather information relating to the Army in the Vietnam War, before retiring a second time in 1971.

General Pattison squinted. "Don't give me that, Twichell. I know how hard you tried to get out of this job. Now do a good job for me and I'll take care of you."

I went to work and performed basically busywork for a couple of months while I was familiarizing myself with the office routine and getting to know members of the staff. There were some really nice people there, including Charles B. McDonald, the author of *Company Commander*.[17] He and I became good friends. After about three months, General Pattison called me back into his office and said, "There's a downsizing going on Army-wide, as you know. Your job has been eliminated. What would you like to do?"

My perspective had not changed, so I replied, "I wanted to go to DCS-Ops in the first place, so see if you can get me there now?"

General Pattison said, "I'll give it a try." He called me the next day and informed me, "They're downsizing, too; no vacancies at all."

All this assignment turmoil happened in 1971. It was the beginning of President Nixon's draw down from the Vietnam War. I softened my position somewhat and said to General Pattison, "I'll take any Department of the Army (DA) staff job, which is what I really need."

He replied tersely, "There's no DA staff hiring going on right now. What else would you like to do?"

I responded, "Well, I have a year left on my doctoral degree program. I'd like to go back to graduate school."

General Pattison was decisive. "You got it." He let me keep my office at the Office of the Chief of Military History (OCMH), which included use of the copy machine and their library, along with a team of talented historians that gladly served as readers to vet the manuscript.

That's how I wrote my dissertation. During that year, I kept going to work at OCMH, but dressed in civilian clothes. I kept working in the same office, and a year later, I had my dissertation done.

After I turned in my dissertation, I took a week of leave in June of 1971 to take my wife to Europe as a reward for typing the manuscript

---

17   Charles B. MacDonald, *Company Commander* (Washington, D.C.: Infantry Journal Press, 1947).

error free. Then I was on a plane to Vietnam for my second combat tour. Before I left for Vietnam, I accomplished my oral exams at American University. I had been told the orals at American University were fairly grueling, and I was prepared for that. I remember the event clearly. I entered a room, and seated before me were all of the professors I had worked with. They asked me only one question and I answered it succinctly. They talked briefly amongst themselves, and then the head of the department faced me and declared, "That's it. Let's go to my house for champagne." And so we did.

I did not know at the time that my committee was submitting my dissertation for the Allan Nevins Prize, which is a competition nationwide that includes all the major universities for the best dissertation in American history each year.[18] There are normally a couple hundred dissertations submitted. The panel of readers in my year included Barbara Tuchman and Arthur Schlesinger, Jr., among others. I didn't know any of this when I went off to Vietnam.

My first assignment in Vietnam was with the 101st Airborne Division, stationed along the Demilitarized Zone (DMZ). The unit was in the midst of drawing down and going home when I arrived, and by the middle of my tour the 101st Airborne had redeployed from Vietnam. They left me there as an advisor to one of the Vietnamese regiments that took over the area of operations of the 101st Airborne. This made sense because I was already familiar with the area and didn't have to relocate to a different region. One day, in March of 1972, I was standing in an observation tower about a mile short of the DMZ. I'd been on the job for about six weeks. I had my binoculars in hand, because we had heard reports that there were things going on across the DMZ. My driver was posted with a radio next to my jeep, which was parked at the base of the tower. He called up, "There's someone coming to see you, sir!"

---

18 The Allan Nevins Prize is awarded annually by the Society of American Historians for the best-written doctoral dissertation on a significant subject in American history. The award-winning work is published by one of a consortium of distinguished publishing houses that support the prize, carries a monetary award, and is named in honor of the society's founder.

I looked back down the Street Without Joy, which was our name for Highway 1, the highway that ran up the coast of Vietnam. About ten miles away there was a Jeep coming up the highway about sixty miles an hour with a rooster tail of dust behind it. Soon the Jeep reached the tower and screeched to a halt. Out jumped a "headquarters type," with spit-shined combat boots and starched fatigues. He yelled from below, "I have a telegram for you here, sir. It's from General Westmoreland."

General Westmoreland had left Vietnam and was currently the Chief of Staff of the Army.[19] Westmoreland was writing his autobiography, and Charles B. McDonald, from my old office in Military History, was the ghost writer for "Westy's" memoirs. When the Allan Nevins Prize was announced, the staff at OCMH heard about it right away, including Charlie McDonald. He went to Westy and said, "This guy is in Vietnam. The Army desperately needs credibility with the academic community. We've got to get him home for the award."

The Army pulled out all the stops. They got me on a plane and flew me to New York City. My wife rented a tuxedo and met me there. We took a room in the Americana Hotel.[20] I was the guest of honor at the Harvard Club that night. My dinner partners were Barbara Tuchman and Arthur Schlesinger, Jr. I received a guarantee of publication and a check for a thousand dollars.[21] The next morning, I got on a plane and went back to Vietnam to do some more fighting. The day after I returned to Vietnam, on March 30, 1972, the Easter Offensive hit us hard. My entire unit was decimated. I left Vietnam for good shortly thereafter. It was a psychological roller coaster.

The actual publication of the Allen book turned out to be a challenge in light of Vietnam and the Army's public perception at the time. One of the rules of the Nevins Prize is that each year a different publishing company (Doubleday, St. Martin's Press, Random House,

---

19   General Westmoreland was replaced by General Creighton Abrams in June 1968, shortly after the Tet Offensive. General Westmoreland served as Chief of Staff of the Army from 1968 until his retirement in 1972.

20   In 1979, the Sheraton Corporation acquired the Americana Hotel. It is currently named the Sheraton New York Times Square Hotel.

21   Heath also candidly admitted that he spent every penny of the award on a lavish New York City party for his friends and family.

Heath Twichell receiving the Allan Nevins Prize for best dissertation in American history from Arthur Schlesinger, Jr., 1972. *Photo courtesy the Heath and Mary Twichell Private Collection.*

etc.) gets first choice at the winning manuscript. Never in the history of the prize—it has been running continuously since 1961—has a dissertation ever been turned down by all of the dozen or so associated publishing houses. But the publishers turned the book down because it was a military subject that put the U.S. Army in a somewhat favorable light. So I waited. Each publishing house wrote me and said, "No, we can't use it, but we'll pass it on to the next."

The editor for the last one said, "I'm sorry, we can't do this either; it's just not commercial. But I would be glad to send it over to Rutgers Press because I know someone over there who I think might be interested in it." At that point, in 1974, I was at Ft. Bragg as a Logistics Officer for the 82nd Airborne Division, and about to assume command of the 1st Battalion, 508th Infantry Regiment.[22] I had little time or energy to be fussy about publication.

So they sent the manuscript to Rutgers and I enjoyed a really great relationship with the editor at Rutgers Press. They did a good job for me. That's how the Allen biography got published; but they only published a thousand copies.

■ ■ ■

The tale of Heath Twichell's relationship with Henry Allen, from his first "encounter" with the historical figure to the publication of Twichell's award-winning dissertation, illustrates the human elements of inquiry—his discovery, his growing determination to understand this man, the personal relationships he developed, and his interactions with various research mentors reveal the often-enigmatic process of research. Timing and circumstances are equally significant, and they impact historiography in ways that historians seldom fully recognize. For example, Twichell's book almost went unpublished, owing to the political-social milieu of the Vietnam War era. Moreover, the details of Allen's life and expedition, in some cases relayed through aging descendants, may have been lost had Heath not recovered them when he did. The question of how Twichell's research will influence what history enters national and regional history narratives and how that history is perceived has yet to be answered. In the meantime, his story provides a rich case study for students of historiography, in its illumination of how a researcher's process and personal circumstances, as well as the sociopolitical context of a given era, impact both the author's interpretation of the history and whether that work will be published. This story also demonstrates how research is perpetuated, and is therefore dedicated to Terrence Cole, reflecting his gift of inspiring and connecting students in the process of academic discovery, continuing the great circle of historical research and mentorship.

22　Heath was a 1956 graduate of the United States Military Academy and served twenty-four years as an Infantry Officer before retiring in the rank of colonel in 1980.

BIBLIOGRAPHY (PARTIAL)

Allen, Henry T. *My Rhineland Journal*. Boston: Houghton Mifflin, 1923.

———. *The Rhineland Occupation*. New York: Bobbs-Merrill, 1927.

Allison, W. B., et al. "Testimony before the Joint Commission to Consider the Present Organization of Certain Bureaus in 1886" in Allison Commission, Senate Miscellaneous Document 82, 49th Congress: 1st session, 2345.

Henry T. Allen Papers, Manuscript Division, Library of Congress, Washington, D.C. http://lccn.loc.gov/mm78010504.

MacDonald, Charles B. *Company Commander*. Washington, D.C.: Infantry Journal Press, 1947.

Sherwood, Morgan B. *Exploration of Alaska, 1865–1900*. New Haven: Yale University Press, 1965.

Twichell, Heath. "The German Army and Disarmament during the Weimar Period" (master's thesis). American University, 1964.

———. *Allen: The Biography of an Army Officer, 1859–1930*. New Brunswick, NJ: Rutgers University Press, 1974.

INDEX

Page numbers in italics refer to figures.